IRIS MURDOCH AND THE SEARCH FOR HUMAN GOODNESS

Iris Murdoch and the Search for Human Goodness

edited by
Maria Antonaccio
William Schweiker

THE UNIVERSITY OF CHICAGO PRESS
CHICAGO & LONDON

MARIA ANTONACCIO is assistant professor of religious ethics at Bucknell University, and the author of a dissertation on Iris Murdoch at the University of Chicago. WILLIAM SCHWEIKER is associate professor of theological ethics at the University of Chicago Divinity School, and the author of *Mimetic Reflections: A Study in Hermeneutics, Theology, and Ethics* and *Responsibility and Christian Ethics*.

The University of Chicago Press, Chicago 60637
The University of Chicago Press, Ltd., London
© 1996 by The University of Chicago
All rights reserved. Published 1996
Printed in the United States of America

05 04 03 02 01 00 99 98 97 96   5 4 3 2 1

ISBN 0-226-02112-2 (cloth)
ISBN 0-226-02113-0 (paper)

Library of Congress Cataloging-in-Publication Data

Iris Murdoch and the search for human goodness / edited by Maria Antonaccio and William Schweiker.
    p. cm.
    Includes bibliographical references and index.
    ISBN 0-226-02112-2 (cloth).—ISBN 0-226-02113-0 (pbk.)
    1. Murdoch, Iris—Ethics. 2. Didactic fiction, English—History and criticism. 3. Good and evil in literature. 4. Ethics in literature. I. Antonaccio, Maria. II. Schweiker, William.
    PR6063.U7Z714 1996
    823'914—dc20   96-12925
                                                                    CIP

The paper used in this publication meets the minimum requirements of the American National Standard for Information Sciences—Permanence of Paper for Printed Library Materials, ANSI Z39.48—1984.

For Iris Murdoch

Contents

ACKNOWLEDGMENTS ix
INTRODUCTION xi
Maria Antonaccio and William Schweiker

PART ONE
ISSUES IN THE HISTORY OF THOUGHT
1 Iris Murdoch and Moral Philosophy   3
   Charles Taylor
2 Love and Vision: Iris Murdoch on Eros and the Individual   29
   Martha C. Nussbaum
3 Iris Murdoch and the Many Faces of Platonism   54
   David Tracy

PART TWO
MORALITY, ETHICS, AND LITERATURE
4 "We Are Perpetually Moralists": Iris Murdoch, Fact, and Value   79
   Cora Diamond
5 Form and Contingency in Iris Murdoch's Ethics   110
   Maria Antonaccio

6   The Green Knight and Other Vagaries of the Spirit;
    or, Tricks and Images for the Human Soul;
    or, The Uses of Imaginative Literature   138
            Elizabeth Dipple

            PART THREE
    MORALITY, METAPHYSICS, AND RELIGION
        7   On the Loss of Theism   171
            Franklin I. Gamwell

8   Murdochian Muddles: Can We Get Through Them If God
            Does Not Exist?   190
            Stanley Hauerwas

        9   The Sovereignty of God's Goodness   209
            William Schweiker

            APPENDIX:
        Metaphysics and Ethics   236
            Iris Murdoch

        BIBLIOGRAPHY   253
    LIST OF CONTRIBUTORS   259
            INDEX   261

Acknowledgments

The conference that formed the context for the present volume grew out of conversations between the editors, Maria Antonaccio and William Schweiker, on current debates in theological and philosophical ethics about human existence, the good, and moral identity. The conference was supported through the Divinity School of the University of Chicago under the auspices of the D. R. Sharpe Lectureship on Social Ethics. The lectureship, in the words of its benefactor, is meant to provide "the opportunity for the best and most creative minds to explore society's social needs and present an ethical standard for modern life." More pointedly, Sharpe wrote that the "distinctly modern problem is whether there are ethical principles sensitive to the religious and cultural heritages and enlightened by contemporary knowledge adequate for the evolving needs of society in its search for purposeful life on this planet." It was fitting, then, that a conference dedicated to exploring the work of Iris Murdoch, a thinker concerned with conceptions of the human good in contemporary Western cultures, should be conceived in terms of the D. R. Sharpe Lectureship. As the papers collected in the volume aptly show, the relation between the moral and religious life remains central to current ethics. We express our profound gratitude to the Divinity School for the support of this conference through the D. R. Sharpe Lectureship. We are happy now to be able to offer these essays to a wider audience through the publication of this book.

Many persons were important in making the conference and book possible. We wish to thank Dean Clark Gilpin of the Divinity

School for his support of the conference. We also thank Sandra Peppers and Timothy Childs of the Divinity School for help in organizing the conference and W. David Hall for his assistance. We owe a special debt of gratitude to James J. Thompson, Darlene Weaver, and Marsha Peeler for the preparation of the manuscript. Our heartfelt thanks are due to all of the participants in the conference and the labor they contributed to this volume. Finally, we express our deepest gratitude to Dame Iris herself, who not only attended the conference but engaged the participants with characteristic insight and good will. Without the support and work of all of these persons, this book would not have been possible.

Maria Antonaccio
Bucknell University
William Schweiker
University of Chicago

Introduction

Maria Antonaccio and William Schweiker

This volume stems from a conference held at the Divinity School of the University of Chicago from May 11 through May 13, 1994, which brought together eminent scholars from a variety of fields to explore the significance of the work of Iris Murdoch for contemporary thought. At the center of the conference and all of the essays collected here is the problem of how we can and ought to picture the human insofar as any account of human life entails moral, metaphysical, and religious claims. In this respect, the book, while taking its inspiration from the work of Iris Murdoch, seeks to address questions of wide significance in current life. How ought we to understand human existence? What are the ways human life has been pictured in our traditions and cultures? How do conceptions of human life inform ways of life? In this introduction, it is our purpose to clarify the significance of Murdoch's work and briefly to indicate the contribution of the essayists.

I. The Significance of Murdoch's Thought

The work of Iris Murdoch occupies a distinctive place in the field of contemporary moral inquiry. As a noted philosopher and one of the most gifted and prolific novelists of the twentieth century, Murdoch has anticipated and shaped many of the issues central to recent ethics, including the relation between human identity and ideas of the good, the effect of the modern critique of religion on moral life and thought, the relation between ethics and literature, and the contemporary debate about liberalism. Over the past forty years Murdoch's diverse writings have influenced a generation of moral and religious thinkers, many of whom have contributed to this volume.

Born in Dublin in 1919, Murdoch grew up in London, receiving her university education at Oxford and later at Cambridge. Since 1948 she has been a Fellow of St. Anne's College, Oxford, where for many years she taught philosophy. Murdoch made her debut as a writer in 1954 and has published 26 novels, a volume of poetry, and several works of drama. Among the honors and awards she has received for her fiction are the James Tait Black Memorial Prize, the Whitbread Literary Award, and the Booker McConnell Prize. In 1987, Murdoch was made Dame of the Order of the British Empire. In addition to numerous essays and treatises on moral philosophy, art, literature, religion, and politics, Murdoch has written several books of philosophy, including *Sartre, Romantic Rationalist; The Sovereignty of Good; The Fire and the Sun: Why Plato Banished the Artists; Acastos: Two Platonic Dialogues;* and, in 1992, *Metaphysics as a Guide to Morals*, a revised and expanded version of her 1982 Gifford Lectures.

As a philosopher and a novelist, Murdoch is centrally engaged with the question of the self and the moral dimensions of every attempt to "picture" human beings. Both her fiction and her philosophy constitute a sustained argument against reductionistic accounts of human life that omit the "valuing" aspect of subjectivity and consciousness. Murdoch's numerous writings defend the integrity of the individual as a unique and unified center of value and significance. She explores the character of human existence with respect to the relation between self-consciousness—the mode of moral being—and the Good. In this way, Murdoch retrieves themes within Platonic ethics in the context of contemporary culture.

One reason for this retrieval of Platonic thought is that in Murdoch's judgment traditional religious beliefs, which insisted on the reality of ultimate goodness and the sanctity of individual life, have lost currency in contemporary life. Moral philosophy must answer for the loss of religious conviction. Although she is, strictly speaking, neither a Christian believer nor a theologian,

Murdoch's thought builds important bridges between secular moral philosophy and religious ethics. While she acknowledges the waning influence of traditional religious beliefs and ideals in contemporary society, Murdoch embraces an essentially religious picture of human beings as fallen and in need of transformation. Religious concepts, techniques, and ideals may be critical in addressing what she regards as the central question of ethics, "How can we become morally better?" It is this question, she believes, that was central to Platonic ethics.

The significance of Murdoch's thought in contemporary ethics can be specified along a number of interrelated lines. First, in terms of conceptions of the human person, or the ways we picture the human, Murdoch's insistence on the relation between the self and the Good challenges various strands of existentialism and liberalism. These forms of thought conceive the individual in terms of the simple capacity or freedom to act, thus severing any connection between freedom and a conception of goodness in the formation of the self. It is important for the reader of this volume to realize that current criticisms of existentialist and liberal conceptions of human existence centering on the naked will owe a debt to Iris Murdoch. Once a student of Sartrean existentialism, Murdoch nevertheless launched one of the first challenges to existentialism within ethics. Yet in doing so, Murdoch did not follow the path of other prominent challenges to existentialist thought, notably that of Martin Heidegger and, more recently, deconstructionism, which turn against any humanistic concern. Rather, Murdoch reopened the question of the relation of the self and the Good seen in Platonic ethics while insisting, with liberals and existentialists, on the moral importance of the individual person. As several of the essays here show, Murdoch's work on moral subjectivity and the individual remains central in current ethics.

The second line of significance in Murdoch's thought follows closely on her claims about the human person and the Good. Against those forms of ethics that insist that morality is something we invent to serve social purposes and that the "Good" is likewise a matter of utility, Murdoch has insisted on the *reality* of the Good. As a moral realist, she argues for the ontological necessity of the Good in ways reminiscent of arguments for the existence of God.

While realism in ethics has been challenged throughout this century, owing in large measure to the importance of language and cultural diversity in the moral life, there is now a resurgence of interest in moral realism. In this respect, Murdoch again anticipated important developments in current ethics. For her, the Good is a necessarily real, magnetic force which draws the self beyond itself in moral concern for concrete other individuals. In making this claim Murdoch not only reopens the question of the status of the Good within the moral life, but also reasserts the importance of the connection between morals and metaphysics. Again, several essays in this book address this theme of moral realism and thus testify to the continuing significance of Murdoch's work.

The final line of significance in Murdoch's work we must note is closely linked to those already mentioned. It has been virtually axiomatic of modern moral philosophy that ethics is autonomous of religious claims and beliefs. Murdoch has in one important respect challenged this assumption. Her understanding of the moral life as focusing on the improvement of life, and thus about some idea of perfection, is consonant with the claims of religious traditions. Thus, while Murdoch rejects a theistic ground to moral philosophy, she nevertheless insists on the importance of various religious ideas and practices in the moral life. Ethics depends on the Good, not God, and yet the moral life needs the aid of traditional forms of religious practice, such as meditation and prayer. Essays in this volume also address the relation between theology and ethics and thereby continue the debate about the connection between religion and morality that spans the long history of Western ethics.

Thus, Murdoch anticipated many developments in contemporary ethics while simultaneously reopening issues in the history of ethics. Her own moral philosophy centers on the individual in relation to the Good, an individual who must undergo nothing less than a spiritual journey in order to become morally better. In developing an ethics capable of presenting this moral vision, Murdoch has engaged debates about the nature of human existence, the meaning and nature of the Good, and, finally, the connection between morality and the divine. Each of these issues is addressed in the essays collected in this volume. In this respect, the essays not only provide careful readings of Murdoch's work, but also ad-

Introduction

vance current thought on a variety of topics. In order to clarify this last point, it is important to recount in more detail some of the main lines of Murdoch's argument in her recent *Metaphysics as a Guide to Morals*.[1] More than any other single book, this work provides the background for the essays of this volume. After reviewing this important work, it will be possible to clarify the structure and purpose of the essays found in this book.

II. METAPHYSICS AND MORALS

Metaphysics as a Guide to Morals is a revised and expanded version of Murdoch's 1982 Gifford Lectures. It is a brilliant, erudite, but sprawling work that proceeds reflectively through an enormous range of topics, including art and religion, morals and politics, metaphysics, imagination, thinkers such as Schopenhauer, Wittgenstein, and Martin Buber, and even deconstructionism. What Murdoch has given us is not a systematic treatise, but what can be described, using her own words, as a "a huge hall of reflection full of light and space and fresh air, in which ideas and intuitions can be unsystematically nurtured" (p. 422). In our judgment, the text is nothing less than a "guide" for a journey which begins with the place of images and pictures in human existence since humans are unique image-making animals (chaps. 1–5), through the dynamics of moral consciousness and the inner life (chaps. 6–12), to matters of the source and status of morality, the reality of the Good, and also the fragility of life or void (chaps. 13–19). Throughout this journey, there is a complex engagement with the problem of how we "picture" ourselves and our world with respect to the moral life and the reality of the Good. This understanding of the text is perfectly consistent with Murdoch's entire corpus. She has always held that metaphysics involves the creation of imaginative concepts and images to guide our reflection on persons and the moral life. It is important to note that the theme of the relation between the imaginary and morality is explored throughout the essays in this book, particularly in the contributions of Martha Nussbaum and Elizabeth Dipple.

---

1. New York: Allen Lane/Penguin Press, 1993.

Murdoch's approach to the question of metaphysics and ethics is complex and has preoccupied her throughout her career. In an early essay titled "Metaphysics and Ethics,"[2] written during her years at Oxford and included here as an appendix to this volume, she criticized the "elimination of metaphysics from ethics" that has characterized British moral theory since G. E. Moore. With one stroke, Moore not only abandoned metaphysics but reaffirmed David Hume's insight that naturalism—the attempt to move from a description of facts to a conclusion about their value—was a fallacy. Murdoch's magnum opus, *Metaphysics as a Guide to Morals*, can be seen in part as an extended, albeit indirect, response to the "naturalistic fallacy," which has virtually defined the practice of moral philosophy in this century by sharply distinguishing fact and value. Indeed, one of the central arguments of *Metaphysics as a Guide to Morals* is that the segregation of fact and value, while originally intended "to guarantee the *purity* of value and the *accuracy* of fact" (p. 50), has eclipsed "an obvious and important aspect of human existence, the way in which almost all of our concepts and activities involve evaluation" (pp. 25–26). Moral reflection, in Murdoch's view, does not consist of two independent operations: first, a neutral description of the facts and, second, a rational assessment of their value. Rather, "in the majority of cases, a survey of the facts will itself involve moral discrimination" (p. 26). The question of fact and value as well as the valuing activity of the self are also addressed in this volume by a number of authors, notably Cora Diamond and Maria Antonaccio.

Readers of Murdoch's earlier collection of philosophical essays, *The Sovereignty of Good*,[3] will recognize this familiar and compelling argument against rationalist and other moral theories, such as existentialism, which treat the Good as a "choosing tag of the will" rather than as the necessary condition for the possibility of moral choice. In *Metaphysics as a Guide to Morals* it becomes clearer that Murdoch is appealing explicitly to a transcendental argument about the Good to defeat the segregation of fact from value. The Good, in other words, is not a "label" that we apply

---

2. In *The Nature of Metaphysics*, ed. D. F. Pears (London: Macmillan, 1960).
3. London and New York: Routledge, 1970.

Introduction   *xvii*

to persons, actions, events, or things according to our choices or preferences. Rather, the Good is—in the Platonic image of the Sun that has dominated Murdoch's ethics—the *light* in which human moral existence is lived and evaluations and choices are made. This argument for the inescapable presence of value in human life is set forth most directly in two chapters on the ontological proof and represents what Murdoch considers to be the indispensable metaphysical dimension of human life. Metaphysics *guides* morals, Murdoch believes, by helping us to picture the way in which morality and evaluation are omnipresent in human life. Once again, essays included in this volume address the question of metaphysics in ethics and also the status of the claims about the Good in the moral life, in particular the contributions by Franklin I. Gamwell and Charles Taylor.

It would be misleading, however, to treat *Metaphysics as a Guide to Morals* solely as a work in moral theory. For Murdoch also seeks to rehabilitate metaphysical reflection about the moral life by drawing both religion and art into close relation with metaphysics. Metaphysics and religion resemble each other, Murdoch believes, in that they treat the "deep structure" of human existence; that is, they treat what is absolute, necessary, or essential in human life and seek to "picture" it by means of concepts, images, or mythical explanations. In this sense, both metaphysics and religion live off the natural image-making capacity of human beings. The danger of metaphysics and religion, a danger long recognized by Platonists of all sorts, is that, like all "image-play," they can be used either to illuminate the deep truth about human life or to perpetuate consoling illusions. The demand of Murdoch's ethical position is that we resist these false consolations as much as possible and strive to make our theories and beliefs answerable to the truth, that is, to the real, which is the sole criterion of the Good. Here, too, the essays included in this volume, particularly those of David Tracy, Stanley Hauerwas, and William Schweiker, explore the relation between metaphysics and religion and are attentive to the place of beliefs, symbols, and narratives in human life, culture, and religious communities.

Murdoch's awareness of the potential dangers of the attempt to seek metaphysical unity where there is in reality none leads her to reflect on two countervailing impulses that challenge metaphysical reflection: *empiricism* (which in political philosophy takes the form of a utilitarian concern for happiness rather than a metaphysical inquiry into goodness as such), and what we might call *negation* (what Murdoch calls "Void"), which is the radical *absence* of Good (empirical or metaphysical) in life. Empiricism challenges the abstract theorizing of metaphysics with a reminder of the ordinary details of lived human experience and the obviousness of certain truths. Philosophy, Murdoch believes, does in fact require not only elaborate theories and "ambitious synthesis," but also "piecemeal analysis, modesty and commonsense," which preserve the particular, contingent, and the individual from absorption into any kind of totalizing theoretical framework. In *Metaphysics as a Guide to Morals*, Murdoch insists that the "life of morality and truth exists within an irreducible incompleteness" (p. 490). In this respect, she attempts to honor the empiricist insight without collapsing metaphysical inquiry into itself.

In contrast to the empiricist challenge, metaphysical ethics also faces the challenge of what Murdoch simply calls "Void," a term she borrows from Simone Weil to refer to the extreme affliction brought about by the total absence of Good in one's life. The experience of Void is in effect a limit-experience for any metaphysics of the Good. It raises the question, "Can one go on talking about a spiritual source and an absolute Good if a majority of human kind is debarred from it?" (p. 499). Metaphysics may founder on the bald fact that "the average inhabitant of the planet is probably without hope and starving" (p. 498). Further, the category of Void brings out the essential paradox of metaphysics as a means of *picturing* the deep aspects of human existence. For metaphysical theorizing faces the conundrum of every effort of human thinking (art, philosophy, theology) to capture the nature of ultimate reality in language, concept, or symbol. Murdoch thus poses the familiar problem of any *via negativa* in reflection in an effort to show us, as she does in all of her work, that whatever theories may tell us, what is most real always exceeds or resists our descriptions of it. Here, too, she acknowledges the point about negation in human life and thought without thereby abandoning metaphysical inquiry. Virtually all of the essays in this volume address this problem, and, moreover, they do so out of passionate concern to speak of the Good in a time of global need, suffering, and struggle for hope. In this respect, the essays link theoretical inquiry with deep moral conviction and concern, as Murdoch herself does. *Metaphysics as a Guide to Morals* in its breadth and richness is thus an extended inquiry into the author's favorite topics. Yet this inquiry, as these essays show, is important, indeed crucial, for current moral and religious reflection. More than many contemporary moralists, Murdoch leads us through arenas of moral reflection while at the same time urging the reader, urging us, to understand this inquiry as a moral journey, a journey meant to make us better. And in this respect, too, the works presented in this book are concerned not only with broad matters of ethics, that is, moral philosophical reflection, but also with the moral life itself.

III. THE CONTENTS OF THIS BOOK

As we have already indicated, the essays address basic themes in the work of Iris Murdoch with the purpose of advancing current thought. They present forays, as it were, into Murdoch's thought from distinct but related perspectives. Taken together they provide a comprehensive account of Murdoch's literary and philosophical corpus as well as chart directions for thought influenced by her work. The advantage to the reader, then, is that she or he can enter this text through the door of any one essay or theme and then read more widely by tracing connections in Murdoch's thought and among the essayists. The volume has been structured to aid in this kind of reading.

Part 1 of the book addresses issues in the history of thought. It is thematically structured around issues in moral philosophy (Taylor), the relation of literature and ethics (Nussbaum), and religion and theology (Tracy). In this respect, Part 1 examines the main themes of the whole book while locating Murdoch's work and the individual authors' inquiries in the history of thought. Part 2 turns directly to issues in ethics and literature. Here there is an inquiry into the problem of fact and value (Diamond), an essay on the relation between Murdoch's ethics and her understanding of literature (Antonaccio), and, finally, an examination of Murdoch's literary corpus with respect to the imaginary (Dipple). Finally, Part 3 explores the connection between metaphysics and religion in terms of the metaphysical status of theism (Gamwell), the use of Murdoch's thought in Christian ethics (Hauerwas), and the moral meaning of the symbol "God" (Schweiker).

This book then is itself a "huge hall of reflection" that the reader is invited to explore. The three parts just indicated, while structurally useful, should not conceal the fact that common themes run throughout essays in various parts of the book and, indeed, the book as a whole. We have attempted to indicate some of these basic themes in this introduction. This book, like Murdoch's thought, has an "unsystematic" coherence with respect to basic themes and concerns pertaining to the ways in which we can, do, and must picture the human.

IV. Conclusion

It is our pleasure to be able to publish this collection of essays. It is often said that contemporary thinkers have abandoned the attempt to understand human life and provide guidance for living as persons and communities in favor of addressing the particular questions arising within the guild of scholars. As a philosopher and artist, Iris Murdoch does in fact continue the age-old quest for understanding, the love of wisdom. So, too, the essays collected in this book, inspired by Murdoch's tenacious wrestling with basic human questions, seek to strike beyond the confines of the academy in thinking about how we ought to see ourselves and how we can and ought to undertake the human adventure.

PART ONE

ISSUES IN THE HISTORY OF THOUGHT

I
IRIS MURDOCH AND MORAL PHILOSOPHY

Charles Taylor

I

I cannot pretend to give an account of Iris Murdoch's contribution to moral philosophy, much less sum it up or give some verdict on it. Her contribution is much too rich, and we are much too close to it. What I want to do, instead, is talk in a more personal vein and say what Dame Iris's work has meant for me. This is inevitably going to be idiosyncratic, and Dame Iris may not recognize herself in my remarks. But I think it does touch on some important issues.

Dame Iris's work had meaning for me partly as someone involved in the world of analytic philosophy. This world has lots of good qualities. But one of its drawbacks is a tendency to narrowness on certain questions. And one of the most marked sites of this narrowness was in moral philosophy. The narrowness concerns more than just the range of doctrines considered, though it also consists in that. But, more fundamentally, it has restricted the range of questions that it seems sensible to ask. In the end it restricted our understanding of what morality is. I have tried to sum this up by saying that Anglo-Saxon moral philosophy has tended to see morality as concerned with questions of what we ought to do and to occlude or exclude questions about what it is good to be or what it is good to love. The focus is on obligatory action, which means that it turns away from issues in which obligation is not really the issue, as well as those where not just actions but ways of life or ways of being are what we have to weigh. Another shorthand way of putting this point is that this philosophy tended to restrict itself to the "right" at the expense of the "good." If issues of the good life were allowed, independent of the issue of what is right, they were seen as a second zone of practical consideration, lacking the urgency and high priority of the moral. (Jürgen Habermas has formulated this priority, which shows that this philosophical temper has gone beyond the Anglo-Saxon world.)

From within this narrow perspective, it could seem that moral philosophy had two main intellectual tasks: (1) to try to work out exactly what the considerations are which tell us which action is right and (2) to try to show that these are the right considerations, against other rival candidates. The first has a place because our sense of what is right starts off fuzzy and powerful, with strong but unclear intuitions; it stands in need of clarification. The second task is the exercise of founding. It is not surprising that within this philosophical climate, the two main contenders were utilitarianism and Kant. For some writers, the main philosophical debate seems to be between these two outlooks. John Rawls, in some sense inspired by Kant, seemed to assume in his original *Theory of Justice* that the rival he had to defeat was utilitarianism. The rest of the philosophical universe was given much shorter shrift. These two schools are popular because they do come up with clear answers to (1) and (2). Moreover, in each case, the answer to the first has the intellectually satisfying property of being a single criterion. Morality can be derived from one source.

Now a countermovement has begun in analytical philosophy in recent years. To some extent, it is the revenge of Nietzsche (Bernard Williams is important here). In another way, it reflects a return of Aristotle. In either case, it wants to restore the wider focus. One way of stating this is to introduce the stipulative distinction, whereby "morality" is used for the narrower domain concerned with obligatory action, and "ethics" for the wider domain, including issues of what is a good or worthwhile life. The influence of Nietzsche is at work here, but using this vocabulary does not mean we have to reject morality; it can be seen as a legitimate part of the larger domain of ethics. What it cannot be anymore for the users of this vocabulary is the whole, or the one ultimately serious domain of the practical, trumping all others.

Iris Murdoch was criticizing the narrowness of moral philosophy well before the present counterwave—and not entirely on the same grounds. Indeed, her reflections would lead us to make a further extension of the ethical, beyond those proposed by neo-Nietzscheans and neo-Aristotelians. Put briefly, while these take us beyond morality to issues about the good life, they stop there. Murdoch seems to me to take this first step, but then one further. Beyond obligatory action, she opens up the question of what it is good to be. But she takes this beyond the question of a good and satisfying life to the consideration of a good which would be beyond life, in the sense that its goodness cannot be entirely or exhaustively explained in terms of its contributing to a fuller, better, richer, more satisfying human life. It is a good that we might sometimes more appropriately respond to in suffering and death, rather than in fullness and life—the domain, as usually understood, of religion.

Put another way, in the terms I suggested above, this takes us beyond the question of what we ought to do to that of what it is good to be, and then beyond that again, to what can command our fullest love. (But I'm already sneaking in a Christian rather than a Buddhist discourse here. There is a disagreement between Dame Iris and me about this, which I want to return to later.) I would like to use an image here: We were trapped in the corral of morality. Murdoch led us out not only to the broad fields of ethics but also beyond that again to the almost untracked forests of the unconditional. (Forest is a Buddhist image.) I want to talk about these two stages, more about the first, because I understand it better, but also some about the second, because there lie many important questions which Murdoch has opened up for us.

II

Let me start with the first liberation: from morality to ethics, from the narrow corral to the wider pasture. In order to liberate ourselves fully, we have to understand what was going for the narrow focus on morality. Two important orders of reason converged to encourage the shift: One was moral, one epistemological.

One can still sense the force of the moral reasons in the rhetoric of contemporary philosophers. If one objects to a utilitarian that one might legitimately put, say, one's own integrity before the obligation to do the act which has the highest utility consequences, one invites the retort that one is self-indulgent and not really singlemindedly committed to human happiness, as one ought to be. We can see here in secularized form the traces of the Christian origins of this philosophy. If Aristotelian ethics starts with the question of what constitutes a good and worthwhile life, and then raises the issue of what one owes to others within this frame, it has seemed to a certain Christian temper, present in all ages but particularly strong during the Reformation and early modern period, that the demands of charity are unconditional, that they override fulfillment. Concentrate not on your own condition, but on practical benevolence.

This temper was strengthened by the cultural revolution which I have called the affirmation of ordinary life, which dethroned the supposedly higher activities of contemplation and the civic life and put the center of gravity of goodness in ordinary living, production, and the family. It belongs to this spiritual outlook that our first concern ought to be to increase life, relieve suffering, foster prosperity. Concern above all for the fullness of life smacked of pride, of self-absorption. And beyond that, it was inherently not egalitarian, since the alleged "higher" activities could only be carried out by an elite minority, whereas leading one's ordinary life rightly was open to everyone.

There is a moral temper to which it seems obvious that our major concern must be our dealings with others, in justice and benevolence; and these dealings must be on a level of equality. One can emphasize more justice (Kantians) or benevolence (utilitarians), but there is a shared perspective which is inimical to the ancient primacy of ethics and which draws us powerfully to the corral.

The second motive is epistemological. It concerns the demands of disengaged reason. I mean here self-monitoring reason, reasoning which can turn on its own proceedings and examine them for accuracy and reliability. We can scrutinize these proceedings to any degree of clarity, even up to the undeniably binding.

This is the great contribution of Descartes, which he expressed in terms of *les idées claires et distinctes*. Disengaged reason is opposed to uses of reason which try to get a good purchase on some domain analogous to perception, but also to discerning the qualities of a piece of music, being able to tell what people are about, how they stand to the matter and to you, and so on. We do not tend to call these "reason," but they have analogies to *to logistikon* of Plato. Disengaged reason means that we cease to rely on our engaged sense, our familiarity with some domain, and take a reflexive turn. We put our trust in a method, a procedure of operation. The sense of freedom and power which goes with this is part of the motivation. This move connects with the primacy of instrumental reason.

In this outlook, the prospect of a single criterion is very exciting. At last the fuzzy intuitions of common sense can be reduced to clarity. What is more, all incommensurabilities, and, hence, difficult decisions, can be ironed out. Utilitarianism both satisfies demand for rigor and homogeneity and also fits well with the disengaged stance of instrumental reason. Think of the rhetorical self-portrayal of disengaged reason, daring to withdraw from the hold of sacred hierarchies, to stand back from them, and assess them coldly, in the light of how much *good* they do. And this good can be clearly measured. Here clarity, rigor, disengagement, and also philanthropy come together. But Kantianism also gets a charge from being rigorous and homogeneous. Part of the immense success of Rawls's *Theory of Justice* when it was first published came from this sense that after all it showed that rigorous modes of reasoning (e.g., game theory) can be of use in ethics.

So we have the complex standing behind morality: the primacy of justice-benevolence with equality, and also disengaged reason, rigor, clarity. Single-term moralities offer us a homogeneous, calculable domain of moral considerations. This seems right to their protagonists (1) because the exaltation of justice-benevolence over issues of fulfillment and the good life simplifies the domain of the moral and (2) because the calculability fits with the dominant models of disengaged reason. Now there is reason to think that principle (2) is not a cogent *argument* but, rather, a good cultural *explanation* for the popularity of single-term theories. Principle (1) is questionable, but one might find it convincing in some form. Even so, this is not a good ground for holding to single-criterion moralities, because even if you grant (1), you still cannot simply put *all* questions to do with justice-benevolence in a single category, to be decided without reference to any external considerations. You cannot just say, as Kant does with his categorical imperative, this set of considerations *always* has priority. This would exclude all questions of importance and put the most trivial demands of justice-benevolence over the most weighty of fulfillment.

Principle (1) is *one* sense that can be given to the slogan, "The right has priority over the good." And analogies and close relations emerge in political theory. So, for example, we entrench rights and we say: Protecting these takes precedence over all other considerations, for example, of the public good, happiness, and so forth. A project is being pursued in this entrenchment which we would all agree with. That is, with really essential rights, there should not be any derogation for mere advantage: No one should condemn an innocent person, or torture someone, or deprive people of the right to speak their minds just because the gross national product will go up or because most people will have more satisfying lives, or live in greater security. But these provisions have to be applied with a sense of how to distinguish the important from the trivial. One of the cases fought under the Canadian Charter of 1982, which won in first instance, was by a man who objected to the Alberta law requiring the wearing of a seat belt.

There are also other reasons for adopting single-term moralities. These deal with (3) questions of fairness and justice between people. And these seem to many people more clear-cut, more capable of satisfying and unchallengeable solution than issues about fulfillment and the good life. These latter seem to allow an indefinite proliferation of possible solutions, whereas issues of justice seem to allow for clear-cut resolution. Anybody can fantasize about possible fulfillments: I can decide that I ought to spend my life like Simon Stylites atop a pillar. Are you sure you can tell me I am wrong? But I cannot just decide that I need your car, and that makes it all right for me to take it. Whether there is anything at all to this, plainly it is what people think. No one thought Rawls was out of his mind to try to decide between different principles of justice with the aid of rational choice theory. (Correction: Some of us did question this, but we were a distinct minority, as the Rawls boom showed.) But people would have been stunned if he had proposed to settle in this way questions of the good life. Modern Western culture has made issues of epistemology central, and this has generated some skepticism about morality. But the skeptical sense falls unequally on the different kinds of considerations. Questions of the good life are more easily declared insoluble than those of justice.

Another reason for distinguishing justice from the good life concerns (4) our respect for people's freedom, another central good of modern Western culture. Determining what constitutes the good life means being able to tell people that they are mistaken when they propose another model for themselves. This is the reason for part of the suspicion of Aristotle among moderns. He is telling us that a certain way of life is the truly human one. That means that people who live other ways are declared wrong. It is thought that a real respect for their autonomy requires being agnostic on their way of life, allowing them the space to design their own lives without forfeiting the respect and even support of their fellows. But plainly this courtesy cannot be extended to issues of justice, as the point above about my needing your car shows. Moral restrictions intervene where we have to direct the traffic between people seeking to fulfill life plans, and give everybody a chance. However, these restrictions ought not intervene *within* the itinerary of any one agent. So a morality showing respect for freedom (itself an issue of justice) will make a sharp distinction between questions of justice and those of the good life, and will moralize the first and leave the second unregulated And so we generate the single-term moralities concerned with justice-benevolence. Clearly (4) is in a relation of mutual support with (3).

There is a variant of (4) which returns as a principle of political theory. Someone may deny (3) as a principle of ethics, that is, they can think that there are universal truths about the good life. Some people are wrong, and are living tawdry and contemptible lives, and we are perfectly at liberty to tell them so. Nevertheless, these thinkers hold (5) that political society must give everyone the space to develop on his or her own, and that this society should not espouse one or another view of the good life. R. M. Dworkin holds something like this. This is a political transposition of a single-term morality. It is a basic definition of liberal society for some, but it does not require that these people hold to a single-term morality.

Staying with moral theory—hence leaving aside (5)—it does not seem to me that (3) or (4) do anything to make single-term moralities more plausible. Indeed, (4) may be thought to be incoherent. If there is a real issue of what is the good life for some person X—and why would there be a reason to take seriously his decisions on it if it weren't?—then why can he not be wrong? But these reasons help explain something else about these theories: their thinness. They have a narrow view of what morality is as a dimension of human life.

Let us try to get at this issue by taking up the question, What is involved in being a moral agent? Everyone would probably agree that a moral agent is sensitive to, responding to, certain considerations, the ones we think of as moral; or, an agent who is capable of responding to these considerations. To speak a dialect of Heideggerese, the agent has moral meanings in his or her world. So what is it to have these meanings? Much contemporary Anglo-Saxon moral philosophy concentrates on the agent's having a sense that she or he ought to do certain things. The focus is on what we are obliged to do. The intellectual interest concentrates on getting clear what the things we are obliged to do have in common. One theory says that they all involve maximizing human happiness; another says that they all involve our not acting on maxims which are not universalizable. Another way of putting this is: Philosophy is seeking here a way of deriving our obligations, seeking a test by which we can see what we are morally obliged to do.

But ethics involves more than what we are obligated to do. It also involves what it is good to be. This is clear when we think of other considerations than those arising from our obligations to others, questions of the good life and human fulfillment. But this other dimension is there even when we are talking about our obligations to others. The sense that such and such is an action we are obligated by justice to perform cannot be separated from a sense that being just is a good way to be. If we had the first without any hint of the second, we would be dealing with a compulsion, like the neurotic necessity to wash one's hands or to remove stones from the road. A moral obligation comes across as moral because it is part of a broader sense which includes the goodness, perhaps the nobility or admirability, of being someone who lives up to it. The obligation to do and the goodness in being are two facets, as it were, of the same sense. Each totally without the other would be something very different from our moral sense: a mere compulsion on one hand, a detached sense of the superiority of one way over another, on the other hand, comparable to my aesthetic appreciation of cumulus over nimbus clouds, not making any demands on me as an agent. Contemporary philosophy has explored one facet at length but has said almost nothing about the other. But this too can be articulated; more can be said about the goodness of different ways of being. Traditionally, philosophical theory has explored this in the language of virtue. But even more important for our moral consciousness has been the portrayal of good and bad lives in exemplary figures and stories. Our moral understanding would be crippled if we had to do without such portrayals. Christian moral theology without the Gospel would be an even stranger affair than it is. Nevertheless, this whole domain of the articulation of the good, whether philosophical or narrative, has been relatively neglected in Anglo-Saxon moral philosophy. Why?

One answer could be the hard-headed reason that we do not need to explore this in order to know what to do. Philosophy should help us clarify obligation. So finding out that what really makes an action obligatory is that it furthers the general happiness is really useful stuff. Just being more articulate about the kind of good person you are when you do this adds nothing. It is a form of self-indulgence. But this will not really stand up. We often need to be clearer on the goods involved in order to deliberate well. Take the domain favored by single-term morality itself: justice-benevolence. There is an internal tension that can arise here, between the two terms. The issue can arise: When should we override justice in the name of benevolence? Should we ever override it at all? Traditionally put, this is the issue of justice versus mercy. To answer these questions, we may find ourselves looking at what kind of good it is to be a just person and what it is to be benevolent. We will be thinking of how to place these two virtues in our lives. This is the case, a fortiori, when it is a matter of thinking how to combine justice-benevolence and the virtues of fulfillment or of the good life. The belief that all the moral deliberation we need can be effected with a calculus of obligated action is another illusion of the erroneous single-term moralities, and only makes sense on condition that their homogeneous domain exhausts the moral. Ethical thinking, to use this term for the broader domain, sometimes also requires deliberation about what it is good to be in order to determine what to do in certain circumstances.

An example is inspired by some arguments of Bernard Williams. Let us say that the course of action with the highest utility consequences clashes with that which my integrity would demand. I am minister of forests in the red-green coalition government. I am also head of the Green party. I am reluctantly persuaded that the least bad course of action really available in the situation is to chain-saw a section of rain forest. But I ask the Prime Minister to relieve me of my portfolio. Let someone else do the deed. Deciding this involves weighing not just actions and their consequences but also qualities of being, that is, assessing the action also by how it fits into a whole life, constituted not only of other actions but also of feelings, commitments, solidarities, and so forth. The same order of considerations is in play if you think that I am just indulging my image here and ought to take responsibility for what has to be done. In either case, I need to get clear on what it is good to be and how important this is relative to the other considerations in play.

Single-term morality perpetrates a drastic foreshortening of our moral world, by concentrating only on what we are obligated to do. But the reduction is even more drastic than I have described hitherto. I spoke of the things it is good to be, of virtues as "life goods" in *Sources of the Self*.[1] I also distinguished there what I called "constitutive goods." By that I mean features of ourselves, or the world, or God, such that their being what they are is essential to the life goods being good. Examples in well-known traditional views are: God having created us and calling us is a constitutive good for Judaeo-Christian-Islamic theism; the Idea of the Good is one such for Plato; for Aristotle, our being animals having logos is one. In these well-understood traditional ethics, articulat-

---

1. Cambridge: Harvard University Press, 1989, chap. 4.

ing the life goods quite naturally leads to spelling out the constitutive goods. And, moreover, getting clear on these helps to define more clearly and vividly the life goods. This is obvious in the theistic case, where among the most important life goods are the love and worship of God. But we can also see it in Plato, where a deeper understanding of the life dominated by reason has to pass through attaining a vision of the Idea of the Good. The truly good person is inspired to model himself or herself on the order shaped by the Good. Similarly, for Aristotle we come to see better how to order the goods in our lives when we understand that we are animals possessing logos.

Now it might be thought that constitutive goods figure only in theistic or metaphysical ethics, that they have no place in a modern humanistic outlook. But this would be a mistake. In a modern humanistic ethic, the locus of the constitutive good is displaced onto the human being itself. In Kant, the sense of the dignity of human life, as rational agency soaring above everything else in the universe, is an example of the identification of a constitutive good in a humanist ethic. My claim is that something like this sense of the dignity and value of human life, of the nobility of rational freedom, underpins the ethical consciousness of our contemporaries and plays the two roles we can see it occupying in Kant's philosophy: it defines why the human being commands our respect when she or he is the object of our action; and it sets us an ideal for our own action.

And just as defining the virtues helps us to deliberate, understanding better as we do what it is good to be, so this understanding can be further aided by clarifying the constitutive goods. We help to clarify what it is good to be by getting clearer on just what is noble or admirable about the human potential. Here again, we have two facets of the same exploration. On one, we are defining the virtues, the qualities of life we want to have; on the other, we are looking at what is, the human being endowed with its potential in its world, and taking inspiration from what we find worthy in this. There is, indeed, an important difference from the earlier theological or metaphysical ethics, insofar as on this second facet these incorporated elements which go beyond human potential, for example, God or the Good. But there is also a substantial overlap, and thinking on these two facets remains part of our moral understanding. We are in some way *moved* by human powers; this forms part of the moral meanings in our world, along with our sense of what it is good to be, and what we ought to do—just as the theist is moved by the love of God.

The foreshortened single-term morality misses not only life goods but constitutive goods. It neglects not just the unarticulated know-how but misses a lot of what we need to articulate in order to know what to do. But there is an even more serious omission. I have been talking mainly as though the point of articulation were to help one see what to do. But some of our articulations not only help us to define better what we want to be and do, they also move us, as I have just indicated. Articulating a constitutive good not only helps us fine-tune what we want to be and do, it also inspires and moves us to want to be and do it. And articulating the virtues can have a similar effect. This is nowhere more evident than in the recounting of the models and paradigms, exemplary people and actions, in real life or story, which both inspire and guide us. Both functions frequently come together in these narrations, which also involve articulating goods of both kinds. Exemplary figures body forth life goods, but in some cases—the Gospels, the life of the Buddha—part of what is being conveyed is a constitutive good.

Moreover, these two functions are in part interdependent. Seeing better what a certain good involves can change your stance towards it—in either direction, of course. It may increase or decrease your attachment to it. Even more important, appreciating what is good about a good can be an essential condition of making finer discriminations about what it means to realize it. This is the point made by Aristotle when he holds that the *phronimos* has to have the right dispositions in order to discern the good. Bad moral dispositions do not destroy our understanding of mathematics, he says, but they do weaken our grasp of the *arche* or starting points of moral deliberation.[2] To put it in more Platonic language, in many situations really to know what to do you have to love the good, and there is thus something self-defeating in confining ethics to the issue of what to do.

---

2. Aristotle, *Ethics* VI, 1140b10–20.

If we give the full range of ethical meanings their due, we can see that the fullness of ethical life involves not just doing, but also being; and not just these two but also loving (which is shorthand here for being moved by, being inspired by) what is constitutively good. It is a drastic reduction to think that we can capture the moral by focussing only on obligated action, as though it were of no ethical moment what you are and what you love. These are the essence of ethical life.

One of the reasons for shying away from all this, besides the many enumerated above, is the confused inarticulacy of modern naturalism. This comes from a deep reticence in talking about foundations and an inability to determine how to talk about them (which obviously strengthens the reticence). After clarifying what we ought to do, utilitarians and contemporary neo-Kantians are left uncertain how to talk about the basis for accepting the whole range of obligations. Sometimes they just shift into another register, like John Mackie,[3] and give a sociobiological account of how it is understandable that we have the norms we do. But that is not articulating the good, because it in no way makes clearer what is good or admirable about what we seek; it just tries to explain in a quasi-scientific way why we seek it. (Although sometimes it is confusedly taken in the latter manner, and then becomes part of the support for a reductive instrumentalist ethic.) Some writers just terminate with the brute fact that our intuitions are what they are.

This is partly because of a confusion about what arguing "foundations" could be. This word is bad, because it implies something to the philosophical ear which is impossible. It implies that you could argue someone who shared absolutely no moral sense at all into morality. "Foundations" means you would have to take him from point zero of moral commitment to the full sweep of obligations you generate by your calculus. This cannot be done, but there is no reason to think that it ought to be, that something terrible is missing because it cannot be.[4] The point of articulating our moral

---

3. *Ethics* (Harmondsworth, Middlesex: Penguin Books, 1977), part 2.
4. I argue this in "Explanation and Practical Reason," in *The Quality of Life*, ed. Martha Nussbaum and Amartya Sen (Oxford: Clarendon Press), 1993.

sense cannot be to provide foundations in this sense, though it can be a very powerful tool in real moral argument. The famous line from Dostoevsky, "If God does not exist, then everything is permitted," is often taken as an assertion that foundations have to be given. If I think God does not exist, I feel I can do anything; then you convince me he does, and I suddenly see that there are moral limits. But I think the sentence can be taken as a statement of the constitutive good that someone (Dostoevsky?) recognizes, without supporting a foundationalist view. What is the difference?

Articulating the good is in a way providing reasons, but not in either of the senses which are generally recognized by much contemporary moral philosophy. Let me outline the two senses. The first is giving a basic reason. I want to speak of a basic reason where we argue for doing A on the grounds that it amounts to doing B, and where this justification is asymmetrical. Basic reasons parallel the structure of purposive action. I am phoning George. You ask why? Because he is going to give me a job. Why do I want a job? Because I need the income to live. The action has several descriptions: (1) phoning George, (2) getting a job, (3) finding the means to live. But these are not on the same footing. The description (3) is basic; I only go for (2) because it amounts in this situation to (3), and similarly with (1). If I could live on the dole or find a job some other way, I would not be phoning. It is one of the self-given tasks of much modern moral theory to identify a basic reason in this sense. Pursuing the greatest happiness of the greatest number is one such. The minister of finance is (1) balancing the budget. She is (quite properly in this context) operating under utilitarian principles, so she is doing it (2) in order to reduce inflation, because (3) she believes that reduced inflation will increase economic well-being. Reason (3) is the basic reason. If you convince her that the conjuncture requires a return to Keynesian policies, she will run a deficit.

So one way of arguing for something is giving a basic reason. But when you have identified the basic reason, and your interlocutor is not moved by it, where do you go from there? It seems you have to set yourself another task: giving him that basic reason, that is, bringing it about that he takes on that basic reason as his own. Now you need to give reasons of the foundationalist sort. But the articulation of life and constitutive goods is reason-giving in neither of the above senses. It does not give a basic reason for a policy described in less-than-basic terms, as increasing economic welfare does for balancing the budget. The two descriptions, pre- and post-articulation, of some life or constitutive good are not related in this way. One gives a fuller, more vivid, or clearer, better defined understanding of what the good is.

On a theistic view, God's will does not stand to loving my neighbor as (3) does to (2) and (1) in the examples above. Or, rather, it does so only in the rather warped Occamite theologies which caused such havoc in early modern thought. In this view, the various actions open to us do not have moral value in themselves, but this is only imparted to them by the command of God. On a less strained and alien view (for instance, Thomist, but not only Thomist), invoking God's will is further expanding what is good about this, which I initially grasp as good by natural reason. So you do not articulate a basic reason here. Nor can you cause another person to acquire a basic reason from a standing start. You have to draw on the interlocutor's moral understanding. How you can nevertheless carry out argument which can bring the interlocutor over to you, I tried to outline in "Explanation and Practical Reason." The distorted understanding of practical reason is one of the grounds which have moved moral philosophy of a naturalist temper to make both kinds of goods an intellectual no-go area. But there also are confusions about what is entailed in the "antimetaphysical" stance of naturalism itself.

Drawing this together, we can see a link between two main lines of criticism offered here of single-term moralities: (1) their attempt to develop high-definition decision procedures, denying the need for phronesis, and (2) their foreshortening of the moral domain. We see what is wrong with the first when we note that our judgments of what to do take place in the context of a grasp of the good which is largely unarticulated. It consists largely of background understanding. Or else it is presented to us in paradigm persons or actions or in internalized habitus. It can be articulated to some degree in descriptions of the good, and this can be very important, both for our knowing what to do or be and because it can move us to do or be it. But these descriptions are only under-the context of background understanding, acquired habits ⎯digms, which can never be transcended or escaped. When we see what the domain is which permits this articulation, we are induced to burst the boundaries of the foreshortened moral world and recognize the relevance for this world of what we are and love, as well as what we do. We thus conceive the place of articulacy in ethical life very differently. We not only see (1) its restricted scope; but also (2) its plurality of function—not only helping us know what to do but also know what we want to be, and even more crucially makes us love the good; and we similarly see (3) that the forms of articulacy are more widely varied, that philosophical definition is one mode, but that our understanding (including philosophical understanding) would be badly impoverished without moral narrative and admiring attention to exemplars.

III

Now I want to talk, all too briefly, about the second move, from field to forest. It is hard to talk about this, and it is, above all, hard to talk about it clearly and in a recognized common language. The forest is virtually untracked. Or, rather, there are old tracks; they appear on maps which have been handed down to us. But when you get in there, it is very hard to find them. So we need people to make new trails. That is, in effect, what Iris Murdoch has done.

We need, partly, new trails because we have changed. We have grown into a different civilization from our medieval and even early modern forebears. We moderns may differ among ourselves as to what has happened in this phenomenon we call "modernity," but it seems agreed by all that something important has changed. It is as though an earthquake has shifted the fields, and we can no longer enter the forest in the same way. Something like this seems to be Murdoch's assumption in *Metaphysics as a Guide to Morals*, because she frequently refers to what we can no longer believe, what is a thing of the past. She writes, for example, "Our general awareness of good, or goodness, is with us unreflectively all the time, as a sense of God's presence, or at least existence, *used to be* to all sorts of believers" (p. 509, emphasis added).

Now I disagree with Murdoch in her actual conclusions here, particularly her ontological proof of the non-existence of God. ("Any existing God would be less than God. An existent God would be an idol or a demon," p. 508.) But the general idea that today we have to start from somewhere other than where our ancestors did seems to me very right. Just what the difference is, we will disagree on, and this is partly because of our different readings of the change we gesture at with the term "modernity."

But that is not the whole story. We also need new tracks because human beings are different. People are constantly blazing new trails, even in so-called ages of faith. We have to accept as an *ultimate surd* that people find very different ways to God, or the Good, or Nirvana, ways that seem to involve incompatible assumptions (hence the need for some disjunctive expression like the ones I have just used to designate the destination), and yet that these are not simply different destinations, like being clever and being rich, but different attempts to articulate the same call. It is obvious that people of great spiritual depth and dedication and, beyond this, people of holy lives, are drawn to very different paths. Someone who wanted to follow all the people they admire today might be tempted to try to take them all. But this is impossible, in that a fuller spiritual life involves engaging on a path, and they are sufficiently different that one cannot be on more than one. This is not to say that there cannot be selective borrowings, as some Christians have learned from Buddhist meditation techniques. It is just that there remain unbridgeable differences, such as whether your focus is God or the Good.

My contention is that this kind of difference cannot be understood simply as one of pre-modern versus modern, but is another manifestation of that puzzling multiplicity of paths which seems to be a perennial feature of the human condition. Many faiths, not least the one I share in, have spent centuries trying to deny this multiplicity. It is now time to discover, in humility and puzzlement, how we on different paths are also fellow travelers. It is in that spirit that I have found Iris Murdoch's work tremendously helpful and illuminating, as much because of as in spite of our differences. And it is in this spirit that I want to try to bring out part of the difference between us, by giving my own account of

Western modernity in its relation to what one might call faith, or in any case what the image of the forest is meant to convey. I am going to try the impossible and say what this image only gestures at. I can think of three ways, and I am going to start with the one which most runs against the civilization of Western modernity.

Entering the forest is acknowledging that life is not the whole story. There is one way to take this expression, which is as meaning something like: Life goes on after death, there is a continuation, our life does not totally end in our deaths. I do not mean to deny what is affirmed on this reading, but I want to take the expression here in a somewhat different (though perhaps related?) sense. What I mean is something more like: The point of things is not exhausted by life, the fullness of life, even the goodness of life. This is not meant to be just a repudiation of egoism, the idea that the fullness of my life (and perhaps those of people I love) should be my concern. Let us agree with John Stuart Mill that a full life must involve striving for the benefit of humankind. Entering the forest is seeing a point beyond that.

One form of this is the insight that there can be in suffering and death not merely negation, the undoing of fullness and life, but also the affirmation of something which matters beyond life, on which life itself originally draws. The last clause seems to bring us back into the focus on life. It may be readily understandable without leaving the fields how one could accept suffering and death in order to give life to others. In a certain view, that too has been part of the fullness of life. But entering the forest involves something more. What matters beyond life does not matter just because it sustains life; otherwise it wouldn't be "beyond life" in the meaning of the act. (For Christians, God wills human flourishing, but "thy will be done" does not reduce to "let human beings flourish.")

This is the way of putting it which goes most against the grain of contemporary Western civilization. There are other ways of framing it. One which goes back to the very beginning of Christianity is a redefinition of the term life to incorporate what I'm calling beyond life, for example, the New Testament evocations of eternal life, and John 10:10. Or, we could put it in a third way: entering the forest means being called to a change of identity. Buddhism gives us an obvious reason to talk this way. The change here is quite radical, from self to "no-self" (*anatta*). But Christian faith can be seen in the same terms: as calling for a radical decentering of the self in relation with God. ("Thy will be done.") This way of putting it brings out a similar point to my first way, since most conceptions of a flourishing life assume a stable identity, the self for whom flourishing can be defined.

So entering the forest means aiming beyond life or opening yourself to a change in identity. But if you do this, where do you stand in relation to the fields? There is much division, confusion, and uncertainty about this. Historic religions have in fact combined concern for field and forest in their normal practice. It has even been the rule that the supreme achievements of those who went beyond life have served to nourish the fullness of life of those who remain on this side of the barrier. Thus, prayers at the tombs of martyrs brought long life, health, and a whole host of good things for the Christian faithful. Something of the same is true for the tombs of certain saints in Muslim lands, while in Theravada Buddhism, for example, the dedication of monks is turned, through blessings, amulets, and so forth, to all the ordinary purposes of flourishing among the laity.

Against this, there have recurrently been "reformers" in all religions who have considered this symbiotic, complementary relation between renunciation and flourishing to be a travesty. They insist on returning religion to its "purity," and posit for everyone the goals of renunciation from the pursuit of flourishing. Some are even moved to denigrate the latter pursuit altogether, to declare it unimportant or an obstacle to sanctity. But this extreme stance runs athwart a very central thrust in some religions. Christianity and Buddhism will be my examples here. Renouncing, aiming beyond life, not only takes you away but also brings you back to flourishing. In Christian terms, if renunciation decenters you in relation with God, God's will is that humans flourish, and so you are taken back to an affirmation of this flourishing, which is biblically called agape. In Buddhist terms, Enlightenment does not just turn you from the world; it also opens the flood-gates of *metta* (loving kindness) and *karuna* (compassion). There is the Theravada concept of the *Paccekabuddha*, concerned only for his own salvation, but he is ranked below the highest Buddha, who acts for the liberation of all beings. Thus, outside of the stance which accepts the complementary symbiosis of renunciation and flourishings, and beyond the stance of purity, there is a third one, which I could call the stance of *agape/karuna*.

I have gone into this to set the stage for my account of the conflict between modern culture and forest-dwelling. There is going to be some corner-cutting and oversimplification, but I believe that a powerful constitutive strand of modern Western spirituality is involved in an affirmation of life. It is perhaps evident in the contemporary concern to preserve life, to bring prosperity, to reduce suffering world-wide, which is I believe without precedent in history. This arises historically out of the affirmation of ordinary life which I referred to above as a consequence related to, but distinct from, the focus on morality. This affirmation originally was a Christian-inspired move. It exalted practical agape and was polemically directed against the pride, elitism one might say, and self-absorption of those who believed in higher activities or spiritualities. Consider the Reformers' attack on the supposedly "higher" vocations of the monastic life. These were meant to mark out elite paths of superior dedication, but were in fact deviations into pride and self-delusion. The really holy life for the Christian was within ordinary life itself, living in work and the household in a Christian and worshipful manner.

There was an earthly, one might say earthy, critique of the allegedly "higher" here which was then transposed and used as a secular critique of Christianity and, indeed, religion in general. Something of the same rhetorical stance adopted by Reformers against monks and nuns is taken up by secularists and unbelievers against Christian faith itself. This allegedly scorns the real, sensual, earthly human good for some purely imaginary higher end, the pursuit of which can only lead to the frustration of the real, earthly good, to suffering, mortification, repression, and so forth. The motivations of those who espouse this "higher" path are thus, indeed, suspect. Pride, elitism, the desire to dominate play a part in this story too, along with fear and timidity (also present in the earlier Reformers' story, but less prominently). In this critique, of course, religion is identified with the second, purist stance above, or else with a combination of this and the first "symbiotic" (usually labelled "superstitious") stance. The third, the stance of *agape/ karuna*, becomes invisible. That is because a transformed variant of it has in fact been assumed by the secularist critic.

Now one must not exaggerate. This outlook on religion is far from being universal in our society. One might think that this is particularly true in the United States with its high rates of religious belief and practice. And, yet, I want to claim that this whole way of understanding things has penetrated far deeper and wider than simply to card-carrying, village-atheist-style secularists, that it also shapes the outlook of many people who see themselves as believers. What do I mean by this way of understanding? Well, it is a climate of thought, a horizon of assumptions, more than a doctrine. That means that there will be some distortion in the attempt to lay it out in a set of propositions. But I am going to do that anyway, because there is no other way of characterizing it that I know. If it were spelled out in propositions, it would read something like this: (1) that for us life, flourishing, driving back the frontiers of death and suffering are of supreme value, (2) that this was not always so; it was not so for our ancestors and for people in other earlier civilizations; (3) that one of the things which stopped it being so in the past was precisely a sense, inculcated by religion, that there were "higher" goals; (4) that we have arrived at (1) by a critique and overcoming of (this kind of) religion.

We live in something analogous to a postrevolutionary climate. Revolutions generate the sense that they have won a great victory and identify the adversary in the previous regime. A postrevolutionary climate is one which is extremely sensitive to anything which smacks of the ancien regime and sees backsliding even in relatively innocent concessions to generalized human preferences. This can be seen, for example, in the Puritans who saw the return of Popery in any ritual, or Bolsheviks who compulsively addressed people as "comrade," proscribing the ordinary appellation "mister." I would argue that a milder, but very pervasive, version of this kind of climate is widespread in our culture. To speak of aiming beyond life is to appear to undermine the supreme concern with life of our humanitarian, "civilized" world. It is to try to reverse the revolution and bring back the bad old order of priorities, in which life and happiness could be sacrificed on the altars of renunciation. Hence, even believers are often induced to redefine their faith in such a way as not to challenge the primacy of life.

My claim is that this climate, often unaccompanied by any formulated awareness of the underlying reasons, pervades our culture. It emerges, for instance, in the widespread inability to give any human meaning to suffering and death, other than as dangers and enemies to be avoided or combated. This inability is not just the failing of certain individuals; it is entrenched in many of our institutions and practices, for instance the practice of medicine, which has great trouble understanding its own limits or conceiving some natural term to human life.

What gets lost, as always, in this post-revolutionary climate is the crucial nuance. Challenging the primacy of life can mean two things. It can mean trying to displace the saving of life and the avoidance of suffering from their rank as central concerns of policy. Or, it can also mean making the claim, or at least opening the way for the insight, that more than life matters. These two are obviously not the same. It is not even true, as people might plausibly believe, that they are causally linked, in the sense that making the second challenge "softens us up," and makes the first challenge easier. Indeed, I want to claim (and did in the concluding chapter of *Sources of the Self*) that the reverse is the case: that clinging to the primacy of life in the second (let us call this the "metaphysical") sense is making it harder for us to affirm it wholeheartedly in the first (or practical) sense.

But I do not want to pursue this claim here. The thesis I am presenting is that it is in virtue of its post-revolutionary climate that Western modernity is very inhospitable to forest-dwelling. This, of course, runs contrary to the mainline Enlightenment story, according to which religion has become less credible thanks to the advancement of science. There is, of course, something in this, but it is not in my view the main story. Moreover, to the extent that it is true, that is, that people interpret science and religion as at loggerheads, it is often because of an already felt incompatibility at the moral level. It is this deeper level that I have been trying to explore here. In other words, to oversimplify again, the obstacles to belief in Western modernity are primarily moral and spiritual, rather than epistemic. I am talking about the driving force here, rather than what is said in arguments in justification of unbelief. That is why I feel I want to demur when Murdoch invokes in *Metaphysics* things in which we allegedly can no longer believe. In one sense, I don't think there are such things. Even the grossest superstitions survive in advanced societies, and these were on the other hand always condemned by minorities. On another level, if we want to talk about things it is *hard* to believe, things that go against the grain, then I think this is true today of forest-dwelling in general, whether one is on their path or mine. Talking about what cannot be believed seems to accept that the revolution is epistemically-driven, whereas I think that the motor of change is elsewhere.

I want to extend a little farther what is involved in this "take" on our age. For those who reject the metaphysical primacy of life, this outlook can itself seem imprisoning. The field is turned into another corral. From my perspective, human beings have an ineradicable bent to respond to something beyond life; denying this stifles. This perspective is, of course, radically at odds with that of secular humanism. But there is a feature of modern culture which fits my perspective. This is the revolt from within unbelief, as it were, against the primacy of life. It is not now in the name of something beyond, but really more just from a sense of being confined, diminished by the acknowledgement of this primacy. This has been an important stream in our culture, something woven into the inspiration of poets and writers, for example, Baudelaire (but was he entirely an unbeliever?) and Mallarmé. But the most influential proponent of this kind of view is undoubtedly Nietzsche. And it is significant that the most important anti-humanist thinkers of our time, for example, Foucault, Derrida, Bataille, all draw heavily on Nietzsche.

Nietzsche, of course, rebelled against the idea that our highest goal is to preserve and increase life, to prevent suffering. He rejects this both metaphysically and practically. He rejects the egalitarianism underlying this whole affirmation of ordinary life. But his rebellion is in a sense also internal. Life itself can push to cruelty, to domination, to exclusion, and indeed does so in its moments of most exuberant affirmation.

So this move remains within the modern affirmation of life in a sense. There is nothing higher than the movement of life itself (the *Will to Power*). But it chafes at the benevolence, the universalism, the harmony, the order. It wants to rehabilitate destruction and chaos, the infliction of suffering and exploitation, as part of the life to be affirmed. Life properly understood also affirms death and destruction. To pretend otherwise is to try to restrict it, tame it, hem it in, deprive it of its highest manifestations, what makes it something you can say "yes" to. A religion of life which proscribes death-dealing, the infliction of suffering, is confining and demeaning. Nietzsche thinks of himself as having taken up some of the legacy of pre-Platonic and pre-Christian warrior ethics, their exaltation of courage, greatness, elite excellence. Modern life-affirming humanism breeds pusillanimity. This accusation frequently recurs in the culture of counter-Enlightenment.

Of course, one of the fruits of this counter-culture was Fascism, to which Nietzsche's influence was not entirely foreign, however true and valid Walter Kaufman's refutation of the simple myth of Nietzsche as a proto-Nazi. But in spite of this, the fascination with death and violence recurs, for example, in the interest in Bataille, shared by Derrida and Foucault. (Bataille was also a pre-war fascist sympathizer.) Jim Miller's book on Foucault shows the depths of this rebellion against "humanism," as a stifling, confining space one has to break out of.[5] My point here is not to score off neo-Nietzscheanism, as some kind of antechamber for Fascism. A secular humanist might want to do this. But my perspective is rather different. I see these connections as another manifestation of our (human) inability to be content simply with an affirmation of life. The Nietzschean understanding of enhanced life, which can fully affirm itself, also in a sense takes us beyond life; and in this it is analogous with other, religious notions of enhanced life (like the New Testament's eternal life). But it takes us beyond by incorporating a fascination with the negation of life, with death and suffering. It does not acknowledge some supreme good beyond life

5. Jim Miller, *The Passion of Michel Foucault* (New York: Simon & Schuster, 1993).

and in that sense sees itself rightly as utterly antithetical to religion.

I am tempted to speculate further and to suggest that the perennial human susceptibility to be fascinated by death and violence is at base a manifestation of our nature as *homo religiosus*. From the point of view of the forest-dweller, it is one of the places this aspiration for the beyond most easily goes when it fails to take us to the forest. This does not mean that religion and violence are alternatives. On the contrary, it means that most historical religion has been deeply intricated with violence, from human sacrifice down to inter-communal massacres, because most historical religion remains only very imperfectly oriented to the forest. The religious affinities of the cult of violence in its different forms are indeed palpable. What it might mean, however, is that the only way fully to escape the draw towards violence is to enter the forest, that is, through the full-hearted love of some good beyond life. A thesis of this kind has been put forward by René Girard, for whose work I have a great deal of sympathy, although I do not agree on the centrality he gives to the scapegoat phenomenon.[6]

On the perspective I am developing here, no position can be set aside as simply devoid of insight. We could think of modern culture as the scene of a three cornered—perhaps ultimately a four-cornered—battle. There are secular humanists, there are neo-Nietzscheans, and there are those who acknowledge some good beyond life. Any pair can gang up against the third on some important issue. Neo-Nietzscheans and secular humanists together condemn religion and reject any good beyond life. But neo-Nietzscheans and forest-dwellers are together in their absence of surprise at the continued disappointments of secular humanism, together also in the sense that its vision of life lacks a dimension. In a third line-up, secular humanists and believers come together in defending an idea of the human good, against the anti-humanism of Nietzsche's heirs.

A fourth party can be introduced to this field if we take ac-

6. René Girard, *The Scapegoat*, trans. Yvonne Freccero (Baltimore: Johns Hopkins University Press), 1986.

count of the fact that the forest-dwellers are divided. Some think that the whole move to secular humanism was just a mistake, which needs to be undone. We need to return to an earlier view of things. Others, in which I place myself, think that the practical primacy of life has been a great gain for humankind, and that there is some truth in the revolutionary story; this gain was in fact unlikely to come about without some breach with established religion. (We might even be tempted to say that modern unbelief is providential, but that might be too provocative a way of putting it.) But we nevertheless think that the metaphysical primacy of life is wrong, and stifling, and that its continued dominance puts in danger the practical primacy.

I have rather complicated the scene in the last paragraphs. Nevertheless, the simple lines sketched earlier still stand out. Both secular humanists and anti-humanists concur in the revolutionary story, that is, they see us as having been liberated from the illusion of a good beyond life and thus enabled to affirm ourselves. This may take the form of an Enlightenment endorsement of benevolence and justice; or it may be the charter for the full affirmation of the will to power, or "the free play of the signifier," or the aesthetics of the self, or whatever the current version is. But it remains within the same post-revolutionary climate. For those fully within the climate, the forest becomes all but invisible. I have been exploring in my own way the terrain that I believe Iris Murdoch has opened up for us. My map is not the same as hers. But then what two maps of largely untracked wilderness can ever be identical? I would like this exploration to be a tribute to the courage and insight of one who was originally, and has remained, one of my teachers.

2
LOVE AND VISION: IRIS MURDOCH ON EROS AND THE INDIVIDUAL

Martha C. Nussbaum

I. BLINDNESS AND LONGING

We live bereft of sight, and filled with yearning. Cut off from the vision of the Good that was ours in another world, we seek to return to that world and that knowledge. In our striving, beauty, and the body's erotic response to the sight of beauty, plays a necessary and central role, since, as Socrates says, "sight is for us the sharpest of the bodily senses. It does not see wisdom—for indeed wisdom would give rise to awesome erotic longing, if it did enter our field of vision and provide a clear likeness of itself, and so too the other objects of our erotic longing. But as things are, only beauty has that lot, to be the most evident and the most erotically arousing" (*Phaedrus* 250D). Those whose vision of the good is dim respond obtusely to their own sexual arousal, giving themselves over to pleasure and seeking only the physical gratifications of procreation or of superficial release (250E).[1] Plato suggests that not only their reaction to arousal but the arousal itself is superficial, focusing on the surface of the bodily form and failing to honor the divine beauty within.[2] But in those who remain closer to the other world the sight of sexual love pierces deeper, catching glimpses of the soul's beauty in the form and features of the body (see 252E7–

---

1. For my account of the diverse scholarly interpretations of this difficult sentence, and my own argument, see "Platonic Love and Colorado Law: The Relevance of Ancient Greek Norms to Modern Sexual Controversies," *Virginia Law Review* 80 (1994): 1515–1651.
2. 250E3: "he does not revere it when he sees it."

253A1). For such people, sexual arousal is a seismic upheaval of the entire soul, whose terrifying disruption of habitual order brings with it a turning toward the good. The sight of the beautiful beloved brings a shudder of awe, which mysteriously turns to a sweating and fever, as the stream of beauty entering through the eyes waters the parched roots of the soul's wings. The wings now begin to grow "over the entire form of the soul" (251B): they belong, that is, to the soul's emotions and bodily desires, as well as to its intellect. And now, indeed, the soul "boils and throbs as a whole," with a feeling like the throbbing in the gums of a teething child when a tooth is about to come through. Madness prevents sleep; the soul is riven between joy and anguish. But when at last the beloved is in the lover's presence, the soul of the lover "channels the stream of desire into herself as through an irrigation trench, releasing the pent-up waters. Then she has a respite from her stings and agonies, and reaps the fruit of the sweetest pleasure this life offers" (251E).

Plato's extraordinary description, with its mixed images of irrigation, of teething, of boiling, of stinging—and with its complex and culturally bold sexual intimations of both activity and receptivity, in which irrigating oneself with the water of the loved one's beauty brings the summit of pleasure[3]—is, we have no doubt, a description of a certain type of personal erotic love, a love in which the body's response to the sight of a beautiful body is linked in mysterious ways with a deeper yearning for the soul that inhabits the body, and for the vision of the Good that this soul appears to offer. This passage has been important to Iris Murdoch in quite a few of her writings, both fictional and philosophical. It has a central place in the argument of *The Fire and the Sun*, receives frequent discussion in *Metaphysics as a Guide to Morals*,

---

3. For sensitive comment on the sexual imagery of the passage, see K. J. Dover, *Greek Homosexuality*, 2d ed. (Cambridge: Harvard University Press), 163–65; for more specific comments on the validation of erotic receptivity, and its culturally anomalous status, see my "Reply to David Halperin," *Proceedings of the Boston Area Colloquium for Ancient Philosophy* 5 (1989): 53 ff., and chap. 7 of *The Fragility of Goodness* (Cambridge: Cambridge University Press, 1986). The language of "reaping the fruit of pleasure" is suggestive of orgasmic pleasure, in the poetic language of Plato's time.

and underlies the plot and action of *The Black Prince*, as well as several other of her novels.

The passage as a whole appears to make four claims about sexual love:

First, love of this sort is a crucial, apparently even a necessary, source of *motivation* for the soul in its search for the vision of the Good. Without the unique role of beauty and sight, without the upheaval of sense occasioned by the physical presence of the beloved, the soul does not search for the Good, and remains in a parched and depleted condition.

Second, love of this sort is a crucial source of *vision*, vision both of the beloved person and of the external impersonal Good, the two being closely linked. The passage makes it clear that the discovery of the inner divinity and the nature of the beloved person and the generous loving actions inspired by this discovery (see 253B, 255B) would not have taken place without the violent erotic reaction of the *whole* soul, therefore not without its sexuality; and sexuality itself, operating as it does here in concert with the emotions and the intellect,[4] serves the person as a reliable indicator of the presence of the Good. The passage also argues that although direct unmediated arousal by the Good is conceivable, it is not empirically possible; as we are, we need the body's response to beauty to stimulate our vision and send it searching for goodness. Blind sexual love is very common, and Plato acknowledges it. But obtuse reasoning is also common; and Plato argues here that reasoning will always be obtuse, unless it is guided by erotic love.

Third, sexual love is not simply a starting point for the mind in its search for the Good, but a lifelong accompaniment to that search. Plato's highest contemplative lovers do forgo full intercourse, on account of Plato's view that that intense degree of bodily pleasure would obscure the soul's vision. But they regularly indulge their sexual desire in caresses that stop short of intercourse. And the many couples who continue to have full intercourse will be rewarded by the gods in the afterlife "on account of their erotic

---

4. I do not mean to imply that there is no tension among these elements; clearly Plato believes that there is, and I shall return to this point. For an excellent discussion of the entire passage, and especially of this tension, see A. Price, *Love and Friendship in Plato and Aristotle* (Oxford: Oxford University Press, 1989).

love ... "; they will spend a "blessed life wandering around in the light with one another," and will regain their wings, with similar plumage (256DE). Plato never suggests that the sexual element in their desire should itself be forgone; in fact, he strongly suggests that it remains throughout life an important component of the search for goodness, both in itself and in one another. In fact, in a culturally remarkable move, he imagines the beloved himself conceiving a reciprocal desire (*anterôs*) for the lover, and depicts this desire as an important part of the younger person's spiritual development.[5]

Fourth, in erotic love of the best sort, the lovers see and acknowledge one another's individuality in two ways: (1) They acknowledge one another as *agents*, each striving toward the Good. A respect for the separate agency or freedom of the beloved, and a wish to foster it, is a big part of what differentiates this generous love from the jealous and possessive loves against which the beloved young person has so frequently been warned (253B, 255B). (2) They acknowledge one another's *qualitative specificity*, in the sense that their love is all about a true perception of and desire for the specific "divinity," or pattern of aspiration, that they discern in the beloved, knowing its presence through its bodily traces.

Given the central importance that Iris Murdoch has frequently given this passage from the *Phaedrus*, we might expect her to endorse its four claims about erotic love. I am not at all certain, however, that she does, and I think it is well worth inquiring what her view actually is. To open that inquiry is my goal in this paper. (I say "to open," since I have no illusion that I will really be able to complete the inquiry, given Murdoch's complexity as both philosophical thinker and artist.) To begin setting up the question, I turn now to a second text, one less centrally discussed by Murdoch than the *Phaedrus* passage, but one that also appears to embody characteristically Murdochian insights into erotic love. Its insights are at odds with those of the *Phaedrus*.

---

5. See David Halperin, "Plato on Erotic Reciprocity," *Classical Antiquity* 5 (1986): 60 ff., and my discussion in "Platonic Love and Colorado Law," 1570–78.

II. The Fog of the World

Dante has passed through the flame that disciplines the lustful, the purifying flame of the Angel of Chastity, whose song is *"Beati mundo corde,"* "Happy are the pure in heart."[6] The last P, the last sign of sin, has been stricken from his brow. Now, as he stands in the Earthly Paradise, the Heavenly Pageant halts before him, as the Prophets sing the passionate words of the *Song of Solomon:* "Come with me from Lebanon, my bride." These words are passionate, and yet it is clear that theirs, like Dante's, is a passion from which sexual lust has been entirely purged away. And now, from that chariot, from within a cloud of flowers, a lady appears before Dante, her veil the white of Christian faith, her cloak the green of hope, her gown the flame red of Christian love. This lady is not unknown to Dante, nor he to her:

> My soul—such years had passed since last it saw
> that lady and stood trembling in her presence,
> stupefied, and overcome by awe—
>
> now, by some power that shone from her above
> the reach and witness of my mortal eyes,
> felt the full mastery of enduring love.[7]

Turning to Virgil, Dante now quotes Virgil's own lines, lines said by Dido when she recognizes that her love for Aeneas is the "same love" that she felt for her dead husband Sychaeus: "I recognize the tokens of the ancient flame," *"Conosco i segni del antica fiamma."*[8]

---

6. I have discussed Dante's views on the ascent of love in my Gifford Lecture 8; some of this material is published in a collection of essays entitled *Virtue, Love, and Form: Essays in Memory of Gregory Vlastos*, ed. T. H. Irwin and M. Nussbaum, *Apeiron* special issue 1993 (Alberta: Academic Printing and Publishing, 1994), 161–78.

7. *Purg.* XXX.34 ff., trans. John Ciardi (New York: New American Library–Dutton, 1989), except in l. 36, where I have replaced Ciardi's "stupefied by the power of holy awe," since no word corresponding to "holy" appears in the original, and it seems wrong to suggest that Dante's youthful love for Beatrice was already holy.

8. Virg. *Aen.* IV.23, *"agnosco veteris vestigia flammae."*

These words of recognition strike the reader as profoundly ambiguous: for if Dante's passion is characterized by shuddering and trembling, by intense erotic longing, and by an upheaval of the soul as intense as the upheaval that shakes the lover in the *Phaedrus*, there is also a very real sense in which it cannot possibly be "the ancient flame," given that flame itself has removed the sexual heat that once suffused it, and given that flame, in Beatrice's gown, now symbolizes a Christian love purified of bodily desire. It is at this point, as Beatrice addresses him, that Dante's own name occurs for the first and only time in the poem:

> Dante, do not weep yet, though Virgil goes.
> Do not weep yet, for soon another wound
> shall make you weep far hotter tears than those!
> ....
> Look at me well. I am she. I am Beatrice.
> How dared you make your way to this high mountain?
> Did you not know that here man lives in bliss?[9]

Now, at the moment when Dante is purified of sin, he is addressed by his own name—as if only now were he being seen and loved in all his individuality. And the object of his passion, she who sees him with loving particularity of vision, she too emphasizes the full individuality in which she stands before him. *"Ben son, ben son Beatrice,"* "I really am, I really am Beatrice." The emphatic linking of the name with its rhyme, *"felice,"* "blessed," indicates, once again, that it is in the context of Christian salvation that individuality is most truly seen and loved.

It is evident that this perception of individuality could not have taken place before the purification of sin. For, as Dante so elaborately shows his reader, "the world is blind" (*"lo mondo è cieco," Purg.* XVI.66). The manifold lures of the world—including fame, honor, money, and sexual gratification—create a "fog" around the sight of the individual,[10] blocking him from truly per-

---

9. *Purg.* 55–57, 73–75. The literal translation of l. 73 is "Really look—I really am, I really am Beatrice."
10. *Purg.* XI.30: *"purgando la caligine del mondo."*

ceiving other individuals, and to a great extent from being truly perceived. The sins that are purged in purgatory are all different forms of false love, in which the soul has taken an excessive interest in objects that are not the worthy or true objects of its love. These false loves get between the individual and a love of persons, who are worthy objects of love. In pride, for example, one attends only to one's own standing; this leads to a failure to notice the needs of those one loves. In envy, one fixes on the possessions or standing of others, again failing to notice who they are and what they need. In anger one is filled with resentment at slights to oneself and so cannot fully attend to the particular history and needs of another. In sloth and gluttony, one's absorption in one's own comfort and gratification make one slow to go to another's need. Lust, finally, is also seen as a deformation of individual love. The suggestion is that the lustful, focusing as they do on their own bodily pleasure and excitement, are imperfectly able to notice and respond to the needs of the person whom they love or even to take in their full particularity. A person who is seen as a vessel of pleasure is not seen truly for what he or she *is*. Dante's reader would recall that Paolo and Francesca, though together in love for all eternity, do not exactly see one another's individual specificity. He speaks of her as a *"bella persona,"* a "beautiful form,"—and she notices that this bodily form is hers no longer. She sees him as a source of *"piacer,"* and calls him *"costui,"* "that one." Never in her long speech does she mention his name. Nor does either recognize the other as a center of agency and freedom. Their love delights in the thought of mutual surrender and passivity.

If, then, we take this passage of the *Purgatorio* in its context, we find it yielding four theses about sexual love, which do not seem easy to reconcile with the claims of the *Phaedrus*.

First, sexual response to the bodily beauty of another decreases motivation to pursue the vision of the Good (and of the individuality of the person) by binding the mind to a false object of love.

Second, sexual love, like other sins, creates a kind of egoistic "fog" around the lover, impeding his vision of the reality of the other and of the Good.

Third, even if sexual desire cannot be avoided as one stage

in human life, love must be purified of bodily desire before true vision of the other person, or of the Good, can be achieved—and this means, as well, before the best form of human love and beneficence can be achieved.

Fourth, sexual love is incapable of fully attending adequately either to the agency or the qualitative specificity of the object of love. It prefers to conceive of its object as passive, surrendering, and as a seat of superficial pleasantness.

These claims conflict with the claims of the *Phaedrus*. One might attempt to resolve the conflict by saying that some cases of sexual love have *Phaedrus* properties and some have the properties that Dante notes. Plato himself lends support to this strategy, since the *Phaedrus* prominently recognizes cases of sexual love that *are* superficial in vision, that do not lead to an accurate view either of the beloved or of the good. But Dante's argument will not admit this reconciling strategy. He makes it very clear that in even the best cases of human sexual love—and we must suppose that his own love of Beatrice is a pretty good case—the sexual element in the love is an impediment and a source of delusion. True sight is recovered the far side of the purifying flames. And if one never had lust in the first place one would be much better off as a perceiver and lover.

My puzzle is that the Dantean view of sexual love is also a Murdochian view. Indeed, without thinking of the *Phaedrus* at all, and well before I conceived of the idea of writing this paper, I find that I wrote a footnote at that point in my own Gifford Lectures, saying, "Dante's conception of the worldly obstacles to particular perception and love is close to the contemporary conception developed by Iris Murdoch in philosophical writings such as *The Sovereignty of Good* and *The Fire and the Sun*, but also in novels such as *The Bell, The Black Prince*, and *The Sacred and Profane Love Machine*." Murdoch, more than any other contemporary ethical thinker, has made us vividly aware of the many stratagems by which the ego wraps itself in a cozy self-serving fog that prevents egress to the reality of the other. Her catalog of sins, in fact, closely resembles Dante's. In the famous example of the mother and daughter-in-law in *The Sovereignty of Good*, it is envy and perhaps also sexual jealousy that causes the mother-in-law to focus on the superficial and unattractive traits of her daughter-in-law. The mother's (M) effort to see her daughter-in-law (D) truly is an inner moral effort that could usefully be compared to the discipline undergone by Dante's souls in purgatory. For if to Sartre *"l'enfer c'est les autres"* (Hell is other people), for Murdoch, by contrast, hell is being walled up inside one's own fat cozy ego without means of egress to the other or to the Good; heaven is the place of true and selfless vision; and purgatory the place of moral effort that attempts to deliver us from the one to the other.

It is frequently suggested, both in Murdoch's philosophical works and in her novels, that sexual desire and the bodily component in love are sins in the Dantean sense, that is, sources of egoistic self-delusion and self-immersion that persistently come between us and the reality of those we love. And if that is so, if, that is, it is so pervasively, then Murdoch cannot endorse the entirety of Plato's vision in the *Phaedrus* as a story about how we recover our wings. She can endorse the special role Plato gives to the sight of beauty, and she can argue that the bodily response to beauty plays a crucial role in motivation and in vision. But she cannot hold that the sexual ferment that the *Phaedrus* actually describes is a valuable part of the search for truth, much less, as Plato strongly suggests, a necessary part.

It is difficult to investigate this issue within Murdoch's philosophical works themselves. For although they do contain many statements that bear both on Murdoch's relation to the *Phaedrus* and on her view of the self-gratifying ego—and some statements, as we shall see later, that usefully suggest a way of relating them— I know of no passage in which the tension between the two views of the sexual is confronted head-on. What I propose to do here, then, is to turn to two of Murdoch's novels in which the relationship between sexual love and truth is a central theme: *The Sacred and Profane Love Machine* and *The Black Prince*. Despite the evident difficulty of finding Murdoch among her characters, I shall claim that we can find in these novels insights about love that may justly be called Murdochian. I shall argue that *The Sacred and Profane Love Machine* appears at first to support a Dantean reading of Murdoch, but ultimately does not do so, since there are crucial elements in the portrayal of love that are more Platonic than Dantean.

A reading of *The Black Prince* further supports the view that Murdoch is actually closer to Plato than to Dante, though she complicates Plato's analysis with a very Dantean account of the "fog" created by envy and anxiety.

After discussing these two cases, I shall then raise some questions for both Murdoch and Plato, suggesting that the way in which both of them connect the love of persons with the love of impersonal goodness may contain too little room for the real-life human individual, with its recalcitrant tendency to refuse identification with any piece of the impersonal good. I shall suggest that while both appear to validate sexual love as a central source of value in human life, neither actually does so in a way that fully accepts the flawed, idiosyncratic, lumpy, surprising human individual. Both, in their accounts of erotic achievement, somewhat impatiently bypass this individuality in search of the good. And I shall suggest that the reason for this is not that Murdoch really agrees with Plato in his dismissal of the material and the accidental, his exaltation of the abstract philosophical vision of the good. Murdoch holds, instead, that the vision of the accidental comic and surprising *is* of highest importance, but that neither personal love nor philosophy can achieve it. The flawed and the comic particular can be lovingly embraced only by the vision of art.

III. Sacred and Profane

The plot of *The Sacred and Profane Love Machine* is, at first look, Dantean, focusing, as do many of Murdoch's plots, on the havoc caused by egoistic self-deception. Blaise Gavender has for years lived calmly with his wife Harriet and his son David, while maintaining another household with his lover Emily McHugh, who has also borne him a son. The strong erotic desires that connect Blaise with Emily have also led him to rationalize his guilt and conceal from himself the badness of his violation of his wife's trust. Indeed, he even feels that he is totally in the right: "It was ecstatic, sudden, total. As total as Harriet's trust, its cataclysmic necessary counterpart. Sin was an awful private happiness blotting out all else; only it was not sin, it was glory, it was his good, his very own, manifested at last. . . . A combination of pure free creation and pure causality now ruled his life. . . . This was not just intense sexual bliss, it was absolute metaphysical justification" (pp. 71–72).[11] This highly Dantean passage shows sexual desire creating a fog around Blaise, preventing him from naming his situation correctly. Even the word "sin" must be replaced by the words "glory" and "good," since otherwise Blaise could not fully enjoy the "sexual bliss" Emily offers him. Both his motivation to pursue the good and his vision of the good are obscured. Nor, the reader senses, does his desire allow him fully to take account of the pain of Emily, who lives a very miserable life for many years. He is able to see her as his glory and his justification; but desire actually prevents him from acknowledging her needs as a person—for desire could not survive the pain that would come of that acknowledgment. And when the affair is revealed to Harriet, Blaise's self-deceptive stratagems only become more devious and more complicated. The fantasy of pardon from his saintly wife sustains him in continuing his adultery. The self-serving conviction that it will be best for everyone if he continues to maintain two households propels him on into further complexities of deception, as he attempts to convince each woman that he does not desire or make love to the other.

At the same time, the novel's parallel plot, the story of the writer Montague Small, reinforces, or so it seems, its Dantean vision of the erotic. For Monty, mourning for his dead wife Sophie, is in the grip of an erotic obsession so intense that it obscures from view the good of all others and of his own good as well. Listening again and again to the tape recording of Sophie's voice, Monty allows all other voices to move around him unheard. And the marriage that we enter through his memories was itself a marriage in which the suddenness of particular erotic love unsettled the equilibrium of the entire world, creating an egoistic fog of jealousy that prevented Monty from seeing anything truly, including and especially his intensely loved Sophie. His motivation to recognize her particularity and her agency has been entirely cut away by the paralyzing anxiety of jealousy, to the point that her last days, as she dies of cancer, are spent in an ugly exchange of recriminations

11. Iris Murdoch, *The Sacred and Profane Love Machine* (New York: Penguin Books, 1974). All citations from the novel are taken from the Penguin edition.

in which his hatred of all obstacles to her love gets the better of his love for her. The voice Monty hears again and again on the tape recording is a voice taunting him with the fantasy of her other lovers—and it is as that taunting voice, rather than as a person, that he remembers her.

The undermining of love by sexual desire and sexual anxiety reaches its logical conclusion in Monty when he murders his wife. For the reader learns, late in the novel, that he strangled her as she lies on the sofa taunting him:

> It is simply the litany of her doomed pain, Monty told himself, as he had told himself many times in the last weeks, as Sophie reviled and tormented him, casting her anguish off on to him like an acid shower. He made his usual effort to be quiet, not to quarrel with her.... But once more he failed. "All right, I wish I'd never married *you*! I wish I'd had a decent loyal wife and not a whore who went to bed with all my friends!" "You have no friends, you don't know how they mock and despise you, all of them." ... "Oh, shut up, Sophie, go to bed." "They all mock you, Richard mocks you." "Shut up!" "You didn't know I made love with Richard." "It's not true." "It is true, here in our bed, we mocked you ... " "You'd invent anything to hurt me, wouldn't you?" "I hate you, I hate you, I hate you."
>
> Monty caught his breath. The memory had risen like a noxious atomic cloud in the midst of his sailing thoughts. He checked himself, made himself rigid, while the hysterical voices went on and on in his mind. He had made them silent at last, seizing her throat. It had been like an embrace. He had to make her silent. He threw himself upon her and silenced her and held her, wanting to hurt her, wanting to dominate and hold that awful consciousness which filled him with so much pain and so much wild awful pity. (pp. 324–25)

Even the part of Monty's love that does seem to contain a true and highly concrete perception of Sophie is defeated at last by the blinding force of his sexual obsession.

All this is true. And these are no isolated moments in Murdoch's fiction, which contains many more examples of the defeat of vision by desire. And yet in this novel, I feel, there is also Platonism. Sexual desire is linked not only with obtuseness and cruelty, but also with self-discovery and deep self-expression. Blaise's passion with Emily is selfish; but the reader is made to feel that there is also truth in his claim that the passion is a kind of glory and a source of revelation: "The world in its detail was revealed at last to an indubitable insight. His whole being was engaged, he was identified with his real self, he fully inhabited his own nature for the first time in his life" (p. 72). The novel shows how this feeling can serve as a screen, concealing from Blaise the cruelty of his actions; but the conflict is complex precisely because there is truth, we know, in Blaise's feeling that his and Harriet's marriage has inhibited self-discovery for both parties, at the same time offering neither any deep insight into the soul of the other. The fact of his deep erotic passion for Emily does promote genuine exposure and mutual knowledge in a way that the calmer relation did not. When Blaise and Emily are together at last, late in the novel, Emily concludes, "Didn't I tell you that your real self lived with me?" And although the reader can perfectly well see how that description can serve to distance or deny Harriet's pain, the reader also feels its truth. "He had married Harriet to rescue himself from his peculiarities, and that had seemed to be the formula for happiness" (p. 285). Of course, the reader now knows, it has not been. And when Blaise and Emily make love in the newfound knowledge that they are going to spend their lives together, the authorial voice comments on their passion directly, in a manner far more Platonic than Dantean: "Intense mutual erotic love, love which involves with the flesh all the most refined sexual being of the spirit, which reveals and perhaps even *ex nihilo* creates spirit as sex, is comparatively rare in this inconvenient world. This love presents itself as such a dizzily lofty value that even to speak of 'enjoying' it seems a sacrilege. It is something to be undergone upon one's knees. And where it exists it cannot but shed a blazing light of justification upon its own scene, a light which can leave the rest of the world dark indeed" (p. 261). Here we find Plato's imagery of illumination, awe, and wonder, Plato's idea of a spirituality that manifests itself in the surface and movements of the body. Indeed, Murdoch seems more charitable to the sexual than Plato himself, since she allows that sexual intercourse itself, not merely the bodily response to the sight of beauty, can intimate and express spiritual values.

What, then, has gone wrong? The suggestion of the novel is that sexuality is linked with pain and upheaval and self-deception because people all too often flee the sharp knowledge it conveys, seeking a sort of egoistic comfort that stops short of true self-exposure. In this sense it turns out to be Blaise's premature self-insulating marriage, not his love affair, that is the primary locus of egoistic self-deception, and we see that middle-class morality itself can be a source of comforting cozy self-protection, whereas sexuality can, at least in some cases, bring the turning round of the ego to the true sight of the world.

As for Monty, what we discover when we reflect again is that this is a man who desperately seeks to conceal from himself his own deepest thoughts, desires, and vulnerabilities. His series of successful detective novels protects him from the painful self-discovery involved in real art. His cynical detective hero, the thin chocolate-eating Milo Fane, is a substitute persona that masks the real softness and vulnerability of Monty. The entirety of his career is anxious egoistic self-protection. This being so, when deep love does grab hold of him, turning him inside out so that the reality of another's being does matter to him, what should we expect? He cannot really endure it. The sight of love is too sharp, too painfully direct, for this particular man to endure it without terrible anxiety. Jealousy and even, eventually, hatred are the forms taken by his intense love in combination with self-protective need. The instability and pain of the marriage are not, then, to be blamed on its sexual intensity, which was the one thing that jolted Monty out of himself in the first place, but on the habits of self-comfort that love challenges.

And even in Sophie's death there is more complexity than I have acknowledged. For if we return to the paragraph I have quoted, we discover that his murderous embrace, though inspired in part by the desire to hurt and to dominate, is inspired also by "wild awful pity." And as we look back on all his memories of those dreadful weeks, we recognize that the intensity of conflict between the couple grows out of the inability of either one to tolerate the advent of premature death. Sophie, hating her own death, also hates being seen as a dying person, immobile, wasted, helpless; her taunts express a hatred of helplessness, just as his jealous rages express a rage against the world that she should be taken from him. And his embrace really is a kind of euthanasia, and what Murdoch's reader must acknowledge is that the euthanasia of a beloved person is not always a morally cozy event in which loving motives are decisively supreme, but can be a most ugly mixed event, and yet be euthanasia, and be loving for all that. When he finds himself able to recall his deadly act, Monty finds himself able, as well, finally to *see* Sophie, to let her be in the world: "'Sophie,' he said aloud. 'Sophie. Sophie. My darling. Rest now. Forgive me.' She was part of him for ever. Only here within him did she now exist. His love for her was still alive and would live always and would change as live things change" (p. 325). If there is something disquieting in this reconciliation—we know that its necessary condition is that Sophie is in fact dead, does in fact now exist not separately, tormentingly, but only inside of Monty—there is also, confusedly mixed up with what is disquieting, the real vision of love.

In short, there is Platonism here, but with an implicit reproof to Plato for having been too simple in his account of *eros,* and this in two ways. First, Plato has ignored the manifold motives people have to avoid love, to conceal and protect themselves, not to recognize it when it arrives. These motives complicate love and make it filled with conflict, although they do not remove its illuminating power. Second, Plato has forgotten, it would seem, that people suffer manifold accidents and that the sight of the illness or death of a loved one brings rage and hate as well as pity. These insights complicate Platonism, but they do not restore us to Dante's picture: for the sexual element in love is, after all, if in a very qualified way, seen as a source of genuine insight.

IV. Anxiety and Madness

These suggestions of a complex Platonism are confirmed in *The Black Prince*—perhaps Murdoch's most self-consciously Platonic love story. In fact, this wonderful novel might well be introduced by Murdoch's own comments on Plato in *Metaphysics as a Guide to Morals:*

> Love, as the fruit and overflow of spirit. Plato's visions may seem far away from the mess of ordinary loving, but they shed light, we can understand. Falling in love is for many people their most intense experience, bringing with it a quasi-religious certainty, and most disturbing because it shifts the centre of the world from ourself to another place. A love relationship

can occasion extreme selfishness and possessive violence, the attempt to dominate that other place so that it be no longer separate; or it can prompt a process of unselfing wherein the lover learns to see, and cherish and respect, what is not himself. There are many aspects to this teaching; for instance, letting the beloved go with a good grace, knowing when and how to give up, when to express love by silence or by clearing off. This negative heroism may be very enlightening, aided by the palpable satisfaction of having behaved well when one desired to behave otherwise! (pp. 16–17)[12]

So much may be said of Bradley Pearson's own love story.[13] For years, the center of Bradley's world has been himself: his sterility as an artist, his envious friendship with Arnold Baffin. His passion for Julian opens his eyes—as the mysterious editor of his manuscript remarks, vindicating Bradley against the older Julian's denunciation of the erotic (p. 414). Anxiety and envy close Bradley in, but passion opens him up.

In fact, as he looks back on his love, Bradley persuasively, and in a very Murdochian way, argues that not love but egoistic anxiety is the root of all the vices: "Anxiety most of all characterizes the human animal. This is perhaps the most general name for all the vices at a certain mean level of their operation. It is a kind of cupidity, a kind of fear, a kind of envy, a kind of hate. Now, a favoured recluse, I can, as anxiety diminishes, measure both my freedom and my previous servitude. Fortunate are they who are even sufficiently aware of this problem to make the smallest efforts to check this dimming preoccupation. . . . The natural tendency of the human soul is towards the protection of the ego" (p. 183). Now of course anxiety may arise in the context of love, as it does for both Monty and Bradley. It may even manage to poison love. But it is not identical to erotic love, and in a very real sense the two are antagonists. Erotic love gives Bradley wings of joy, a sense of the blotting out of self, a turning away from customary fears: "A common though not invariable early phase of this madness, the one in fact through which I had just been passing, is a false loss of self, which can be so extreme that all fear of pain, all sense of time (time is anxiety, is fear) is utterly blotted out. The sensation itself

12. Iris Murdoch, *Metaphysics as a Guide to Morals* (New York: Allen Lane/Penguin Press, 1993), hereafter referred to as *Metaphysics*.
13. Iris Murdoch, *The Black Prince* (New York: Viking, 1973).

of loving, the contemplation of the existence of the beloved, is an end in itself" (p. 244). And although love ultimately brings with it the torment of jealousy, and although this initial loss of self does prove to that extent "false," it is evident that Bradley is freed from egoistic self-preoccupation, to the extent to which he is, thanks only to the intensity of his desire, not in spite of it. His experience of love does include the virtuous actions Murdoch names—letting the beloved go with good grace, knowing when to give up, behaving well when one wishes to behave otherwise. In fact, although he does not praise himself, we understand well that love has brought him to a virtuous action extreme in its consequences—for it is clearly for Julian's sake that he conceals the true facts concerning her mother's murder of her father, and takes the conviction and sentence with staggering courage. It is also thanks to love that he becomes a real artist, for we are to think that the manuscript we read is his first humanly rich and truly perceptive work of art. It is subtitled "A Celebration of Love," and its editor, P. A. Loxias, is a proxy for the god Apollo himself.

There are certainly doubts about the Platonism of Bradley's love. We wonder, for example, how truly he sees Julian. She once remarks, with some justice, "You say you love me, but you aren't *interested* in me in the least" (p. 266). Both her agency and her specificity seem to be to some extent disregarded. We wonder, too, about the relationship between the physical expression of love and its more illuminating moments, for in sex Bradley becomes self-preoccupied and anxious in a way he has not been until then, and the eventually successful lovemaking is dark and impersonal, not clearly suggestive of clear vision of the other or the good. (Perhaps here Murdoch is echoing Plato's own reservations about complete intercourse.) Nor is his love for Julian internally stable, as is the love depicted in the *Phaedrus*. These doubts linger, as they must in the comic and tragic confusion of a real life love, so different really from the purified carefully arranged world of the philosopher.

But the Platonism of Murdoch's "Celebration" of the erotic has the last word. For in the postscripts at the end of the novel Julian herself, grown older but hardly wiser, expresses the negative Dantean view: true vision is "very very cold." "Erotic love never inspires art. Or only bad art." "Love is concerned with possession and vindication of self. Art with neither. To mix up art with Eros, however black, is the most subtle and corrupting mistake an artist can commit" (p. 410). Love, she argues, is inherently narcissistic, antithetical therefore to the outward-reaching truth-directed vision of good art (p. 411). This view of the world and of Bradley Pearson is, however, repudiated, first of all, internally, since the self-conscious arty prose of Julian Belling rings false, gives us the sense of a stunted personality and imagination. More important, it is repudiated by Apollo himself, who makes fun of her "very *literary* piece," and asserts that erotic love *can* open the lover's eyes to the truth.

V. The Erotic and the Absurd

Murdoch's picture of *eros* is, then, more Platonic than Dantean, though it complicates Platonism with a complex diagnosis of the roots of self-avoidance. Through sexual love her characters do find themselves jolted out of themselves, prepared to search, at least, for the real good that is in the world that surrounds them. But there are questions that ought to be raised about Plato's project, and Murdoch's Platonism, as a response to the fact of personal sexual love. For the rest of this paper I turn to a somewhat halting articulation of these problems.

Plato's generous and splendid conception has a great problem as an account of human love. In loving the image of the divine good in a person, there is a sense in which we love the human particular in spite of itself. The dedication to a god may be, as it is in the *Phaedrus*, a profound part of what an individual really is; but still, it is only a part. Individuals are lumpy, comical, surprising. As agents they do not fly off straight to the good but do and say many things both mundane and absurd. Nor is their qualitative specificity limited to what the Platonic lover sees and cherishes. It includes, as well, many flaws, faults, and lapses, many inexplicable ungeneralizable bits of manner and tone of voice and gesture and history. It includes, above all, the surprising fact of having a particular body that shows not only the traces of the soul but also the sheer fact of itself. The *Phaedrus* tells us nothing of the love of bodily particularity, since the body, from the first, is seen as a sign of something deeper. We hear about the gleaming countenance of the beloved, which gestures beyond itself to the good. We do not hear about the way this particular person makes jokes, or the way he eats his dinner, or his characteristic choice of words and phrases, or the smell and taste of his neck. And although the love described is sexual through and through, we do not hear anything about its sexual particularity. The mythic abstractions of the good and the bad horse get between us and the personal quite specific caresses that two real people with real personal histories and idiosyncratic, somewhat unruly, bodies will be likely to exchange. The reason for this, quite clearly, is that Plato is not at all fond of these features of human love and thinks of love as uplifting only to the extent that it sets its sights elsewhere. Indulgent as he is to the couple who value the bodily element in their relationship, he clearly thinks them deluded insofar as they do consider this the "greatest of pledges." And his distaste shows up in his highly distanced and distancing abstract description of them, not humanized by the sight of awkward particularity, therefore not replicating the sight that we may imagine the two have of one another.

What of Murdoch here? One might now suspect that Murdoch's Platonism, like Plato's, sets her in an ambivalent relationship to the sight of the human, that her intense love of the good militates against a loving embrace of the living particular in its everyday nonsymbolic realness. Insofar as the good itself is love's focus, there is bound to be much that is unsatisfying in a mere human being. We see this in the loves that Murdoch describes: for both Blaise and Bradley, insofar as they love in the reverential inspired Platonic way, do look beyond the real people whom they love to the obscure image of a metaphysical source of that reverence and awe.

On the other hand, it is perfectly clear that the vision of all that is human, including the comic and the absurd, is not alien to Murdoch's art. In fact, Murdoch repeatedly insists on the connection of art to the ordinary and the funny. Tyrants fear art, she argues, because "it gives weight and interest to what is various, obvious, and ordinary. Tyrants fear funniness. . . . The absurdity of art, its funniness, its simplicity, its lucidity connects it with ordinary life and is inimical to authoritarian mystification" (*Metaphysics*, 90–91). When Julian Belling, in her Postscript to Bradley Pearson's narrative, defends a purified unerotic cold art, Loxias the editor characterizes this view as both naive and fearful: "Art, my dear Mrs Belling, is a very much tougher and coarser plant than you seem to be imagining in your very *literary* piece. . . . Why are you so anxious to divide that great blackamoor in two, what are you afraid of?" (*Black Prince*, 413–14). Indeed a great part of Murdoch's case for art as opposed to moral theory and psychological theory is that it *can* tell the truth about that "whole entity" (*Metaphysics*, 492) the human being, with all the idiosyncrasy and contingency of detail that really do characterize any real life. "We tame the world by generalizing," as Pearson says (*Black Prince*, 81), and it is art that gets at the details, therefore the awkward truth, of the substance of our lives. It does so in large part, in fact, by being funny, since the funny is "a great redeeming place of ordinary frailty" (*Metaphysics*, 91). This means that Murdoch's own art is very unlike Plato's: both are playful, but hers is a play of the awkward detail, the odd physical fact. We might put this in another way: Murdoch's art can depict more about the human particular than her characters can see, insofar as they are Platonic lovers.

All this is true. And in this sense we might say that Murdoch is more like Proust than like Plato. In the life and vision of art, we attain to a specificity of perception that life itself generally denies us. In art we see the whole human being, whereas in the rest of life we cannot both embrace the real and pursue the good. And yet, for Murdoch as for Proust—who is himself a Platonist at heart and who refers to both the *Symposium*'s metaphor of ascent and to the *Phaedrus* as sources of inspiration for his account of love—Platonism profoundly shapes the work of art. It is indeed true that for Murdoch art can present the whole human being, the absurd and idiosyncratic alongside the splendid. On the other hand, her severe allegiance to the Good colors the way in which these features of daily life are seen. It is not easy to express this response clearly, but I frequently feel, reading Murdoch, that she wishes to discipline her characters, and that she does not really like them as they are. There is the faithful rendering of the daily and the comic and the vulgar, and there is also—very much as in Proust—a mind behind it all, somewhat detached from the daily, loc with considerable irony and more than a little distas commitment to the idea that "What is needed . . . is tion of our desires, a re-education of our instincu. (*Metaphysics*, 503)—an idea that she illustrates by reference .. the *Phaedrus'* account of the struggle of the two horses—leads often, in the fiction, to a slight disdainfulness toward characters who do *not* re-educate their instincts. Her insistence that "The inhibition of unworthy fantasies is perhaps the most accessible discipline" (*Metaphysics*, 503) makes her impatient with characters who live immersed in such messy and uneducated fantasies and even seem to like them. And this makes me often feel, as reader, that Murdoch does not altogether like *me*, that she would have me be quite other than I am.

I can perhaps make this response more precise by suggesting that the artist who is the clearest antitype to Murdoch is James Joyce.[14] Murdoch does not much care for Joyce, to judge by her almost complete failure to mention him. (The one mention in *Metaphysics* lists him in a group of thinkers who are important as background to Derrida [p. 290]—hardly a good sign, given Murdoch's view of Derrida, which I share.) I think that the reason for this is not difficult to see. It is that Joyce is the great anti-Platonist of art. He is not an anti-Platonist in the superficial sense that he mocks or condemns the Platonic search for good. To do that would already be to be inside the Platonic project. Joyce is anti-Platonist in the far more fundamental sense that he simply does not see the reason for the Platonic ascent. It is much too much fun down here below, with the body and its smells and its odd deflections from rationality, with the outhouse and the crumbs of Plumtree's Potted Meat and the joy of being and making a mess. Joyce, I think, really loves

---

14. See my Gifford Lecture 10, published in a shorter form as "The Transfiguration of Everyday Life," *Metaphilosophy* 25 (1994): 238–61. Joyce, in *Ulysses*, connects Aristotle with Bloom and the Jewish tradition, in connection with the acceptance of the essentially enmattered nature of the human being. In the paper cited, I note that this parallels, in fact, a debate about the role of matter inside the tradition of Aristotle interpretation, in connection with which Hilary Putnam and I recently claimed, only slightly facetiously, that by establishing that, the body was the fitting home.

sexuality in a way in which neither Plato nor Murdoch actually does, much though they give it high praise. For they praise it as a route to something else, whereas Joyce made a big point of inverting the direction of signification. *Ulysses* ends with the word "yes," he explained in a letter, because that word stands for a woman's cunt.[15] In other words, the body is not the route to metaphysics; metaphysics, insofar as it has a function, is a route to the body. As the letter goes on, in opposition to Goethe's Mephistopheles, the "spirit who always says 'no'," Joyce introduces not the redemption of Faust and his ascent into heaven, but, instead, Molly Bloom, of whom he writes, *"Ich bin der [sic] Fleisch der stets bejaht,"*[16] "I am the flesh, which always says 'yes'." And lest we be tempted to see this as an announcement that Molly is a Platonic symbol of the affirmation of life, we are forced to notice that Molly's flesh says "yes" in a quite ordinary way, which Joyce depicts with a most unPlatonic specificity and a most undisciplined delight.

Ulysses knows well that much of human life consists in fantasy. It knows, too, that this is especially true of the sexual life, that there would probably not be any sexual arousal at all without it. As Bloom says, watching Gertie McDowell limp down Sandymount Strand, "See her as she is spoil all. Must have the stage setting, the rouge, costume, position, music."[17] But in its chaotic profusion of styles the text itself gives fantasy a loving embrace. Far from seeking to discipline or educate its characters the text both takes them as they are and announces that it is itself no different from them. In saying Molly's "yes" to sexuality the text is not saying "yes" to a spiritual discipline that will lead to the regrowth of the wings; it is just saying "yes" to the real life of sex, with its fantasies and its absurdities, its longings for the good so incongruously coupled to the unruly behavior of genital organs.

Joyce put a name to the intellectual basis for his art. He put many many names, of course, but there is one that stands out for

---

15. Letter cited in R. Ellman, *James Joyce* (New York: Oxford University Press, 1982), 501.
16. Presumably Joyce knew he was making a gender mistake and did so deliberately, in order to make the parallel closer with *"Ich bin der Geist, der stets verneint."*
17. James Joyce, *Ulysses* (New York: Modern Library, 1992), 370.

Love and Vision

me, that helps me to think about Murdoch's Platonism. That name is Aristotle. In his 1904 poem "The Holy Office," written just after a visit to Paris, during which Joyce spent a lot of time in brothels and much of the rest reading the *De Anima* in French translation, he wrote the following exuberant lines:

> Myself unto myself will give
> This name Katharsis-Purgative . . .
> Bringing to tavern and to brothel
> The mind of witty Aristotle . . .
> Ruling one's life by common sense
> How can one fail to be intense?

As the poem continues, Joyce develops the central image: his frankly sexual art is a kind of Aristotelian sewer-pipe that will drain off the censorious metaphysics of the Irish Catholic church as he knew it, to leave the body in peace and health:

> But all these men of whom I speak
> Make me the sewer of their clique.
> That they may dream their dreamy dreams
> I carry off their filthy streams . . .
> Thus I relieve their timid arses,
> Perform my office of Katharsis . . .
> And though they spurn me from their door
> My soul shall spurn them evermore.

This poem gives me a way of focusing my comments about Murdoch. Murdoch is, I think, in a very serious sense, the sort of Platonist metaphysician against whom Joyce here rebels. Not that she is an otherworldly metaphysician, but she is a Platonist metaphysician about the Good nonetheless. For her, there is a real sense in which the fantasies and the follies of much of our sexual life are sewage; and art of the truest kind is the great cleansing Platonic sewer-pipe that will in a certain sense carry all that off— in the Proustian sense that it will give it back in a form scrutinized by the discipline of purified desire. Joyce, by contrast, joyfully inverts the image. His sexual art is itself an Aristotelian sewer-pipe that will drain off Platonic metaphysics, leaving us to be ourselves. Joyce's holy sacrament is the Aristotelian purgation of all Platonic forms. Murdoch's "holy office" is the sacrament of purifying one's attention so that the good becomes evident. And this means that my original question, Is Murdoch Plato or Dante, now has a certain sort of answer: for she is both, insofar as both are united in their departure from Joyce's Aristotle, with his indifference to purifications, his calm delight in the body.

Murdoch ends her Gifford Lectures with a praise of spiritual discipline, of "our experience of the unconditioned and our continued sense of the holy" (*Metaphysics*, 512). I chose to end my Gifford Lectures with *Ulysses* and Molly Bloom, with the sun on Howth and the rhododendrons and the fantasy of Mulvey and the real semi-ignored presence of Poldy and the fantasy of Poldy and the Yes inside the fantasy and the Yes to the fantasy. In Murdoch's presence I feel reproved for this choice, as if a wiser and more disciplined person were saying, "How childish, how self-indulgent." This guilty response probably betrays the fact that I have undisclosed Platonist sympathies that are to some extent at odds with the view that I on the whole put forward. The beauty of Murdoch's more severe picture elicits those sympathies in a powerful way.

But since I have confessed to residual Platonism, let me end by suggesting that in Murdoch there seems to be residual Aristotelianism—a sense, at times, that the real physical being of the object is out there somewhere and the better for not being seen with the purifying scrutiny of art. Such moments of sympathy and yielding are especially powerful sources of generosity and vision in her work, at odds though they may well be with the spirit of Platonism that on the whole animates it. Let me therefore end by simply quoting one such passage, which is among the passages in Murdoch that, recalcitrant Aristotelian, I most cherish. It is the end of Bradley Pearson's Postscript to his own narrative, in *The Black Prince*:

> And I would not wish it to seem at the end that I have, in my own sequestered happiness, somehow forgotten the real being of those who have figured as my characters. . . . And Julian. I do not, my darling girl, however passionately and intensely my thought has worked upon your being, really imagine that I invented you. Eternally you escape my embrace. Art cannot assimilate you nor thought digest you. I do not now know, or want to know,

anything about your life. For me, you have gone into the dark. Yet elsewhere I realize, and I meditate upon this knowledge, that you laugh, you cry, you read books and cook meals and yawn and lie perhaps in someone's arms. This knowledge too may I never deny, and may I never forget how in the humble hard time-ridden reality of my life I loved you. That love remains, Julian, not diminished though changing, a love with a very clear and a very faithful memory. It causes me on the whole remarkably little pain. Only sometimes at night when I think that you live now and are somewhere, I shed tears. (p. 392)

3
IRIS MURDOCH AND THE MANY FACES OF PLATONISM

David Tracy

I. THE UNLIKELY RETURN OF PLATO

There is something both strange and courageous in Iris Murdoch's decision to develop a form of Platonism in the late twentieth century. Among the ancients, Aristotle, that sometime Platonist, can always return even if in our own period, though Aristotle returns not as a metaphysician but more often as a practical philosopher.[1] But Plato? Consider his critics. For many philosophers in the Continental tradition from Nietzsche through Heidegger to Deleuze, Plato is where the Greeks took a wrong turn—either away from the honest aesthetic world of tragedy (Nietzsche) or away from the non-forgetfulness of Being in the pre-Socratics (Heidegger) or away from the more daring language studies of some of the Sophists (Deleuze). At the same time as these not insignificant Continental criticisms are leveled at Plato, for many Anglo-American analytical philosophers, Platonism—especially in the modern form of a Hegelianized Platonism as in Bradley—is exactly the kind of muddled, vague, overambitious, implausible kind of philosophy that analytical philosophy in its earliest, more strictly observant mode was supposed to undo forever. In that perspective, only a few of Plato's arguments—analyzed through conceptual analysis and decontextualized from their concrete settings in the

---

1. See, for example, Stephen Toulmin, *Cosmopolis* (Chicago: University of Chicago Press, 1990), and Martha Nussbaum, *The Fragility of Goodness* (Cambridge: Cambridge University Press, 1986).

complex form of his dialogues—seem of much logical interest. Even many of the present internal critics of analytical philosophy, such as Richard Rorty, Bernard Williams, or Alasdair MacIntyre, do not return to Plato or Platonism. They are more likely to turn either to rethinking the relationship of philosophy and literature (Rorty) or tragedy (Williams) or tradition (MacIntyre) than to attempt to recover any notion of the Good in Plato.

Nor are most contemporary theologians more likely to recover Plato or Platonism. The Thomists—even the transcendental ones like Rahner, Coreth, and Lonergan—are more likely to find Plato on the Good as an interesting but dispensable way-station on the road to Being and God—and Thomas Aquinas. The Barthians have never found much to approve of in Plato or the Platonists. It is almost enough for Karl Barth to remember that Schleiermacher was one of the great Plato translators and scholars to find that door closed. Barth's successors seem so concerned to restore the realistic narrative form of theology that Plato's experiments with other forms seems, one gathers, profoundly irrelevant to their researches. The process theologians are, to be sure, always ready to quote Whitehead's famous statement that Western philosophy is a series of footnotes to Plato. However, even they seem less interested in noting, as Whitehead himself did note, that Whitehead's *Process and Reality* can be read as a modern scientific rewriting of Plato's *Timaeus*.

There are, of course, philosophical and theological exceptions to this general picture. Most notably, some contemporary French thinkers—especially Emmanuel Levinas and Jean-Luc Marion—have reread and rethought aspects of the Platonic heritage while critically retrieving it. Levinas's insight into Plato is notably similar to, yet finally different from, Iris Murdoch's reading of Plato. For Levinas, Plato helps one to break out of totality (including the totality of any Platonism, especially that of the last great neo-Platonist, Hegel) into infinity.[2] Plato does this, for Levi-

---

2. See especially, Emmanuel Levinas, *Totality and Infinity,* trans. Alphonso Lingis (The Hague: Martinus Nijhoff, 1969), reflecting on Plato's famous expression in the *Republic* 6, 509B "The good beyond being" (*agathon epekeina tes ousias*).

nas, through his brilliant move in the *Republic* to the "Good beyond Being." Levinas's critique of Heidegger on Plato, as well as his insistence that ethics, not ontology, is first philosophy, is surprisingly similar to Murdoch's critique of Sartre.[3] Both involve, moreover, a rethinking of the Good in Plato as a necessary resource for contemporary ethics. Even more striking is Jean-Luc Marion's recovery of the Platonic notion of the Good in his book *God without Being*.[4] Marion rethinks the category Good in relationship to the notion of gift (grace) articulated, for Marion, above all, by the Christian Platonists beginning with Dionysius. This move allows Marion to challenge Thomism and most metaphysical namings of God as Being in favor of the Good as the primary cataphatic name for God, as in Dionysius and Bonaventure, but not in Thomas or Suarez.[5] Indeed, like Levinas's reading of Plato on the Good, Marion's reading of Dionysius on the gift bears striking similarity to and just as striking difference from Murdoch's reading of the Platonic Good as a resource for contemporary thought. Iris Murdoch's reading of the Good, with her fascinating metaphor of the Good as

---

3. For Levinas here, besides the discussions in *Totality and Infinity*, see also *Otherwise Than Being or Beyond Essence*, trans. Alphonso Lingis (The Hague: Martinus Nijhoff, 1981) and the discussion of Heidegger in *Ethics and Infinity* (Pittsburgh: Duquesne University Press, 1985). See also Adrian Peperzak, *To the Other: An Introduction to the Philosophy of Emmanuel Levinas* (West Lafayette: Purdue University Press, 1993) and Edith Wyschogrod, *Emmanuel Levinas: The Problem of Ethical Metaphysics* (The Hague: Martinus Nijhoff, 1974). On Sartre, see Iris Murdoch, *Sartre: Romantic Rationalist* (Cambridge: Bowes & Bowes, 1953) and *Metaphysics as a Guide to Morals* (New York: Allen Lane/Penguin Press, 1993) 154–56, 260–61, 266–67. Notice, for example, Murdoch's frequent appeals to Simone Weil's understanding of "attention" (as here "a just and loving gaze directed upon an individual reality") in contrast to Sartre's "gaze" at the other, for example, in Iris Murdoch, *The Sovereignty of Good* (New York and London: Routledge, 1970), 34–35. It is puzzling that Murdoch's work does not refer to Levinas, with whom, in my judgment, she has much in common, despite obvious and important differences. A critical comparison of the two thinkers on the "other" and "ethics" would be a valuable contribution.
4. Jean-Luc Marion, *God Without Being*, trans. Thomas A. Carlson (Chicago: University of Chicago Press, 1991), esp. 215–17.
5. Ibid., esp. 32, 74–82. See, however, the important qualifications on Thomas Aquinas in the preface to the English edition, xix–xxv.

distant, impersonal, powerful magnetic power[6] could prove one of the most important inner-Platonic challenges to the contemporary French philosophical debate over the Good as gift—a metaphor bearing both more personal and more readily theistic overtones. This French philosophical retrieval of and new debate upon Plato and the Good is surely the conversation which Iris Murdoch (with her criticisms of Sartre and Derrida and her affinity for Simone Weil) could profitably address (and vice versa).[7] For therein lies a genuine internal challenge to her critique of God and the Good and the greatest internal difference to her magnetism model for Plato's understanding of the Good. In the meantime, there have been other retrievals of Plato and the many kinds of Platonism in our period. In hermeneutical philosophy, for example, Hans-Georg Gadamer's most significant critique of his mentor Heidegger lies in their conflict of interpretations on Plato. Moreover, Gadamer's interpretation that there is a fundamental agreement between Plato and Aristotle on the meaning of the Good for ethics deserves far more attention from the many neo-Aristotelians of our day than it ordinarily receives.[8]

In Christian theology, moreover, the increasing influence of Hans Urs von Balthasar has led to a widespread rereading of Plato and the Platonists (Christian and non-Christian) by many contemporary Christian theologians. Surely von Balthasar—especially in his great studies of Plotinus and Dionysius, of Bonaventure and Dante[9]—is right to insist that Platonism has provided Christian

---

6. The metaphor occurs throughout *Metaphysics as a Guide to Morals*. See, e.g., chap. 15, "Martin Buber and God," on the reasons why Murdoch argues against "personal" (i.e., "God") language in favor of the impersonal (magnet-like) language of the Good. See also the essay "On 'God' and 'Good'," in *The Sovereignty of Good*, 46–77.

7. On Derrida, see *Metaphysics as a Guide to Morals*, esp. 185–216. For Derrida himself on ethics, see his important recent development of a "Messianic ethics" in his *Specters of Marx*, trans. Peggy Kamuf (London: Routledge, 1994).

8. Hans-Georg Gadamer, *The Idea of the Good in Platonic-Aristotelian Philosophy*, trans. P. Christopher Smith (New Haven: Yale University Press, 1987).

9. For von Balthasar on form, see Hans Urs von Balthasar, *The Glory of the Lord: A Theological Aesthetics*, vol. 1: *Seeing the Form* (San Francisco: Ignatius Press, 1982). For the separate studies, see "Dionysius and Bonaventure" in vol.

theology far more of a sense of participation and an insistence on the centrality of form in a Christian theology than the Scholasticism and Reformation theologies which largely replaced Platonism. Among contemporary theologians, John Macquarrie and Bernard McGinn have also developed arguments grounded in the kind of careful scholarship,[10] at once historical and constructive, which a revival of Plato and Platonism in contemporary theology most needs. These new movements have surely retrieved aspects of Platonism for contemporary needs. They are clearly important in themselves and, as readings of Plato and Platonism, promising for the future of any theology prepared to rethink the understanding of God beyond both classical theism and beyond modern forms of deism, pantheism, and even panentheism. And yet, even these new Platonic theologies need to meet the kinds of challenge of Plato and Platonism which Iris Murdoch's affirmation of the Good and negation of God so brilliantly address.

I have no idea if Murdoch's strategy is a deliberate or instinctive one but, as I read her, in both her novels and her philosophical books from *The Sovereignty of Good* through *The Fire and the Sun* to *Metaphysics as a Guide to Morals,* she replies to the critics of Plato by employing a clever strategy first named by another troubled Platonist in another deeply troubled age, Augustine of Hippo: the strategy of despoiling the Egyptians. Most contemporary defenders of Plato choose one or another of his critics (usually within the disciplines of philosophy or theology) and move their argument

---

2: *Studies in Theological Style, Clerical Styles,* ed. John Riches, trans. Andrew Louth et al. (San Francisco: Ignatius Press, 1984); "Dante" in vol. 3: *Studies in Theological Style, Lay Styles,* trans. Andrew Louth et al. (San Francisco: Ignatius Press, 1986); "Plotinus" in vol. 4: *The Realm of Metaphysics in Antiquity,* ed. John Riches, trans. Oliver Cavies (San Francisco: Ignatius Press, 1989). For good studies of this important contemporary Christian Platonist theologian (my description, not his), see John Riches, ed., *The Analogy of Beauty: The Theology of Hans Urs von Balthasar* (Edinburgh: T & T Clark, 1986); and David L. Schindler, ed., *Hans Urs von Balthasar: His Life and Work* (San Francisco: Ignatius Press, 1991).

10. John Macquarrie, *In Search of Deity: An Essay in Dialectical Theism* (New York: Crossroad, 1985); Bernard McGinn, *The Presence of God,* vol. 1 (New York: Crossroad, 1991).

forward. Fair enough. But Murdoch's multi-layered strategy, especially but not solely in *Metaphysics as a Guide to Morals*, is a more expansive, daring and subtle one. She attempts to turn the critics—or, at least, their major intellectual resources—into new resources for her own Platonic understanding of the human search for the Good as well as the Platonic understanding of the Good as the impersonal, distant, unavoidable reality magnetically drawing all to itself, especially through beauty and love as both are provoked by and provocative of the Good.

This is clearly Murdoch's strategy in the signal case of Freud and the Freudians.[11] Outside the strictly philosophical and theological debates and indeed influencing them as well (as Paul Ricoeur persuasively argues)[12] is the all-pervasive influence of Freud in our culture. For our culture is one where, as W. H. Auden justly observed, Freud is no longer so much a position as a whole climate of opinion. Part of that climate is the belief—widely shared by practically all of us—that traditional notions of the human search for the Good (including the Platonic pilgrimage from appearance to reality, that is, to the Good become a therapy for the soul) may finally prove too optimistic, even too naive, a portrait of the profound ambiguities in the human situation. Recall how Peter Brown[13] compares the shock which Augustine gave to the Platonists of his day by his disturbing portrait of the self always trapping itself in its own egoistic madness to the shock which Freud gave

---

11. See the many discussions of Freud carefully indexed in both *The Sovereignty of Good* and *Metaphysics as a Guide to Morals*. This interest in and use of Freud occurs throughout the novels; see, especially, *A Severed Head* (London: Chatto & Windus, 1961). I have been especially guided for Murdoch's use of Freud as a novelist by the studies of Deborah Johnson, *Iris Murdoch* (Bloomington: Indiana University Press, 1987), esp. 14–18, passim, 33–40; and Elizabeth Dipple, *Iris Murdoch: Work for the Spirit* (Chicago: University of Chicago Press, 1982), esp. 93–94, 152–57, 272–73. Deborah Johnson's study is also very instructive for analyzing Murdoch's work from a feminist perspective, including discussion of feminist critiques of Freud and Freudianism.
12. Paul Ricoeur, *Freud and Philosophy*, trans. Denis Savage (New Haven: Yale University Press, 1970).
13. Peter Brown, *Augustine of Hippo* (Berkeley: University of California Press, 1967), 261.

to the optimistic Victorians, or, one may add, which Freud still gives to those able to see past so many of his domesticating ego-psychology successors.

Iris Murdoch never domesticates Freud's steady, indeed relentless, insistence on the powerful reality of the unconscious on all consciousness nor his vision of the fragility of the ego in any search for the good life—or, even, as in *Civilization and Its Discontents* in any human search for a decent, civilized life. It would be difficult to name a contemporary novelist (think of *The Severed Head* as merely the most explicitly Freudian of Murdoch's tales[14]) who takes Freud more seriously in his unyielding portrait of the self-deception of the ego, especially as the ego searches for the good. Recall, for example, how in *The Severed Head* this very contemporary Freudian narrative, without loss of its tragic sense, becomes suffused—and to an extent, diffused—by a brilliant Murdochian comedy of errors. For Iris Murdoch insists, in her novels as much as her philosophy,[15] that Freud was entirely right to see libidinal energy at the base of all artistic and spiritual experience. Freud was right again to show how ideals of the good (such as self-sacrifice) can sometimes function as illusions hiding deeper sado-masochistic drives.

But what Murdoch also shows is that these Freudian insights are devastating only to those forms of Platonism and understandings of the search for the Good which have forgotten Plato. It is not just Freud, it is Plato who insists that eros is a sort of universal energy, a profoundly ambiguous force which can work either for destruction or for the good. What Murdoch shows is not merely the Freudian tone of Plato's analysis of eros and the Good but, just as paradoxically, the Platonic tone of Freud's analyses of eros, of the soul, and of therapy. Indeed, Freud was never reluctant to admit his affinity with and, at times, his debt to his mentor. He declared his debt to Plato for the exposure of the illusions created by the ego, as well as for the self's need for a therapy that moves beyond the fragile, self-deluding ego to the full reality of the self or soul.

---

14. See the analyses of Deborah Johnson, *Iris Murdoch*, esp. 17–18.
15. See, especially, *Metaphysics and a Guide to Morals*, 20–24, for one of her many intriguing Plato-Freud comparisons.

It is Plato who first enunciated the classic Freudian portrait of the full horror of our situation in his extraordinary picture of the tyrant as the one who does in reality what the rest of us do in dreams.[16] It was Plato who insisted that only a full-scale therapy of the soul could be trusted to allow anyone to happen upon an occasional glimpse of the Good.[17] A glimpse, notice, no more than that, no union with the One as with Plotinus and many later Platonists.

Of course, neither Murdoch nor any other good interpreter of eros and the Good would claim that Plato and Freud share the same view of our situation. But Iris Murdoch does show their affinities by her careful interpretation of central factors in both Plato's and Freud's different but oddly related notions of the need for therapy in the soul before any objective truth or goodness can be claimed. Her argument is that Plato is never as optimistic on the search for the Good as many later Platonists may now seem in a post-Freudian age.[18] She shows this by both philosophical argument and, perhaps above all, by showing how such a search for the Good moves forward in and through the strange, tragic-comic interactions of the characters in her novels. Her personae, so contemporary and yet so ancient, seem driven by the madness of the ego and its self-delusions and illusions on what constitutes the genuine good, even as they find themselves magnetically attracted to the Good. It is this unique combination of Freud and Plato on eros and the Good, therapy and truth, that renders Murdoch's philosophical novels so captivating and her late twentieth-century philosophical retrieval of Plato's Good so important a post-Freudian candidate for serious contemporary philosophical and theological reflection.[19]

---

16. I am indebted for this insight to David Grene in a course jointly taught on *Republic*.
17. Plato, *Symposium*, 210E.
18. This was already, of course, the insight (vis-à-vis Porphyry and Plotinus) of that deeply troubled Platonist, St. Augustine.
19. This also renders Murdoch's philosophy curiously analogous to the debates among the earlier Frankfurt thinkers (especially Adorno and Horkheimer) on the exemplary role of Freudian psychoanalytical theory for a contemporary philosophical "critical theory."

II. FORMS OF THOUGHT AND THE FORM OF THE GOOD

The other charge against Plato, most forcefully articulated by Heidegger, is that Plato initiated the ontotheological reign of metaphysics. To my knowledge, Murdoch does not directly address this central contemporary attack on Plato and Platonism—an attack, as noted above, first forged by Nietzsche, sharpened by Heidegger and resharpened, in our own period, by Jacques Derrida.[20] Although Murdoch addresses other issues raised by each of these (for her) daimonic and poeticizing philosophers, she addresses their central charge against Plato very indirectly indeed.[21] In fact, in *Metaphysics as a Guide to Morals* she basically ignores this charge only to attempt to show both by her interpretations of Plato's experiments with genres and forms for rendering the Form of the Good[22] and by her own experiments with genres and forms how plausible and, one might add, now non-ontotheological Plato's account of the Good may be.

It is, for example, no small matter that Plato chooses the dialogue form to articulate his philosophy.[23] Indeed, if Plato's Seventh

---

20. See the study, *Iris Murdoch*, by Deborah Johnson for an illuminating analysis of what can be called the implicitly feminist elements (especially in the portraits of male and female characters) in Murdoch's novels.
21. Indeed, Murdoch's description and critique of these "daimonic" philosophies intensifies in her readings in *Metaphysics as a Guide to Morals*. Her reading of Derrida is especially severe—and, in my judgment, uncharacteristically unfair at times. Perhaps a reading of Derrida's recent work on ethics (e.g., *Spectrs of Marx*) might help to modify Murdoch's reading.
22. This analysis of Plato's own artistry despite his famous banishment of "the poets" already begins in Murdoch's study, *The Fire and the Sun: Why Plato Banished the Artists* (Oxford: Oxford University Press, 1977). Note the even stronger case made throughout *Metaphysics as a Guide to Morals* on Plato on the Good in comparison with the earlier analyses of *The Fire and the Sun* and *The Sovereignty of Good*.
23. For a more detailed defense of my position here, see David Tracy "Argument, Dialogue and the Soul in Plato" *Witness and Existence: Essays in Honor of Schubert M. Ogden*, eds. Philip E. Devenish and George L. Goodwin (Chicago: University of Chicago Press, 1989), 91–106. For further studies here, see Paul Friedlander, *Plato: An Introduction*, vol. 1, trans. Hans Meyerhoff (Princeton: Princeton University Press, 1969), 154–71, 230–36; Hans-Georg Gadamer, *Dia-*

Letter is genuine (as I believe it is), Plato not only meant, he said, that to understand his philosophy all we have are the dialogues.[24] Elenchus, dialectic, and dianoia are, to be sure, crucial even for the Plato who holds noesis as beyond all those discursive forms of reasoning. But Plato did not leave us a treatise, that is, a systematic collection of arguments like the splendid treatises of Aristotle, some Aristotle's own creation, some lecture notes of his students. Nor did Plato have collections of almost Koan-like meditations ready to be arranged by others into the fascinating form of Plotinus's *Enneads*. This difference between Plotinus and Plato is possibly because for Plotinus a union with the One is possible, whereas for Plato all we can hope for is an occasional glimpse of the Good (*Republic*), or the Beautiful (suddenly in *Symposium*), and possibly the One (in *Parmenides*).[25]

Above all, the form of a Platonic system—the kind of systematic form of neo-Platonism that was forged so brilliantly by Proclus and perfected centuries later in Thomas Aquinas's *Summa*[26]—was never a temptation for Plato. Indeed, I personally doubt if Plato ever gave a lecture on the Good at all.[27] There is no other text for Plato's philosophy. It is all in the dialogues. On my

---

logue and Dialectic: Eight Hermeneutical Studies in Plato, trans. P. Christopher Smith (New Haven: Yale University Press, 1980).

24. Plato, *Seventh Letter,* 341 B-E. See the eloquent and persuasive reading of the importance of this letter for understanding Plato by David Grene, *Greek Political Theory: The Image of Man in Thucydides and Plato* (Chicago: University of Chicago Press, 1967), 95–124.

25. On Plotinus, see Pierre Hadot, *Plotinus on the Simplicity of Vision,* trans. Michael Chase (Chicago: University of Chicago Press, 1973). I have already cited the relevant passages in *Republic* and *Symposium*. The Question of 'The One' in *Parmenides* (so influential on the neo-Platonists) remains extremely difficult to interpret with anything like surety, especially on the question of whether 'The One' of that uniquely dialectical dialogue is really analogous to the Good (in *Republic*) or the beautiful (in *Symposium*)—hence my cautionary adverb "possibly" here.

26. For the influence of Proclus in the systematic form of the *Summa,* see W. J. Hankey, *God in Himself: Aquinas' Doctrine of God as Expounded in the Summa Theologiae* (Oxford: Oxford University Press, 1987), esp. 1–19.

27. F. M. Cornford, *The Unwritten Philosophy and Other Essays* (Cambridge: Cambridge University Press, 1967), 28–47.

reading, the Seventh Letter, whether written by Plato himself or not, is hermeneutically true: What we possess for understanding the philosophy of Plato, including his understanding of the Good, are the dialogues. And I believe we can show that the dialogues are all any interpreter of Plato, including Aristotle, ever had.

Happily, as some analytical philosophers still refuse to see but Iris Murdoch so clearly does, the dialogues more than suffice. For in Plato's dialogues one can find not only formal arguments (some good, some bad, some middling) but also arguments as they actually occur for concrete human beings in concrete settings with real conversation partners. The link between argument and character in the dialogues helps any careful reader to learn that an understanding of the Good will come about only for those engaged in a therapy of their souls, a therapy which clarifies the world of intelligibility (for example, through mathematics), a therapy which takes one to a world of developing ideas and forms by constructing ever finer and more complex hypotheses through ever more demanding dialectical arguments before a noesis of the true can occur. In the greatest dialogues there is a world where the beauty of particular persons and particular art objects is both affirmed as an emblem of the Good and suspected as a distraction from the pure search for the Good. In the dialogues lives a world where myths are both demythologized and invented wholesale, sometimes to forge a dialectical point (as in the Myth of Er at the end of *The Republic*), at other times to become the principal form of logos itself (as in *The Timaeus*, that brilliantly dialectical myth which is perhaps Plato's greatest vision of how the Good has been made concrete in both cosmos and history).[28]

---

28. It is true that myth is usually demythologized in the early aporetic dialogues. However, beginning with the myths of the dramatic middle dialogues, especially *Phaedrus, Republic,* and *Symposium,* and culminating in the extraordinary dialectical-mythic *Timaeus,* one cannot justly claim that Plato is only a demythologizer. In fact, Plato is also one of the great remythologizers. In one sense, it is, of course, anachronistic to discuss Plato in terms of modern (i.e., post-Romantic) notions of myth. As is well known, in Plato (including *Timaeus*) *muthos* and *logos* are often used interchangeably, not as contrast terms. This is important to recall, even though the hermeneutical point holds: Plato develops (in the examples cited above), for philosophical purposes, what one can justly name "myth."

The wondrous middle dialogues—especially *Phaedrus, Symposium,* and *Republic*—seem modeled as dramas of the intellectual journey of the soul to the Good and the Beautiful. They function, for Plato, as alternatives to the dramas of the soul in Homer and in the tragedians (especially Aeschylus).[29] But the early aporetic dialogues and even, perhaps, the less dramatic, more dialectical later dialogues like *Parmenides* and *Sophist* seem not so much dramatic in structure as mimetic; that is, as Aristotle suggests, the dialogues of Plato may be modeled not on the dramas of the tragedians but on the ancient mimes. This is not an insignificant point, especially, as I shall suggest, for understanding the form not only of Plato's dialogues but also Iris Murdoch's own Platonic philosophy. For the ancient mimes, as David Grene has argued,[30] were, in their genre or form, very much like many of Plato's dialogues. The mimes, unlike the dramas, do not drive to a dramatic closure. The mimes, unlike the dramas, occur in the midst of everyday life where inquiring human beings simultaneously search for the good and delude themselves. At all times, however, we are involved in some troubled journey from birth to death and, if fortunate, discover some way to move, at least on occasion (e.g., when in the presence of a beautiful body provoking love), from appearance to reality. The mimes are not dramatic in form and not necessarily significant in content. They are often, to use the more familiar word, aporetic. They give glimpses of the Good in the midst of everyday life to ordinary thoughtful, troubled, and both self-deluding and honestly searching human beings.

Surely David Grene is suggestive in recalling Aristotle's usually overlooked comment that the mime was the model for Plato's dialogues or, at least, the genre for the large majority of the dia-

---

29. There is a striking affinity, at times, between the sensibilities of Aeschylus and Plato: witness the role of *peitho* (persuasion) and necessity in the *Oresteia* and, in Plato, in abstract (and mythic) terms in *Timaeus*. For some fruitful reflections in the Plato-Aeschylus comparison, see F. M. Cornford, *Plato's Cosmology: The Timaeus of Plato Translated with a Running Commentary* (London: Routledge & Kegan Paul, 1948), esp. 361–64.

30. In a public lecture delivered at Hobart and William Smith Colleges (Geneva, New York) in April 1990. This important study will be published in a forthcoming article.

logues. Indeed, most of the Platonic dialogues are like the mimes in the sense of how questions (such as what is courage) occur to human beings in very ordinary circumstances as they try to make some sense of their lives and catch some glimpse of something else, some ideal, some reality greater than themselves which is magnetically drawing them forward.

To return to Iris Murdoch's retrieval of Plato for the present: Some critics have suggested that Iris Murdoch's Gifford Lectures, *Metaphysics as a Guide to Morals,* lack the systematic character they expected or at least desired. This systematic drive seems more present in the briefer but more methodical arguments of *The Sovereignty of Good* and the highly focused interpretations of Sartre in *Romantic Rationalist* or of Plato himself in *The Fire and the Sun.*[31] However, on my reading at least, it is no disparagement of those earlier fine works by Murdoch to say that they lack not merely the ambitiousness but also the elaborate subtlety of form of *Metaphysics as a Guide to Morals.*

The latter book—even more than Murdoch's explicitly Platonic dialogues in *Acastos*[32]—seems to me more faithful to the kind of form needed for rendering a Platonic theory of the Good in the late twentieth century, that is, the century that has read not only Plato and the great Platonists but also Freud and feminists and such powerful philosophical critics of Plato as Nietzsche, Heidegger, and Derrida. For *Metaphysics as a Guide to Morals,* in spite of its occasional appearance of meandering formlessness, seems less a treatise and more like the great mime-like Platonic dialogues. From the very beginning of this strange and attractive book one finds oneself in the midst of a wider and unhurried conversation on unities and forms, on the Good and the search for the good, on illusion and the ego, or art and love and death and the Void— on questions, in short, which any thoughtful human being is likely at some point to ask or at least wonder about. In this meditative and meandering book, one sometimes finds oneself in the midst of

31. This is especially true of the relatively "tight" argument of *The Sovereignty of Good.*
32. Iris Murdoch, *Acastos: Two Platonic Dialogues* (New York: Penguin Books, 1988).

extended arguments (for example, the chapters on consciousness) or of brilliant extended interpretations (for example, the wonderful chapter restoring Schopenhauer to the serious philosophical consideration he deserves and almost never receives).[33] At other times, the reader finds not extended argument at all but brief and telling reflections with favored Murdochian conversation partners who seem to keep returning like characters in a novel into the odd conversation which is this strange, novel-like, philosophical book. At times the same characters seem to leave all too abruptly, again as in novels, mimes, and life (Wittgenstein, Kant, Simone Weil, and, of course, Plato). Sometimes something like closure may occur to a particular train of thought. More often, the argument dissolves or ends abruptly, as when the reflections on the need in our day for meditation, or at least for keeping silent, becomes the abrupt advice, "Teach it to your children." End of discussion. This is rather like the ancient mimes, that is, rather like ordinary life and its conversations. And through it all the somewhat labyrinthine search for the Good[34] yields to a magnetic pull for an occasional glimpse of something real, distant, unavoidable, transcendent, pure, oddly believable—the Void, the Infinite, perhaps the Good. In spite of the final brief summary,[35] there is in fact no dramatic closure to this open-ended dialogue-like work. Iris Murdoch, as a philosopher, has indeed found her proper form for articulating her particular vision of the Good, for she remembers what some of the critics seem to forget: both Plato's mime-like dialogues and her own mime-like novels, to which I now briefly turn.

The complex, again often meandering, sometimes self-disrupting order of Iris Murdoch's novels seems to suggest that any

---

33. *Metaphysics as a Guide to Morals*, 57–80.
34. I am tempted to suggest that the nearest Platonist in terms of a labyrinthine form to Murdoch is her Irish predecessor John Scotus Eriugena. Note, also in non-Platonic Irish works, the labyrinthine beauty of the *Book of Kells* or the endlessly complex forms of *Ulysses* and *Finnegan's Wake* in that wondrous Aristotelian-Thomist James Joyce. Most Platonists and almost all Aristotelians prefer a clearer, more straightforward form, except, it seems, Irish ones (such as Eriugena, Joyce—and Murdoch?).
35. "Metaphysics: A Summary" in *Metaphysics as a Guide to Morals*, 504–13.

ordinary realist ordering of both experience and understanding in a novel as in life and thought is, in fact, a falsification. The shifting and mixed genres of her novels also seem faithful to a vision of the slippery, indeed treacherous, nature of realistic language. As several literary critics have observed, the multi-voiced (one might also say Bahktinian) character of her novels rejects any single narrative voice in favor of many. This mime-like set of characteristics suggests how Iris Murdoch may have found the modern novel more congenial to her Platonic view of the human search for the Good than the form of the ancient dialogue. Indeed, the most widely acknowledged strengths of her novels bear striking family resemblances to some of the classic strengths of the Platonic dialogues: the sharply focused detail of the settings, the moments of interaction become extremely tense between the characters, the frequent surprises, intellectual and emotional, the play between the ideas and arguments themselves with the self's mixture of understanding and egoistic self-delusion.[36] At the same time, her novels, like Plato's aporetic dialogues, tend not to reach closure but to dissolve or sometimes explode or implode as the truth at stake becomes both unavoidable and unbearable, both undeniable and unavailable.

Her modern psychological novels—like Plato's ancient dialogues—demand an active response from the reader. Unlike the form of treatise, the dialogue's very open-endedness in form demands the reader's response. Unlike the realistic[37] novel which

36. See Elizabeth Dipple, *Iris Murdoch: Work for the Spirit*, esp. 36–80; Deborah Johnson, *Iris Murdoch*, 20–56.
37. Here I am once again informed by Johnson's feminist and Bakhtinian reading in her short but illuminating study of Murdoch's fiction. Johnson, in her turn, seems most influenced by the French feminist critic Luce Irigaray for her fascinating study of multiplicity and subversion in Murdoch's novels. Besides Johnson and Dipple (my principal literary guides to Murdoch's fiction), see also A. S. Byatt, *Degrees of Freedom: The Novels of Iris Murdoch* (London: Chatto & Windus, 1965) and Peter J. Comradi, *Iris Murdoch: The Saint and the Artist* (London and Basingstoke: Macmillan, 1986). In terms of Murdoch's novels, my own readings here are especially indebted to *The Black Prince* (New York: Viking, 1973), *The Sacred and Profane Love Machine* (New York: Viking, 1974) and *The Sea, The Sea* (New York: Viking, 1978). Among her more recent novels, *The Message to the Planet* (New York: Viking, 1990) and *The Green Knight* (New

Iris Murdoch's novels both so resemble and dissolve, her novels' characteristic open-endedness demand an active questioning response on the part of the reader. Alasdair MacIntyre is right to insist "Iris Murdoch's novels are philosophy but they are philosophy which casts doubt on all philosophy, including her own."[38] I would only add to this astute observation: and so does her philosophy when its mime-like form, its modern novel-like genre replacing the mime-like dialogues of the ancients, is taken as the signal clue to the philosophical content of her philosophy as glimpse of the Good in the midst of actual human life. One can probably never separate form and content as readily as most philosophers and theologians are still wont to believe.[39] Not only Derrida and Nietzsche but also Plato knew that. So did Augustine and Kierkegaard. So does Iris Murdoch—which is part of her great strength as both philosopher and novelist. Indeed, it is often difficult and sometimes impossible to know in her work where literature ends and philosophy begins or where philosophy ends and art begins. And that paradox can now be acknowledged for what it always was: a strength, not a weakness, especially for any thinker concerned to render a plausible view of the Good not as historical subject but as contemporary need and reality.

III. The Good and the Return of Spiritual Exercises

A major difficulty for modern westerners in reading the texts of the ancients and medievals in Western culture as well as the texts of other great cultures (for example, not only classical but also contemporary Buddhist texts in East Asian, South Asian and even now Western forms) is the habitual belief of modern Western philosophers and even theologians that theory should be separate from practices, especially practices as specific as an ancient thinker

---

York: Viking, 1994) have been especially helpful to me in my attempts to compare her philosophical and novelistic works.
38. Cited in Johnson, *Iris Murdoch*, 86, from MacIntyre's review of Elizabeth Dipple's exemplary study of Murdoch, *Iris Murdoch: Work for the Spirit*.
39. I have argued this, with proper reference to relevant philosophers and theologians, in "Literary Theory and Return of the Forms for Naming and Thinking God in Theology" *Journal of Religion* 74, 3 (1994): 302–19.

meant by the phrase "spiritual exercises."[40] The ancients (and the monastic medieval schools, although not the Scholastics!) would have found such a separation of theory and practical exercises not merely strange but self-destructive for true philosophy. Philosophy was for the ancients, above all, a love of wisdom, a unity of thought and a way of life. The philosopher as philosopher was unclassifiable in ordinary life, as ordinary life is usually understood. The unclassifiable character of the philosopher-sage determined, as Pierre Hadot maintains, all the major philosophical schools as well as all noninstitutionalized philosophic movements (skepticism, cynicism) of the entire Hellenistic period from the third century B.C.E. (when the "sorting out" of the schools as schools occurred) to the third century C.E. (when the classic neo-Platonic synthesis of Aristotelian and Stoic schools with Platonism was achieved).[41]

Exercises for philosophy (thus the word) were understood by all the ancient schools as analogous both to the exercises employed by an athlete for the body and to the application of a medical cure. In contemporary post-Freudian culture one could expand the analogy (Murdoch clearly does) to the exercises needed to appropriate one's feelings in therapy.[42] Among the ancients, such exercises include intellectual exercises: recall the use of mathematics to help the exercitant to move from the realm of the sensible to

---

40. See the ground-breaking work of Pierre Hadot, *Exercises spirituels et philosophie antique* (Paris: Etudes Augustiniennes, 1983). See also the insightful introductions and studies of Hadot's work by Arnold Davidson in his introduction to Pierre Hadot, *Plotinus*, 1–17 as well as the Spring 1990 issue of *Critical Inquiry* and his brilliant and erudite introduction to the English-language publication of Hadot's *Spiritual Exercises*. See Pierre Hadot, *Philosophy as a Way of Life: Spiritual Exercises from Socrates to Foucault*, ed. with intro. by Arnold J. Davidson, trans. Michael Chare (Oxford: Blackwell, 1995). I have been gratefully both introduced to and instructed by Davidson's readings of Hadot in my own interpretation here and elsewhere.
41. The other side of the story, as it were, may be found in Martha C. Nussbaum's study of how philosophy could function, for the ancients, as therapy, in her recent book *The Therapy of Desire: Theory and Practice in Hellenistic Ethics* (Princeton: Princeton University Press, 1994).
42. For a clarification of this suggestion, see Bernard Lonergan, *Method in Theology* (New York: Herder and Herder, 1992), 30–34.

the realm of intelligible in Pythagoras and Plato (and Lonergan).[43] These exercises also encompassed more obviously spiritual exercises, including the use of images, of memory training (recall both Hadot and Murdoch on Wittgenstein),[44] of reflection on the basic doctrines or beliefs of the school as well as exercises above all of increasing one's attentiveness, or awareness, or awakeness. Through all such exercises the exercitant can clarify her or his relationship to the ultimate norm, for example, a Stoic's exercise of attention to one's personal relationship to the *Logos* pervading the entire cosmos. Among the ancients, in sum, all reflection on the relationship between theory and practice must be understood from the perspective of such exercises, especially but not solely meditation. Even on the very limited basis of this summary of Hadot's analysis of ancient spiritual exercises and ancient theory, it is clear that Murdoch's contemporary Platonic philosophy explicitly and brilliantly corresponds to the ancient insistence on the role of intellectual exercises for personal intellectual self-appropriation.[45]

This detour into ancient philosophy surely does not suggest that Iris Murdoch wishes to promote a new institutionalization of a Platonic school for therapy of the soul in the search for the Good. In her portraits of our human condition in her novels as well as in

---

43. See Bernard Lonergan, *Insight: A Study of Human Understanding* (New York: Philosophical Library, 1957), 3–33. On the ancients, see Bruno Snell, *The Discovery of Mind* (New York: Harper Torchbook, 1960).
44. *Metaphysics as a Guide to Morals*, esp. 25–36. For further studies in this relationship, see Michael McGhee, ed., *Philosophy, Religion and the Spiritual Life* (Cambridge: Cambridge University Press, 1992).
45. I have suggested how Bernard Lonergan's work can also be read in this way in "Bernard Lonergan and the Return of Ancient Practice," in *Lonergan Workshop*, vol. 10, *The Legacy of Lonergan*, ed. Fred Lawrence (Boston: Boston College, 1994). I fully concur in Iris Murdoch's admiration of Simone Weil for the latter's exemplary way of uniting intellectual and spiritual exercises. One should also note that Michel Foucault, in his last work (partly influenced by Hadot's studies of the ancients), was also attempting a new "experiment" of unifying thought and life. For Hadot's appreciation and reservations on Foucault's use of his work, see "Reflections on the Ideas of the 'Cultivation of the Self'" in Pierre Hadot, *Philosophy as a Way of Life*, 206–15.

appeals to various kinds of exercises in *Metaphysics* *[as a Guide to] Morals*, Murdoch clearly believes that we need not a [new theory?] but rather more attentiveness to the practices we [are?] already actively engaged in or passively engaged by. Throughout her work she reminds us of the ethical and metaphysical import of our most everyday practices. For example, our ordinary human interactions, as her novels show, are often our best opportunity for both self-delusion and for spotting those self-delusions as we feel, through the very attractions and confusions of our interaction with others, the magnetic pull of the Good.[46] A second example: Erotic love can wrench us from our usual self-interest to face some other reality, even possibly the Good.[47] A third example: Art can, at times, free us to consider the possibility, as Murdoch nicely says, of "a pure transcendent value, a steady visible enduring higher good, and perhaps provides for many people, in an unreligious age without prayer or sacraments, their clearest *experience* of something grasped as separate and precious and beneficial and held quietly and unpossessively in the attention. Good art which we love can seem holy, and attending to it can be like praying. Our relation to such art, though probably never entirely pure, is markedly unselfish."[48]

Not only love and beauty are signals of the presence of our attraction to the Good. As the ancients insisted, intellectual practices function this way as well. Mathematics and dialectic direct our attention out of ourselves by their demand that we acknowledge, by intellectually entering, a world of pure intelligibility. Indeed, learning anything really well—any genuine painstaking work of scholarship or any careful attention to learning another language well, for example[49]—takes us immediately out of ourselves to a different kind of call and demand. That call is to a sense of objectivity as our paying virtuous attention to particular realities outside ourselves. Moreover, as Iris Murdoch's many appeals to

46. Perhaps the point, as well, of Stendahl's observation, "We can achieve everything in solitude save character."
47. *Metaphysics as a Guide to Morals*, 20–25.
48. *The Fire and the Sun*, 76–77.
49. The examples are Murdoch's own in *Metaphysics as a Guide to Morals*.

Simone Weil suggest,[50] explicitly spiritual exercises are also available to anyone. Above all, we can cultivate moments of tact, silence, attentiveness to the world outside ourselves as ways of decreasing our natural egoism. We can learn to pay attention in nature and in scientific inquiry to the image of necessity as law to nature. Such careful attentiveness to nature can help exhibit the futility of selfish purposes. Such attention can promote as well an attentiveness to the Void—that unavoidable reality which opens suddenly in and through our very language use.[51]

Iris Murdoch's hope for the reunion of thought and exercises is not focused upon a Kantian abrupt call for the will to abide by duty or upon a Kierkegaardian leap of faith or a radical transformation or conversion of the self from evil to good. Instead, her hope is directed to a slow shift of our attachments, a painstaking education of desire—an education like that which Plato foresaw as our best, perhaps our only, hope for both living and thinking well. Even metaphysics for her serves not only an intellectual but a spiritual purpose, another great barrier against our natural egoism.[52] There is no shortcut to enlightenment.

The words most frequently used in Murdoch's account of spiritual exercises—detachment and attention—suggest not so much Stoicism or Christianity as a new kind of Platonized Buddhism. Clearly, Christianity's classic narrative of creation, fall, and redemption is deeply embedded in Iris Murdoch's imagination of the human drama. How else to account for her appeal, even after her denial of a personal God, to a Christ-mysticism which discloses the approachable, even consoling, aspect of the Good?[53] Indeed, it is striking how suspicious Murdoch is of almost any conso-

---

50. See, especially, *Metaphysics as a Guide to Morals*, passim, esp. 500–506.
51. Derrida's work, in my judgment, can also be read in this direction. Such a reading could, for Murdoch, allow for a more positive assessment of Derrida than she gives in *Metaphysics as a Guide to Morals*, esp. 185–216.
52. Indeed, this seems to be a principal point of Murdoch's "Metaphysics: A Summary," 504–12 as well as the title of the work itself, *Metaphysics as a Guide to Morals*.
53. Murdoch seems most influenced here by Simone Weil's Christ-mysticism although perhaps Murdoch's own Quaker background is also influential here.

lation in religion.[54] Her problems with Jewish, Christian, or Muslim understandings of God seem to me to have less to do with familiar metaphysical difficulties than with what can only be called a problem of sensibility or even spirituality. She fears that any acceptance of a personal God, unlike the impersonal Good, will eventually console us in ways that allow us to escape once again facing reality—reality as what must be endured, what breaks through our egoism and fantasizing imagination by its unrelenting necessity.[55] For her, a belief in God can function as another veil created by our anxiety to hide away what is terrible and absurd in life and reality.

Surely an observer of any of our Western religions will agree that such a scenario can be the case. Moreover, Christian, Jewish, and Muslim thinkers can be thankful for Murdoch's pushing them in the direction of greater austerity of thought and practice. There is a need in our period, I have long believed as a Christian, for what might be named a more Buddhist sensibility of greater detachment in Christian God-talk.[56] Meister Eckhart now seems, even to many of his fellow Christian theologians, to have developed a far more believable God-language even on inner-Christian grounds than that of his more consoling orthodox critics. Even when a Christian theologian like myself turns away from both Buddhist *sunyata* and the Platonist impersonal Good to God, a turn to the practice of radical detachment after the death of all modern theisms is profoundly necessary for any adequate contem-

---

54. This 'hermeneutics of suspicion' upon all consolation in religion (in both Weil and Murdoch) seems to me profoundly true in its suspicion of how false the consolations of a 'personal God' often are and how cheap the all too 'consoling' grace of religion can be. Nevertheless, the spiritual states of peace, quiet, serenity (all of which Murdoch endorses) are not far from authentic spiritual understandings of 'consolation' in the monotheistic traditions.
55. On necessity, see Simone Weil's wondrous essay, "The Iliad, Poem of Might" in *The Simone Weil Reader*, ed. George A. Paniches (New York: David McKay, 1977), 153–84.
56. See David Tracy, "The Buddhist-Christian Dialogue," in *Dialogue With the Other: The Inter-Religious Dialogue* (Leuven: Eerdmans/Peters Press, 1990), 68–94. Also David Tracy, "God and Emptiness: Response to Abe Masao," in *God and Emptiness*, ed. Christopher Ives (Maryknoll: Orbis, 1990).

porary Christian theological understanding of the relationship of God and the Good.[57]

A final question here: Is the Good best conceived through Iris Murdoch's metaphor as a magnet powerfully attracting us despite ourselves? Or is Platonic Good best conceived through the metaphor of gift, the other great Platonist metaphor which I and others now attempt to retrieve? That question needs to be asked first, I believe, in order to provide the necessary refinement of a contemporary Platonic entry to the question of God and the Good. In the meantime even those like myself trying to grasp the full power and range of the reality of the Good as gift[58] can also affirm the power of the metaphor of the Good as a magnet, forcibly drawing one to itself despite oneself, attracting us by its beauty, its objectivity, and its goodness. That magnetic force of the Good is just what any thoughtful reader can experience in these remarkably complex novels that read so like good philosophy and these stunning, meandering philosophical books that read so like good novels. In both lurks the magnetic power which allows us even now an occasional glimpse of the Good.

57. I hope to expand upon and defend this position in a forthcoming book on naming and thinking God.
58. Jean-Luc Marion, *God Without Being*, 47–49, 101, 106, 161–78, 227.

PART TWO

MORALITY, ETHICS, AND LITERATURE

4
"WE ARE PERPETUALLY MORALISTS": IRIS MURDOCH, FACT, AND VALUE

Cora Diamond

In the 1950s, philosophers in the analytic tradition accepted as virtually unquestionable two closely related ideas, that it is a logical error to attempt to infer any evaluative conclusion from factual premises, and that there is a fundamental distinction between fact and value.[1] In 1956, in her essay "Vision and Choice in Morality,"[2] Iris Murdoch criticized these ideas; she was among the first to do so.

I start with her discussion of fact and value in that early essay. I then look at R. M. Hare's response to that essay, in *Freedom and Reason*,[3] and I move on to a more general discussion of the issue between Murdoch and Hare. Does Hare's supposedly neutral account of the logic of ethics embody, as Murdoch suggests, his own fundamental moral concepts? In the final two sections of the paper I turn back to some further questions about the distinction between fact and value, tied to Murdoch's recent book *Metaphysics as a Guide to Morals*.[4]

---

1. The quotation forming part of the title of this essay comes from Samuel Johnson's "Life of Milton." I take the quotation from Samuel Goldberg's *Agents and Lives: Moral Thinking in Literature* (Cambridge: Cambridge University Press, 1993). See Part IX below for some further discussion of the quotation and Goldberg's use of it.
2. *Proceedings of the Aristotelian Society*, supp. vol. 30 (1956): 32–58, referred to hereafter as "Vision and Choice."
3. Oxford: Clarendon Press, 1963.
4. New York: Allen Lane/Penguin Press, 1993; referred to hereafter as *Metaphysics*.

79

I

In "Vision and Choice," Murdoch suggests that the power of the then current view "derives from a feeling that it constitutes a defence against the fallacy of naturalism"—and that leads her to examine whether indeed naturalism *is* a fallacy. Arguments in which moral conclusions are drawn from non-moral premises are supposedly fallacious because they would depend on a suppressed evaluative premise or on an attempt to define moral terms in non-moral terms (p. 53). There is something valuable in such critiques, and we should follow Murdoch here to see what it is. She considers the example of a person who argues that such-and-such a thing must be all right to do, since statistics show that people constantly do it. A philosopher who accepted the standard argument against ethical naturalism would point out that a premise—what is customary is right—has been concealed. Once the premise has been thus exposed to view, the arguer might indeed go on to accept a definition of rightness in terms of what is customary, and the analytical philosopher would then criticize *that* step. But Murdoch makes clear that "the exposure of the premise" may itself suffice to "destroy the appeal of the argument," which, as she says, "may depend . . . upon the hearer's imagining that he has got to accept the conclusion or deny the plain facts." She herself then goes on to say that she would endorse many arguments of that type, "whose purpose is solely to achieve such exposure" (ibid.).

Murdoch then turns to the claim by analytical philosophers that it is impossible to define moral terms in non-moral terms. This she takes to be more interesting than their contention that naturalistic ethical arguments frequently contain suppressed premises. But it is worth looking longer at the case of suppressed premises. In Murdoch's account, what is the matter with suppressing a premise in a moral argument may be that the hearer of the argument will not grasp the possibilities open to him, will think that he is forced to the conclusion by undeniable facts. The "hearer" need not be someone other than the arguer himself; that is, we may use arguments of this type when we justify to ourselves things which we want to do but which we cannot clearly square with conscience. That the thing we are tempted to do is all right because generally done might be particularly likely to figure in such thinking. What is going on in such cases may be a kind of evasion, a kind of refusal to take responsibility: One wants the undeniable facts of what is customarily done to have fixed the moral rightness. So an argument exposing the suppressed premise exposes also the issue of responsibility. We can then explain the aim of the kind of argument that brings to attention such suppressed premises in terms of responsibility. Iris Murdoch's discussion of cases of suppressed premises in moral arguments connects directly with Stanley Cavell's discussions of moral rationality in Part III of *The Claim of Reason*.[5] For Cavell, moral rationality centrally includes coming to understand what we are doing (or plan to do, or have done), what we are committing ourselves to, what responsibility we are taking.

Looking at Iris Murdoch's discussion of moral arguments with suppressed premises, we can now see a particular limited kind of agreement with the analytical philosophers of the 1950s and a more important disagreement. She and they can agree that an important kind of flaw in some arguments that proceed from fact to value is the suppression of premises. But, for the analytical philosophers, the need for the further premise is tied to the supposed existence of a logical gap between fact and value; for Murdoch, the need for the further premise and the point of exposing it are tied to a quite different conception of moral rationality, in which there is no logical gap between fact and value, but there is the possibility of a kind of failure in moral thinking, the criticism of which is not an abstract logical matter. If, in such criticism, we ask, "Are you not assuming that such-and-such?" the availability of that question is not dependent on general logical relations between fact and value. The need, if there is a need, to press such a question cannot be derived from the general logical relations between two types of discourse; the recognition of the need involves sensitivity to the possibilities of moral evasion in the particular

5. New York: Oxford University Press, 1979.

case.[6] I have used the notions of evasion and responsibility in explaining Murdoch's views, and these are terms of evaluation of thinking which are as much moral as cognitive.

What we reach then by taking further Iris Murdoch's discussion of suppressed premises is an extremely central theme of her moral philosophy, especially as we see that philosophy 37 years later in *Metaphysics as a Guide to Morals*. I mean the theme that thinking is always an activity of ours as *moral* beings. This is the theme of the cognitive as always moral. I shall return to this theme later.

II

Murdoch had summarized the objections of analytical philosophers to arguments purporting to draw moral conclusions from factual premises: The arguments will turn out either to involve suppressed major premises or to depend upon an illegitimate attempt to define moral terms in non-moral terms. Why, she asks, are such definitions supposed to be illegitimate? In "Vision and Choice," her argument against the analytical philosophers on this is very condensed; it is spelled out and expanded in *The Sovereignty of Good*.[7] What is at stake is a cluster of conceptions. That is, she is calling attention to, and criticizing, the analytical philosophers' conception of moral rationality, their idea of the character of moral concepts, their idea of what it means for us as moral agents to have or exercise freedom, and their idea of what it is for us to be placed in situations requiring moral attention. She tries to show how a totally different mode of understanding of all of these is possible, and that the issues here are not "logical," if that means that they can be settled by some neutral philosophical analysis: They are differences of moral understanding. So, an important part of her argument is that the supposed ethical neutrality of moral philoso-

---

6. Certain familiar kinds of naturalistic arguments, and certain familiar types of examples, may make it appear that all that is involved in the critique of arguments as suppressing an evaluative premise is the identification of a set of premises as "factual" and of the conclusion from them as "evaluative." On this issue see chap. 12 of Cavell, *The Claim of Reason*.
7. London: Routledge and Kegan Paul, 1970.

phy is illusory. She does not use the word "ideological," but her argument could be said to show the ideological character of moral philosophy: It works to exclude certain moral conceptions which it makes appear as logical confusions, discoverable to be confusions by neutral analysis. Among the conceptions thus excluded are, as she points out, that of the Marxist and those of at least some kinds of Christian ("Vision and Choice," 56).

To return to the issue of defining moral terms. For the analytical philosopher who rejects, as illegitimate, naturalistic definitions of moral terms, such definitions would constitute an interference with the freedom of the moral agent. Presented with the facts, a moral agent can describe them in non-moral words, and express his commitment to an evaluative principle, or evaluative framework, through his own choice of criteria for the use of such terms as "good." Here Murdoch reminds us of the importance of moral concepts unlike *good* and *right* and *wrong:* She says that a moral outlook can be shown in ramifications of more specialized concepts, concepts that determine a vision of the world ("Vision and Choice," 54). And if we focus on such concepts we shall perhaps be less attracted to the idea that value cannot be defined in terms of fact. She mentions that moral concepts may determine what we take a situation to be: It is not the case that if the moral concept were withdrawn we should be left with the same situation or the same facts (ibid.).

She is not denying that there are situations in which *some* view of the facts can be agreed on by everyone, and in which people differ in how they apply a moral concept; and the moral concept itself, the application of which is disputed, may be one of those she is referring to as "specialized." (What she refers to as "specialized" moral concepts includes but is not limited to the concepts now frequently described, following Bernard Williams, as "thick."[8]) Thus there might be a dispute in which it is clear to both sides who took what from whom, but one side calls it stealing, and the other vehemently rejects such a description. That "stealing," or "theft," are specialized moral terms does not imply that

---

8. Bernard Williams, *Ethics and the Limits of Philosophy* (Cambridge: Harvard University Press, 1985).

their application will in all cases be fixed by readily ascertainable facts.

III

R. M. Hare's response to this line of criticism by Murdoch (and to related criticisms made by Philippa Foot) is interesting. He recognizes that his understanding of the freedom of a moral agent might appear to be threatened by the existence of cases in which the application of a specialized moral concept cannot be disputed. The apparent threat can be headed off, he argues, by a clear appreciation of how evaluative words with relatively fixed descriptive content operate.[9] Although words like "courage" do, as he puts it, encapsulate moral attitudes, the person who does not accept the attitudes encapsulated in the word can avoid using it. Such a person might find some morally neutral expression to describe the actions which others call courageous; Hare's example is "disregarding one's own safety in order to preserve that of others." This is not, he says, descriptively equivalent to "courageous"; but he does commit himself to the idea that there *could be* an expression descriptively equivalent to "courageous," correctly applied to the same cases but lacking the encapsulated attitude.[10] Hare's position then connects the agent's moral freedom to the possibility of various sorts of uses of moral terms: Freedom is ensured by the possibility of description of any situation in ways which do not commit the agent to some particular moral view. That is, for any descrip-

---

9. Hare's response may be found in chap. 10 of *Freedom and Reason*. The basis for the development of this line of argument is already present in *The Language of Morals* (Oxford: Clarendon Press, 1952), in the distinction there between evaluative words the descriptive meaning of which is primary and evaluative words the descriptive meaning of which is secondary; see p. 121, and cf. also *Freedom and Reason*, 24–25.

10. *Freedom and Reason*, 187–89. For a critical discussion of this kind of commitment on the part of non-cognitivists, see John McDowell, "Non-Cognitivism and Rule-Following," in *Wittgenstein: To Follow a Rule*, ed. Steven Holtzman and Christopher Leich (London: Routledge & Kegan Paul, 1981), 141–62.

Hare's argument is also open to a different sort of criticism, which would question his idea of the moral neutrality of descriptions like "disregarding one's own safety in order to preserve that of others."

tion in terms which do carry a moral commitment, the moral agent has available some alternative description without that commitment, or such a description could be constructed. So Hare does not need to deny Murdoch's point about there being specialized moral concepts, but he rejects her idea that such concepts may be tied to the understanding of what a situation is—tied to it in the sense that that understanding of what the situation is might be unavailable to people who withheld or rejected certain moral concepts. What a situation is, what its features are, is available to any moral agent as a user (possibly an innovative user) of descriptive language. Concepts, on this view, can shape moral understanding only in the relatively superficial sense that there are concepts which encapsulate attitudes, but which we shall not use if we have certain moral principles. Avoiding such concepts can have no consequences for what is possible in the way of moral understanding.[11]

I shall suggest that Hare's reply showed his failure to see what Murdoch meant by a moral concept shaping our vision of a situation, but I shall get to that later. I turn now to Hare's further response to Murdoch's discussion of fact and value in "Vision and Choice." She had argued that a source of the analytical philosopher's insistence on the gap between fact and value was actually a specific *moral* recommendation: a recommendation that the attitudes of others be respected—a rejection of dogmatism, a recognition that we and others inhabit the same perceptible, describable world. Behind this recommendation, she suggested, "lie the moral attitudes of Protestantism and Liberalism" ("Vision and Choice," 52). Her idea that someone's understanding of a situation might be irreducibly evaluative (might be such that to withdraw the evaluation would not be to leave the same facts) goes against the idea that there is an understanding of what the facts are which does not reflect the moral view of either party to a moral disagreement, and that moral argument can therefore take for granted that the parties to it inhabit the same world. Murdoch asks us to consider someone

---

11. In *Moral Thinking: Its Levels, Method, and Point* (Oxford: Clarendon Press, 1981), Hare's account of terms like "courageous" is integrated into his more general discussion of levels of moral thinking; this does not represent a significant change from the response in *Freedom and Reason* to critics like Murdoch and Foot.

whose fundamental moral attitude is radically different from that of the Liberal—someone, for example, who takes reality to have immanent in it moral purposes transcending human purposes, and who thinks that "moral progress consists in awareness of this reality and submission to its purposes" (p. 56). The difference between such a person and someone like Hare is fundamentally a difference in *moral* view. But within moral philosophy the Liberal view is turned into or disguised as a logical theory of moral discourse.

This accusation stung Hare. It called into question his entire project, and indeed the project of analytical moral philosophy: to give an account of *the* logic of moral discourse, an account which is not a mere reflection of any *particular* moral attitudes.[12]

In reply, Hare attempted to show that, although indeed he is a liberal and a protestant, his account of moral language allows for the expression of the most anti-liberal and anti-protestant views: A Nazi fanatic, for example, can be described as holding the principle that anyone with such-and-such characteristics should be exterminated. There is thus no reason why the Nazi could not accept Hare's account of moral language (*Freedom and Reason*, 192–93; cf. 170 on the Nazi and his principles).

As a reply to Murdoch, this is a failure, for two reasons. It misses the point of her criticism, and fails even on its own terms, that is, as an account of Nazi views. I shall explain that first, and then turn to the more important misunderstanding running through Hare's reply.

Hare presents us with a Nazi who has been reconstructed in

---

12. The self-understanding of analytical moral philosophy has undergone some changes since the works that Murdoch criticized. It is no longer fashionable to believe that moral philosophy must be "ethically neutral." But the underlying ideas have not shifted: There is still, in the practice of moral philosophy, the belief that there is a single basic structure of moral discourse or of moral thinking. There is, for example, nothing out-of-date in a moral philosopher taking it that moral thought, if it is to lead to action, must involve the application of some moral principle—otherwise, our thought supposedly cannot (logically cannot) bear on action. Murdoch's writings in moral philosophy have consistently called this sort of assumption into question.

some significant ways, to make his moral views universalizable. His Nazi is not so much an anti-Semite as an anti-everybody-who-has-certain-characteristics. In contrast, the views of real Nazis gave a role to Germany, to Hitler, to "the German National Socialist revolution" (and also to "the Jewish race," and to German race-science) which makes it difficult to claim that they were genuinely universalizable. The requirement of passionate devotion to Germany and its "revolution" was not the application to Germany of a universal principle requiring passionate devotion to one's country. Germany was conceived as a unique object of devotion, and Hitler as playing a unique role in its destiny. Real Nazis did not have "ideals" in Hare's sense; they can, from his point of view, be said only to have desires, since the defining difference for him is the presence, in the expression of the views in question, of unremovable proper names. In Nazi rhetoric, even apparently universal claims, like "The artist creates for the people," carried quite clear implicit references to Germany. The distance between uninvented Nazis and Hare's fictional Nazi-with-universal-principles helps to show the force of Murdoch's criticisms in this way: Hare's claim to be able to represent every moral view can be seen, in the case of the Nazis, to involve treating real Nazis as not having moral views, and inventing fictional Nazis who accept universal principles corresponding to some elements in Nazi ideology but whose view of the world, and whose attitude to universality, are quite different from those of real Nazis. The example of the Nazis in fact brings out how the rejection of an Enlightenment conception of rationality, tied to universality in science and ethics, can be at the heart of a moral view.

We can now turn to the question how Hare's reply to Murdoch involved deep misunderstanding of the criticism itself.

An image of Wittgenstein's is helpful here. If we use a certain fixed method of projection to represent on plane B the shapes that are on plane A, we can make inferences from the different shapes that have been drawn on B to the original shapes on A. But suppose we have quite a different procedure: We decide to represent every shape on A by a circle on B, no matter what the shape on A is. The mere fact that a representation on B is a circle tells us nothing at all about the figure represented. That the representation is a circle is simply the established norm of the mapping.[13]

Now Iris Murdoch's argument in "Vision and Choice" went roughly like this: It is possible for a philosopher to represent *all* moral thought, no matter how different in character, as the formation and application of universal rules governing choices. She never doubted that Hare could take any moral view whatever and give some representation of it that fitted his general account. Such a way of proceeding is, she said, philosophically unilluminating (pp. 44, 45, 46–47, 51–52, 57). The philosophical pointlessness of representing very various modes of moral thought using a single model that fits well only some is emphasized by Murdoch not once, not twice, but five times. When she described Hare and other analytical philosophers as having accounts of the "logic" of moral discourse that reflect their particular moral attitude, her point was clearly not that other moral views could not be represented by their theories. The point was that the method of representation itself was what embodied the moral attitude of analytical philosophers; the model itself embodied their liberal or protestant views. So it is no reply to that argument to demonstrate, as Hare tries to do, that Nazi or other non-liberal views can be represented by his model. Putting this point now in terms of the analogy with Wittgenstein's argument about the circles: If it is argued against you that your philosophical account of morality ignores the characteristic features of certain kinds of moral view, if (that is) the charge against you is that you are representing a great variety of different shapes as "circles," it is not a reply to show how views very different from your own can be represented, like your own, as "circles"; it is not a reply to insist that *every* moral view can indeed be represented as a "circle."

We have seen that Hare, in his discussion of these issues, takes as his examples of people who do not share his liberal protestant views, those who accept principles that he rejects, like the principle requiring that Jews be exterminated. Murdoch, throughout her article, had attempted to articulate a *totally different kind* of contrast between approaches to morality, not at all a difference

---

13. L. Wittgenstein, *Philosophical Grammar* (Oxford: Blackwell, 1974), 204–5.

in the content of principles. She had tried to show that a view of *what we are as moral agents* could itself be a moral view ("Vision and Choice," 57); and that a view of *what the world is like* could be a moral view (p. 47). People differ greatly, she had noted, in their moral understanding of the world: "There are people whose fundamental moral belief is that we all live in the same empirically and rationally comprehensible world and that morality is the adoption of universal and openly defensible rules of conduct. There are other people whose fundamental moral belief is that we live in a world whose mystery transcends us" and that morality is the exploration of that mystery in so far as it concerns each individual (p. 47).

Analytical moral philosophy has embodied what she described as the fundamental moral belief of the first sort of person in its account of the logic of moral discourse. If that is indeed her argument, it really is somewhat extraordinary that Hare should have replied that his theory can cover principled versions of Nazism, clericalism, militarism and so on. The issue, as framed by Murdoch, concerned the very idea of a mode of understanding of the world as *itself* a kind of moral belief. But at this point we have gone beyond anything that Hare could indeed argue for. There is, as he conceives matters, no such thing as a person's moral being or moral life apart from his development of universal principles and his application of those principles in action and in principled argument. That that itself should be takeable as a *moral* belief of his is outside the range of discussion constituting moral philosophy. He rejects a conception of himself as someone whose moral being can be seen in what he finds reassuring or unsettling in the describability of the world; he rejects that notion of a person's "moral being."

Let me put this argument another way. Murdoch had argued that Hare's theory contained a built-in moral view, and that it excluded certain sorts of moral views. These excluded views differed from Hare's, Murdoch suggested, not in what principles they contained but in how they understood the character of the world and the nature of moral agency. In his reply, Hare reformulated the criticism. In his version, what it would mean for a theory of ethics to exclude a moral view is simply for that theory to exclude certain principled positions; but his theory, as he can show, excludes no principled moral positions. But that reply itself, and his conception of what he is replying to, have built into them a particular conception of moral agency. In formulating his reply, he assumes that a conception of moral agency cannot itself embody a moral view. But the criticism to which this was supposedly a reply was the criticism that one's understanding of moral agency could be part of one's general moral approach. In Hare's response we can see the circularity to which Murdoch drew attention in the 1956 essay: What counts as part of the sphere of morality is defined by the analytical moral philosopher in a way that does not allow the moral assumptions in the definition to be recognized or challenged ("Vision and Choice," 33).

Hare's response to Murdoch's criticism is an attempt to secure the central value that is built into the account, namely, freedom—freedom as he conceives it. The idea that someone's (Hare's or anyone else's) fundamental conception of the world or of human agency might belong to that person's moral being would threaten that central value. The threat arises from the fact that those fundamental conceptions of the world and of agency are not principles, are not moral beliefs in Hare's sense at all. They are not evaluative commitments, tied to acting in this or that way whenever the facts are of such-and-such a sort; hence, our freedom to formulate principles, and to commit ourselves to them with an understanding of their consequences, would not reach to such "moral beliefs." If such beliefs form a fundamental part of someone's moral being, then our moral being is not at its roots characterized by freedom in Hare's sense. That then is why there cannot, on Hare's account, be such a thing as a moral belief which is not a belief about what one should do in some describable situation or type of situation. To allow the possibility of such a belief would undermine the account of freedom. Further, Hare cannot allow that the definition of moral belief is itself something about which there might be disagreement tied to a different *moral* understanding. Hence, I think, his misrepresentation of the disagreement between himself and Murdoch, as if what he had been criticized for was excluding certain kinds of principled views.

IV

At this point I want to turn to a feature of the disagreement between Murdoch and Hare about which I have said little. Murdoch argues that analytical philosophers like Hare fail to see the shaping role moral concepts have in our thought. Fundamental moral differences, as she points out several times in "Vision and Choice," are frequently or indeed usually conceptual differences. Her disagreement with analytical moral philosophy involves a disagreement about the character of moral concepts themselves. The argument is tied closely to the points that I have been discussing; for the fundamental "moral beliefs" that she ascribes to philosophers like Hare involve a group of related concepts like that of the rationally comprehensible, describable factual world. She speaks of that idea both as a concept and as a "general conceptual attitude" ("Vision and Choice," 44, 48).

Hare's disagreement with these ideas of Murdoch's is complex. Perhaps the most important element of it is his view that a "conceptual apparatus" is something which one adopts; and adopting such an apparatus is distinguishable in principle from adopting a moral view, a system of moral principles (*Freedom and Reason*, 187). He recognizes that there are moral concepts like *courage* which encapsulate moral attitudes. But this leaves him free to deny that moral differences are genuinely conceptual differences. The difference between a person who is willing to use the concept *courage*, who accepts the encapsulated attitude, and a person who rejects the attitude and who might thus opt out of using the concept altogether is really a difference in moral principles. It is a difference concerning what people *ought* to do, and it can be formulated entirely without using the concept of *courage* or any concept which encapsulates an attitude. All moral differences are differences of principle and could at least in theory be expressed in a language without "specialized" moral concepts. (See *Freedom and Reason*, the whole of chap. 10, especially 10.7. These ideas are developed further in *Moral Thinking* but are not changed in any fundamental way.)

Here again, I want to argue that Hare's reply fails to come

into contact with Murdoch's objection. His idea of what moral concepts can be like takes for granted a particular way of thinking of words in relation to the world, the world open to factual description; but Murdoch had tried to show, throughout the essay, that that understanding was not forced on us. Here (borrowing and extending an image from "Vision and Choice," 40) is a description of the way of thinking about concepts which she rejected: Any concept, evaluative or descriptive, is like a ring laid down over a certain area of fact. What determines the area of fact overlaid by a descriptive concept is meaning-rules (so these rings are fixed in place), while what determines the area of fact overlaid by a primarily evaluative concept will be our decisions of principle (so these latter rings are "movable and extensible"). A secondarily evaluative concept like *courage* would, on Hare's view, be tied to a particular area by meaning-rules, but people who rejected the moral views associated with the concept would be able to describe the relevant area in some other way, without commitment to any evaluation. Murdoch rejected not only the ring-picture of moral concepts but also the idea of moral disagreement dependent on it. A moral concept need not be thought of as like a (more or less) movable and extensible ring laid down to cover some area of fact; it may be "like a total difference of *Gestalt*" (see "Vision and Choice," 40–41). The disagreement with Hare about what moral concepts are like was closely tied to the contrast between vision and choice running through the essay as a whole: Moral differences need not be seen as Hare sees them, as differences of choice which remain even when we share an understanding of the facts; they are frequently differences of vision (ibid.).

In her later writing on ethics, Murdoch gives some examples of how moral concepts may shape our understanding of a situation. (See, e.g., *Sovereignty of Good*, 17–23, 25, 31–33.) In Parts V–VIII I discuss two other examples.

V

Consider first G. K. Chesterton's account of his understanding of life.[14] He views the world as filled with the wonder of fairy tales; life is understood as an extraordinary adventure. "This world," he says, "is a wild and startling place" (p. 58). That *Gestalt* (to use Murdoch's word) went with a great tenderness towards the world, a sense of modesty, and a willingness to submit to what might appear to be odd limitations—limitations, though, tied to the totally odd kindness to oneself of one's being alive in this wild and startling world. A profound antipathy towards knowingness and immodesty is also connected to Chesterton's understanding of life. I have chosen this example because I wanted to explain what is meant by Murdoch's remark that a moral concept need not be like a ring laid down to cover a certain area and may be more like a total difference of *Gestalt*. I wanted an example for which her phrase "a general conceptual attitude" would be particularly appropriate.

What now is the contrast between a conceptual attitude like Chesterton's and a concept like *courage*, as Hare conceives the latter? The "goodness of being in a fairy-tale" (if that is one's image of *being alive*) does not have any direct ties with any particular descriptive content. It has connections with how one ought to live, what one ought to do, but not the sort of connections which Hare takes the concept of courage to have. By the linguistic conventions governing its use, the word "courageous" is tied, according to Hare, both to certain sorts of situation and to certain evaluations; and that is exactly why he thinks that one might choose, if one rejected those evaluations, not to use the word at all (or to use it only in inverted commas). But the concepts figuring centrally in Chesterton's view of life are not applied via descriptive criteria to certain sorts of situation. They may indeed cast light on *various* situations; but how they will do that is not tied to any linguistic convention. Further, and perhaps most important here, the "general conceptual attitude" that we are speaking about is not some-

---

14. G. K. Chesterton, "The Ethics of Elfland," in *Orthodoxy* (Garden City, N.Y.: Doubleday, 1959).

thing *chosen* by Chesterton. The image of *conceptual choice,* which is central for Hare's understanding of moral thought and moral agency, could be fitted on to Chesterton's use of concepts only by doing violence to its character, only through a refusal to take seriously the genuine variety there is in the forms taken by moral thought. Life as adventure in a fairy tale was, for Chesterton, the best way of putting something that was for him a kind of perception; it reflected convictions that underlay any conscious understanding of the world ("Ethics of Elfland," 53, 64–65). It preceded, in a sense, anything that was for him a matter of choice or of principles governing choice; it gave him a language, and images, in which he was able to think about what some choice might mean. The difference between Chesterton and those who do not share his view of the world is indeed a moral difference, but it is not, at its roots, a difference of moral principles, a difference about *what we ought to do.*

On Hare's account of rationality in the use of words, both descriptive words and evaluative words are universalizable (see, e.g., *Freedom and Reason,* chap. 2). They are applied to a thing or situation *in virtue of* some feature or features of what they are applied to: In any application there is at least implicit some principle governing what a *consistent* application of the term would be (i.e., specifying that *in virtue of which* the term could also be applied to other things). Rational use of descriptive or evaluative terms is, one could say, "in virtue of"-use. The meaning-rules for descriptive terms fix that in virtue of which they can be applied; so do the meaning-rules for "specialized" evaluative terms like "courageous"; the features in virtue of which a non-specialized evaluative term is applied are determined through our own choice of moral principles. That is the picture of the nature of concepts which Murdoch rejects. Indeed, her rejection of it is reflected in her claims that linguistic philosophers did not take linguistic method seriously, that they "mistrusted" language ("Vision and Choice," 42–43). Their mistrust of language is the mistrust of any use of language about the world which cannot be fitted in to the "in virtue of" model. Chesterton's account of his moral understanding of life, and of the relevance to it of fairy tales, involves uses of words, uses of metaphors and stories, which cannot be accommodated by the "in virtue of" model.[15] It thus exemplifies the life of language, that is, the life mistrusted by linguistic philosophers.

In the next three sections I look at another example, in order to develop that last point, the point that the life of language, the life of our concepts, is kept from view in Hare's kind of account of moral thought. The example I shall consider is one of this century's great works of moral reflection, Alexander Wat's *My Century*.[16]

VI

In his foreword to *My Century*, Czeslaw Milosz comments on the quality of the consciousness of the book's narrator (p. xxv). This notion, of quality of consciousness, is of central importance in all of Iris Murdoch's philosophical discussions of ethics. And so it is particularly appropriate to illustrate her views by a work in which the narrator's quality of consciousness is particularly striking. To describe it as a book of moral reflection on the events of this century is not to say that it has such reflection as its content, but that that is what it achieves through the telling of the narrator's experiences, and through his extraordinary ability to bring experiences, events, and moral ideas into connection with each other.[17]

15. This point can be brought out if we look at Hare's own method of argument. In the case of any descriptive or evaluative term, we are supposedly able to tell the person who applies the term to something X that he is committed to applying the term to anything that is like X in the relevant respects. (See, e.g., *Freedom and Reason*, 18.) But Chesterton's application to life of the expression "wild and startling" is not application in virtue of some feature which life supposedly has, even a feature which only life has. It is a rendering in words of a fundamental kind of responsiveness to life. For an examination of some related issues, see my "Secondary Sense," in *The Realistic Spirit* (Cambridge: MIT Press, 1991).
16. New York: Norton, 1990.
17. *My Century* has also the character of a *Bildungsroman;* we see the moral education of the narrator through the experiences and events he lives through; the kind of consciousness evident in the narrative is what has been made possible by that education. The book thus has some resemblances to *David Copperfield* and to *Great Expectations*, in both of which the moral consciousness of the narrator is shaped by the events he retells. In *David Copperfield*, the art of the narrative itself is meant to be seen as an exercise of the capacities which we see the

The basis of the book is taped conversations, in which Wat recounted to Milosz his experiences as a writer and leftist in pre-war Poland, and his war-time experiences in prison and out of prison in Poland and the Soviet Union. (There are some, very limited, interpolated references to Wat's post-war experiences in Poland.) The book as a whole enables the reader to see how moral concepts can develop and change within a person's life. I am not here concerned with explicit uses of moral concepts, but with their implicit presence in the narrative. This is hard to show with a short excerpt, because the implicit presence of moral concepts in short passages depends to a great extent on the relation of those passages to numerous others. The excerpt I shall look at is about the second visit to Warsaw of the surrealist poet Paul Eluard. On his first visit to Warsaw in 1948, Eluard, Wat, and Wat's wife Ola had formed a close friendship. Eluard was suffering deeply from the death of his wife, and spent almost all his time at the Wats' place, confiding in them what he was going through. Wat describes Eluard's return a year later: "And so Eluard arrived, and an interview with him appeared in the press. This is what he said: [']when my wife died, I wrote many sad, tragic poems, poems full of despair. But Comrade Thorez told me one cannot poison the soul of the proletariat with sadness. And he was right. Now I have reworked the endings of those poems.['] Ola asked him if that were an authorized interview, and he confirmed that it had been. We almost broke off relations with him. Broniewski, for example—I'm not talking about Broniewski at the end when he was already a ruined man—Broniewski would not have been capable of acting like that. Nor would any of us have been" (*My Century*, 26).

What interests me is the connection between that passage and a number of moral concepts. As I suggested, the way in which those concepts are present in the passage is inseparable from the character of the book as a whole, the many narratives of different

---

narrator developing; and, although the relation between Wat the poet and Wat the narrator is submerged in *My Century* (it comes to the surface in an interpolated sketch found in Wat's papers, included in chap. 23), I think there is a significant parallel with the structure of *David Copperfield*. The narrative shows us Wat discovering what it can be, or rather what it can be for him, to "dwell poetically on this earth." (See especially p. 205.)

people yielding to, and not yielding to, the pressures of communism, including here the narrator's own sins (his weak and clumsy play-acting with communist officials, his clumsy lies, his clumsy self-betrayal), and his own courage. And there are also many narratives of friendship—friendships strained, maintained, betrayed. "We almost broke off relations with him." Well, how does what is possible in one's relations with another person depend on what he has shown himself to be capable of? And how may the strains which bring a friendship almost to the breaking point be connected with what it means to write, to be a writer—the place of courage and truth in the writer's understanding of his aims? Nothing of this is laid out explicitly in the book. The presence in the passage which I have quoted of the concepts of friendship, integrity, courage, and truth is entirely dependent on the character of the whole narrative, with its movements back and forth, its human understanding, its own courage and truthfulness. The moral force of the descriptions in the book derives from the narrator's extraordinary capacity to let the many events and experiences described in it bear on each other. My claim then is that the book as a whole, and passages like the one which I have quoted, show us how experience may change the kind of reach into someone's moral being which concepts like integrity, courage, or friendship may have. The book, that is, puts before us something one might call a conceptual achievement, something at once cognitive and moral.

The achieved moral understanding of the book is not a matter of a shift to some new or modified moral principles. Take the passage I have quoted, and consider two possible ways of interpreting it. One might read it as having implicit in it some moral principle: "*Go on* with friendships in circumstances of such-and-such types; *give up* seeing someone if the person has behaved badly in such-and-such ways." And Eluard's behavior might then be seen as almost but not quite leading to a breach of the relationship, in accordance with such principles. I do not want to maintain here that the Wats did not *have* principles of such a sort, but I want to read the passage as involving something quite different from principles, namely, their sense of what friendship is in people's lives and in their own life, and what it is for it to be possible humanly to continue "seeing" someone, as we say. There *are* things that would have made it impossible to speak to a person like Eluard again,[18] not because one had principles about what sorts of people one ought not to speak to; there are things that alternatively might only make one feel the change that had been worked in the past relationship, a change that made the relationship as it had been, that close friendship, no longer possible. The Wats *do* go on with some relation to Eluard; there is still the complex sense of the man they *had* known, and been intimate with, and some tie still to him, together with the *distance* from the person Eluard has shown himself to be. The very brief descriptive paragraph which I quoted shows a kind of complex exercise of responsibility, but responsibility not explicable in terms of principles. There is the responsibility to what there had been in the past, the human ties that had been made there; there is also the responsibility involved in placing, within a range of significances, what Eluard had done in *letting* the Party destroy whatever truth, whatever "interiority," had been in his poems, the placing of what he had done by reference to the weaknesses of Broniewski, the Polish poet and friend of the Wats, and by reference to the strains and pressures that Wat and his Polish writer-friends themselves were under.

VII

The example of Wat's thought can help us to see the inadequacy of Hare's idea of what a concept is. To make that clear I need first to spell out some of Hare's ideas about critical moral reflection and about moral experience.

For Hare, what a word is as we use it is no different (apart perhaps from psychological associations) from what it would be if it had been coined right then on the spot and tied to some set of linguistic rules. (A use of a term cannot have, internal to it, a critical reflective understanding of moral life.) Any kind of genuine or critical moral reflection involves moving outside the range of

---

18. There is, for example, Eluard's behavior a year later, described by Milan Kundera in *The Book of Laughter and Forgetting* (Harmondsworth: Penguin Books, 1986), 66.

meanings embodied in the specific moral vocabulary one is using. Critical moral reflection, for Hare, depends on the purely formal logical structure of moral words; and, indeed, so far as the moral concepts of ordinary life are allowed by someone to have a role in his moral reflection, the *status* of such reflection as genuinely critical is compromised. That that is Hare's understanding of moral reflection emerges especially clearly in his criticisms of John Rawls and of the Rawlsian procedure of seeking "reflective equilibrium." Since "moral intuitions" are allowed to have a role in the Rawlsian procedure, the procedure, according to Hare, can do no genuine work as a form of moral argument. (See *Moral Thinking*, 75–76; cf. also 172.)

Hare's conception of moral experience plays an important role in this argument. He takes what he calls "moral intuitions" to be shaped by our upbringing and past experience; but past experience, so far as it is relevant to moral life, is for him nothing but experience of having chosen in accordance with this or that principle, in circumstances with such-and-such features (*Moral Thinking*, 40). Hare's view allows it to be possible for someone to work with a different notion of courage at 40 from his notion of courage at 20, but the only way the notions could differ (apart from psychological associations) would be in the descriptive criteria for their application. It would remain conceivable at least in principle that someone should have just started off moral life with the descriptive criteria for courage which he actually wound up with only after twenty years of experience. And, further, the justification for regarding the later notion as an improvement would itself have to be framed at a level at which there was no essential use of any conception of courage; at that (reflective) level the only issue would be which principle dealing with the relevant sorts of case would be preferable. Moral life, life with the concept of courage, in a sense *drops out;* it has no necessary role in moral reflection. Critical moral reflection, on Hare's view, depends (as I mentioned) only on the purely formal logical features of moral evaluation. Hare's view here rests entirely on the idea of what a concept is, say a concept like courage. For experience to lead to a changed understanding of courage would be for the associated principles of conduct to change, and it is logically possible that one could have started with whatever the principles are that one had in fact come to through experience.

VIII

Surely there is something seriously wrong with that account of moral experience and moral life. What is present in Alexander Wat's descriptions of the events of his life is an understanding of courage and cowardice, of friendship and betrayal, an understanding of life which is not a matter of his having arrived at this or that principle. Wat's sense of life, his responsible evaluative understanding, colors the narrative. Another way of putting this would be to speak of the moral presence which the reader is aware of: a moral presence, a *reflective* moral presence, a shaping sense of what the events which Wat has been through mean. The moral concepts internal to the narrative belong to that particular moral understanding: It would be nonsense to suggest that *whatever* their content is, those moral concepts "could in principle" be the moral concepts of, say, a clever 15-year-old who could go through the logical rigmarole of what Hare calls reflective moral thinking. (I am not denying that the clever 15-year-old might have any principles you like, of the form "do-this-whenever-so-and-so," but I am suggesting that having principles of that sort is not what it is to have a moral concept, not what it is for it to play a role in one's thought.) The life of the moral concepts at work in Wat's narrative involves a very acute sense of how the currents of life reveal themselves in what at any point one finds possible, what one finds impossible. Wat's perceptiveness in regard to the currents of life is itself a matter of how masses of experience are brought to bear on the particular scene he is describing, or the particular remembered occurrence.

The experiences in question are not just Wat's own experiences. At one point he refers to seeing the world as Adam did, with that freshness of perception (see *My Century*, 210, but also the rest of chap. 23). The moral color of the narrative as a whole derives from Wat's own particular freshness of perception, but also from the freshness of perception of the many writers who sustained him in prison, including Proust and Machiavelli.

Let me summarize these points. Hare has a particular idea of what moral reflection must be. It cannot (on his account) be a deepening of "specialized" moral concepts like *courage*, but requires a kind of critical examination of principles, without ties to any specialized moral concepts. This model of moral reflection depends on an idea of what a concept is, what kinds of impersonal connection with the world conceptual thought can have. Hare's insistence that moral differences are never at their roots conceptual differences is presented by him as a matter of the logic of moral thought, but in fact takes for granted a particular idea of what a concept is. What he is rejecting is the idea of modes of awareness of the world that may color our understanding of events and shape our moral perception. So far as Hare *can* take account of such awareness, it would count only as a kind of emotional detritus left behind by upbringing and experience. Rational moral reflection involves *detachment* from such experientially shaped modes of awareness; the moral agent has a kind of freedom dependent on the capacity for such detachment. The word "intuition" plays an important role in Hare's scheme: The word is tied to elements of moral thought not arrived at through critical reflection on principles. The word itself, as Hare uses it, reflects his idea of what is internal to the free rational moral self and what is, through external things like upbringing, accidental to it. The kind of moral understanding developed through experience, which we see in Wat's book and which is profoundly particular, is being conceptually excluded by Hare, in part through the use of the term "intuition" in making external to the rational moral agent the things that go to shape a person's particular mode of moral response.

An important consequence of this idea of moral life is a reduced conception of what might be meant by self-understanding. A further consequence is a reduced conception of the kind of moral activity involved in thinking about real or imagined events which present one with no immediate need to act. The only moral activity which can be present in such situations is that of the formulating of practical principles; and principles which one comes to through considering fictional cases may, Hare believes, be unsuitable for general use. So there is also, in Hare's thinking, a short route to suspicion of novels.[19] The idea of describing events, real or imagined, as *itself* a moral activity, as itself an exercise of moral concepts, is out of reach: it is incompatible with Hare's idea of what moral concepts are. When moral life is tied too closely to notions of choice and of freedom exercised in the capacity to choose, other forms of moral activity become invisible. The quotation which provides the title of this paper reflects Iris Murdoch's different view. "We are perpetually moralists": that is, our thought about *anything* is the thought of a morally live consciousness, a consciousness with its own moral character.

IX

The quotation from Samuel Johnson, "We are perpetually moralists," is used by the critic Samuel Goldberg in a discussion of ethics and literature strongly influenced by Iris Murdoch.[20] He gives this fuller quotation from Johnson: "We are perpetually moralists, but we are geometricians only by chance. Our intercourse with intellectual nature is necessary; our speculations upon matter are voluntary, and at leisure."

Goldberg notes that Johnson's choice of the word "moralist" reflects his kind of Christianity; but the point that Johnson was making does not depend on that word, or on any kind of religious view. The "key fact" we can take Johnson to be emphasizing is that in all understanding of ourselves and other human beings our moral nature is involved. It is a mistake, Goldberg argues, to tie evaluation solely to choice: choice is only one of the numerous modes of activity in which our sense of values is evident and deter-

---

19. See the remarks about D. H. Lawrence in *Moral Thinking*, 48. I have discussed Hare's view of the moral interest of novels in "Martha Nussbaum and the Need for Novels," *Philosophical Investigations* 16 (1993): 128–53.
20. Samuel Goldberg, *Agents and Lives: Moral Thinking in Literature* (Cambridge: Cambridge University Press, 1993). "'Perpetually moralists' . . . 'in a large sense'" is the title of the first chapter. The rest of the chapter title comes from Matthew Arnold's remark about the moral bent of English poetry, "a large sense is of course to be given to the term *moral*." See *Agents and Lives*, 2.

minative. It is only one place, as he puts it, "on the whole spectrum of feeling, noticing, foregrounding, selecting, heeding, realizing, respecting, delighting, preferring, ranking, loving, valuing, deciding and all the other modes of reflective and unreflective judging" (*Agents and Lives*, 2–3).

In her recent book, *Metaphysics as a Guide to Morals*, Iris Murdoch reflects on what she there refers to as the "ubiquity of value": our "stream of awareness" is a bearer of moral judgment. She does not mean that we are constantly thinking, "This is good" or "That is evil." Rather, in ordinary consciousness, in our desires, aversions, images, feelings, attachments and perceptions, values are at work, are being shaped and reshaped in ways which never lose their attachment to the common world but which are our own, and which give our awareness its own particular character. Perhaps this is most evident when the particular character of somebody's awareness is of a very striking sort, as I have claimed it is in the case of Alexander Wat. And indeed one important kind of thing a novelist can do is make us more aware of the possibilities of very different modes of awareness. In our cognitive activities we may be aiming at getting things right, but how we carry on these activities, how we understand what "getting it right" might involve or might cost in the particular case, reveals our own nature as moral beings. Our moral nature expresses itself in all our modes of consciousness.

In *Metaphysics*, Murdoch's idea of consciousness as morally colored—the idea that we are always, in how we think and respond, drawing on moral concepts and giving them a use that is our own—is tied to an extremely interesting argument about fact and value.

This is an argument against separating fact and value; and it can be directed against any of the variety of moral philosophies within which there is a sharp distinction between fact and value. It can, for example, be directed against Kant, and I shall consider the argument in the form in which Murdoch does actually direct it against Kant.[21] For Kant, our cognitive capacity is a capacity to make true or false judgments about the phenomenal world. Mur-

---

21. *Metaphysics*, 221–23.

doch ascribes to Kant the view that the phenomenal world is "devoid of value." This is not entirely accurate; there are values which are not *un*conditionally valuable and which lie within the world. But that is a relatively minor point; what is significant is that, as Murdoch reads Kant, our nature as moral beings is not actively engaged in our judgments about what is the case. Cognition is not tied to consciousness conceived as "densely coloured," consciousness as always ours not just as moral beings but as moral beings with our own characteristic kinds of moral colorings in all our responsiveness. A Kantian separation of fact and value, as Murdoch sees it, makes impossible a realistic representation of consciousness.

Here there is a link with Murdoch's conception of the realistic novel. The traditional realistic novel is committed to a realistic portrayal of character, and therefore of the mode of awareness of its characters. Since awareness is morally colored, every realistic novel is in a sense an argument against the separation of fact and value. A character cannot be represented as a living human being unless his awareness of facts has internal to it his mode of moral responsiveness.

There is a further element in the Murdoch argument. If *thought* is seen as inherently or ubiquitously moral, then we need to reject the idea that moral thought is a *department* of thought, and moral discourse a *department* of discourse. But that departmental conception of morality characterizes contemporary moral philosophy.

X

If analytical philosophy no longer accepts as unquestionable the idea of a gap between fact and value, this has much to do with Iris Murdoch's earlier writings. *The Sovereignty of Good,* especially, is often treated as groundbreaking in this regard.[22] But Murdoch's recent writings show that there is still a great distance between her approach and that of contemporary analytical philosophy. This fi-

---

22. See, for example, Hilary Putnam, *Realism with a Human Face* (Cambridge: Harvard University Press, 1990), 166.

nal section of my essay is about that distance, about what we still need to learn from her.

First, there is what I just called the departmental conception of morality: the standard philosophical view of morality as a topic, a branch of discourse and thought alongside others. Murdoch's recent work constitutes a great challenge to this conception.

Secondly, there is her awareness, as a novelist and a thinker about novels, of how the realistic novel involves a portrayal of character profoundly at odds with ideas central in contemporary moral philosophy. The conflict can, though, be ignored very easily by philosophers. I mentioned earlier Murdoch's criticisms of the philosopher's will to impose a particular model on all cases. One can, in accordance with such a model, see the moral significance of novels entirely in terms of choices, principles, and factually describable situations within which the principles are applied or fail to be applied. But there is more at stake in this mode of thinking about novels than merely the imposition of a single model on cases it does not fit. For there is also the issue of philosophy's own characteristic kind of moral being: the kinds of awareness that philosophy encourages, the particular moral color of the awareness of philosophers, as it can be seen in writings on ethics. Murdoch is right to bring to our notice the particular moral style of philosophical attention: its direction *away* from the moral color of an individual's awareness, and *to* choice and principles of choice in a world conceived as simply there for cognitive judgment. So I take one important achievement of Murdoch's writing to be the bringing to notice of the *particular* moral style of analytical philosophy, the *particular* range of moral concepts fundamental to it. For analytical philosophy to learn from Murdoch here would be for it to become much more reflective about its own methods, assumptions, and modes of response.

The third point about Murdoch's distance from contemporary moral philosophy involves the fact-value distinction itself. In 1956, she and analytical philosophy were far apart on this issue of the "gap" between fact and value. Analytical philosophy has moved in the direction of the better ground she then pointed out. But we have not moved to the right place; she is still pointing us to better ground. That is what I now want to show.

I start from the argument of hers that I summarized in Part IX. The philosophical idea of a separation of fact and value goes, she says, with an unrealistic understanding of consciousness. For consciousness is always morally colored; moral activity is present in all cognitive awareness. For Murdoch, this is an argument against the traditional post-Kant-and-Hume distinction between fact and value. Her argument can, though, lead us to see a kind of distinction between fact and value, but not the distinction we thought there was. My argument for this comes in two stages.

Stage 1. Consider the discipline of history-writing. Considered as a discipline, it involves practices of justifying assertions, explanations, or conclusions by kinds of evidence, by consideration of alternative views, by raising objections to one's own interpretation and demonstrating how the evidence can be used to reply to such objections. There are, that is, in the discipline of history ways of establishing facts and of establishing understandings of facts, but these ways are tied to *a particular subject*. There is a close connection here between there being *a* subject (or range of subject matter) and there being particular methods, associated with the subject, of justifying claims about facts. Cognitive activity concerned with history *is* cognitive in virtue of history itself being *one* subject among others.

I am not denying that any subject, history or biology or whatever, changes and develops—and, with such changes, the methods of establishing and justifying assertions and explanations in it will also change and develop. All I want, for my argument, is that there are distinct practices of arriving at and justifying factual judgments. Factual judgment-making might be said to be a family of activities, in Wittgenstein's sense.

Iris Murdoch's conception of cognitive awareness is that it is ubiquitously value-laden. Value, or moral value, is not the object of some *branch* of thought or discourse. Moral value is not a subject matter among other subject matters. If we can speak of a ramified family of cognitive practices, of modes of establishing and coming to understand facts, *moral* thought, evaluative thought, is not one member of the family alongside the others. Moral value is not the object of cognitive activity in the way in which historical understanding is an object of cognitive activity. For something to be *an* object of cognitive activity is for there to be some practice or practices of establishing and coming to understand facts belonging to the particular subject matter. The idea of the *ubiquity* of value suggests, then, not that there is no separating fact from value but precisely that there is an important kind of distinction between fact and value. Botany, history, epidemiology are not ubiquitously present to consciousness; and *that they are not* belongs to what it is for there to be investigation of facts of botany, of history, of epidemiology. For an -ology to be an -ology is for it not to be *ubiquitous;* if morals are ubiquitous, they are not facts. End of stage 1 of the argument.

Stage 2. For Murdoch, a central metaphor for moral awareness is *visual* awareness. And it seems that that metaphor can be used to weaken the force of the argument that I have just presented. The use of the visual as a model for the moral might go this way. We *take in* the visual world, and how well we take it in depends on the quality of our attention. The visual world, the object of visual attention, is a model for *the* world *with* its moral colorings, the world that is the object of all cognitive activity—hence the importance of the quality of our attention to reality.

But what notion of seeing is implicit in that model? If we consider a mushroom-fancier on a walk through the autumnal woods, he may be all visual attention. Every possible gleam of a chanterelle will be taken in—but the beauty of the autumn woods may be entirely missed. Or think of the rock climber's perception of the rock wall: He will see routes, fingerholds and toeholds. What he thinks of as *there to be seen* is shaped by the particular activity in which he is engaged; the extraordinary blue of the veronica growing in a crevice is not included.[23] Visual taking-in of things,

23. Cf. Jakob Meløe, "Some Remarks on Agent Perception," in *Perspectives on Human Conduct*, ed. Lars Hertzberg and Juhani Pietarinen (Leiden: Brill, 1988), 89–96. Meløe puts before us a conception of "what there is to be seen" in a particular context in terms of the possibilities offered by the context for actions of the sort with which some agent might be concerned. The novice rock climber, for example, sees very little of "what there is to see" on a rock face, i.e., does not see things which are relevant to possible movements on that rock face. The demands of agency, the interests of agency, determine what is there to be seen.

with acute attention, comes in *kinds,* shaped by particular interests and activities. Such departmentalized visual attention and visual taking-in of reality is not the model that Murdoch wants. What she needs as a model for moral attention is a kind of visual attention that is itself moralized. That is, if we consider the taking in of the visual world with a kind of wonder and freshness of perception, a visual attention which can simply marvel at a shade of blue or at the twistedness of a tree trunk, which can take in the goodness and beauty of the world, then we do indeed have a model of moral awareness of reality. But we can also say that visual awareness is a model of moral awareness only as itself (a kind of) moral awareness.[24] The only model of moral awareness is moral awareness. End of stage 2.

The two-stage argument is meant to lead us to this conclusion. To see value as everywhere present in awareness may indeed be to give up the analytical philosopher's conception of the distinction between fact and value, but we are left with a different understanding of a distinction between fact and value. If value is in a sense ubiquitous, if one wants to speak of it as tied to "quality of consciousness," one *is* distinguishing it from whatever can form *a* subject matter among others. To speak of such a distinction is to make the kind of point Wittgenstein called grammatical. The distinction is not a matter of what forms of inference are correct, or of what kinds of premises moral arguments need to have. On the contrary. If value is said to be ubiquitous, this is in fact tied to the way in which our experience of the world can bear morally on any situation, can shape our vision of what the situation is. There is no limit to how objects of our attention *can* cast light on a situation (no limit that could be set in advance); a fundamental form of moral rationality is the *interpretation of something or other into practical life*—the interpretation into practical life of some fact or person or

---

24. The point may be brought out by the contrast between Meløe's idea of "what there is to be seen" (see note 23 above) and that implicit in Alexander Wat's descriptions of his experiences (*My Century,* chap. 21) of seeing trees while going from one prison to another. He sees the serene dignity, the radiance of trees, triumphing over the "antiworld" of prisons. But all this is "there to be seen" only because his perception is imbued with his moral sensibility. His visual awareness is clearly a kind of moral awareness of the world.

story or proverb or principle.[25] The morally alive awareness of x may enable us to interpret x into the realm of practical life.[26] So, in conclusion, I have argued that Iris Murdoch's discussions of fact and value, if they do (as I think) leave us with a kind of distinction between fact and value, leave us with a distinction that can nevertheless help us make sense of our full human capacity for moral understanding.[27]

25. I discuss this further in "Wittgenstein, Mathematics and Ethics: Resisting the Attractions of Realism," in *The Cambridge Companion to Wittgenstein*, ed. Hans Sluga and David Stern (Cambridge: Cambridge University Press, forthcoming). Even a work on logic—Wittgenstein's *Tractatus*—can be thought of as "ethical," not in virtue of some specific ethical content, but in virtue of the possibility of interpreting it into practical life, of bringing it into contact with a variety of situations not of some type specifiable in terms of any general rule.
26. See Murdoch, *Metaphysics*, 11. Murdoch there speaks of the inspired interpretation into practical life of an ideal pattern, e.g., a Platonic form. Her argument in the book as a whole is that the character of a person's consciousness includes how the attention which he directs towards reality can creatively shape his moral understanding of the situations in which he finds himself. For an interesting parallel, see Joseph Conrad's connection between the character and shades of a person's conscience and the quality of his consciousness (the reflection in consciousness of "self-forgetful attention to every phase of the living universe"), *A Personal Record* (Marlboro, Vt.: Marlboro Press, 1988), chap. 5, 93–96.
27. I am very grateful to James Conant for his helpful comments and suggestions. I also profited greatly from discussions of Iris Murdoch's thought at the Chicago Divinity School lectures on "Picturing the Human."

5
FORM AND CONTINGENCY IN IRIS MURDOCH'S ETHICS

Maria Antonaccio

I. INTRODUCTION

In a time in which the abandonment of metaphysics has become a persistent feature of modern philosophy generally, and modern moral philosophy in particular, Iris Murdoch's latest and most comprehensive philosophical work, *Metaphysics as a Guide to Morals*, raises anew the question of the place of metaphysics in moral inquiry.[1] A revised version of the author's 1982 Gifford Lectures, this work covers an extraordinary range of topics that reflect the breadth of Murdoch's engagement with philosophy, theology, art, ethics, and politics. Central to her reflection about all of these is the problem of how abstract theorizing relates to life, how concepts influence conduct, or as she puts it, "how can metaphysics be a guide to morals?" (p. 146). "The problem about philosophy, and about life," Murdoch writes, "is how to relate large impressive illuminating general conceptions to the mundane . . . details of ordinary personal private existence. . . . How do the generalisations of philosophers connect with what I am doing in my day-to-day and moment-to-moment pilgrimage, how can metaphysics be a guide to morals?" (ibid.). This question marks a central concern not only of this recent work but of Murdoch's thought as a whole, and it is a question fraught with ambiguity.

I wish to thank William Schweiker for many helpful comments and criticisms of this essay.
1. New York: Allen Lane/Penguin Press, 1993; hereafter referred to as *Metaphysics*.

While Murdoch has argued for a retrieval of metaphysical theorizing as essential to moral reflection on human life, her work also shows a persistent suspicion of theory and indeed of all forms of discourse by which we try to capture truth, or to fix knowledge in rigid forms. The problem, as she once noted, is one of "how far conceptualizing and theorizing, which from one point of view are absolutely essential, in fact divide you from the thing that is the object of theoretical attention."[2] Philosophers construct metaphysical systems in an attempt to formalize or unify human life, yet our actual lived experience has no form or unity in itself, but is full of contingent rubble, accident, and unsystematized detail which may resist our attempts at unity.

How can a moral theory encompass these two seemingly contrasting impulses: on the one hand, the urge to create a unified system which illuminates the whole of human life by giving it an apprehensible shape or order, and on the other hand, the recognition that human life in fact has no such order, but is, as Murdoch affirms, "chancy and incomplete"? In spite of its need for systematic elaboration, moral philosophy must not fail to remember the contingent, and to preserve the particular and the individual from absorption into any kind of totalizing theoretical framework. Murdoch argues that the abstract theorizing of metaphysics must be challenged by empiricism, a reminder of the ordinary details of human experience and the obviousness of certain truths.[3] A moral theory, ideally, should combine both elements. But what kind of a theory can accomplish this?

2. Iris Murdoch, "The House of Fiction: Interviews with Seven English Novelists," interviewed by Frank Kermode, *Partisan Review* 30 (1963): 65.
3. As Murdoch states: "Philosophy is perpetually in tension between empiricism and metaphysics, between, one might say, Moore and McTaggart. This argument can take place within the same philosopher. Religion moves similarly between simplicity and elaboration, puritanism and its opposite (to which various names may be given). There are times for piecemeal analysis, modesty and commonsense, and other times for ambitious synthesis and the aspiring and edifying charm of lofty and intricate structures. . . . This task of philosophy is not less but more essential now, in helping to preserve and refresh a stream of meticulous, subtle, eloquent ordinary language, free from jargon and able to deal clearly and in detail with matters of a certain degree of generality and abstraction." See *Metaphysics*, 211.

In this paper I argue that *Metaphysics as a Guide to Morals* offers a profound meditation on what Murdoch calls "the two-way movement in philosophy, a movement towards the building of elaborate theories, and a move back again towards the consideration of simple and obvious facts."[4] As an exercise in metaphysics, the book attempts to give an account of the whole of our moral existence, proceeding systematically through a series of chapters on art, morality, and religion; yet it is also full of empirical observation, frequently departing from its main line of argument in order to comment on particular phenomena of human life. The book itself, in both its style and its subject-matter, enacts the two-way movement in philosophy. I try to show that in *Metaphysics as a Guide to Morals*, Murdoch creates a type of metaphysical theorizing which remembers the contingent and mocks the idea of totality from within.

What is it that motivates Murdoch to insist on the need for both kinds of reflection within moral philosophy itself? In other words, what would be lost if metaphysics were not tempered by empiricism, or if empiricism were not accompanied by a more systematic theoretical impulse? I contend that what is at stake in the two-way movement in philosophy as it appears in Murdoch's thought is the problem of grasping the reality of individuals—human individuals especially but also phenomena of other sorts—a problem which is at the center not only of Murdoch's moral thought, but her theory of art as well. This is why Murdoch contends that a truthful apprehension of individuals requires two kinds of thinking: a unifying kind of thinking, which renders our fragmentary lives more complete by imposing some kind of artful shape on it; and a particularizing kind of thinking, which resists the impulse to order or classify and instead individuates phenomena with a kind of laser beam of attention. This fundamental pattern in Murdoch's thought is evident in the movement between metaphysics and empiricism which structures *Metaphysics as a Guide to Morals*. But it is also illuminated by means of a parallel tension in Murdoch's theory of the novel, the tension between form

---

4. Iris Murdoch, *The Sovereignty of Good* (London: Routledge & Kegan Paul, 1970), 1.

Form and Contingency in Ethics 113

and contingency. The novelist must attempt to create a unified aesthetic whole; yet there is the countervailing need to create individual characters who exist amidst the disunity and randomness that mark ordinary life.

In this respect, the artist creating the work faces a question analogous to that of the metaphysician constructing a theoretical framework. As Murdoch puts it, "At what level of generality am I to operate?.... Great discoveries are made at great levels of generality ... On the other hand, the lack of detail can leave the reader unconvinced that he is really seeing 'human life'."[5] The novelist, like the metaphysician, must unify the work and yet remain true to the contingent stuff of human life, which cannot fully be captured in the pattern of the work. Both art and philosophy must be responsive to the question, What is the fate of the individual or the contingent in theory, in art, and in life? This is the question that I want to explore in this paper.

The argument will proceed as follows. I begin by setting up the basic problem of Murdoch's thought as an attempt to retrieve some kind of metaphysical framework for the moral life and yet still defend the separateness and irreducibility of the individual. In the second part of the paper, I move to an analysis of Murdoch's theory of the novel, arguing that the distinction between form and contingency thematizes the central problem of how to picture individuals in the context of a work of art. In the third part of the paper, I turn to a discussion of *Metaphysics as a Guide to Morals* and attempt to show how an analogous tension, that between metaphysics and empiricism, is operative in Murdoch's moral thought. I contend that her metaphysic attempts to make room for the individual within the formal unity of her moral theory.

II. METAPHYSICS AND THE INDIVIDUAL: THE PROBLEM OF MURDOCH'S MORAL THOUGHT

I would like to begin by placing Murdoch's thought in the context of contemporary attempts to articulate an adequate account of

---

5. Iris Murdoch, *The Fire and the Sun: Why Plato Banished the Artists* (Oxford: Clarendon Press, 1977), 81.

moral subjectivity in relation to a framework of value. On one side of the debate are those thinkers in the Kantian tradition who believe that the self constitutes its world through its acts and choices apart from determination by any antecedent order of value. On the other side are those thinkers descending from Hegel who believe that the aims and purposes of the self are in fact constituted by its natural, social, and historical existence in particular communities. This admittedly rough division of positions is partly what lies behind the recent debate in ethics between liberals and communitarians over whether the self is essentially "unencumbered" or "situated"; a similar division of positions may be seen in the debate between so-called public and narrative varieties of religious ethics. Part of what is at stake in these debates is the nature and scope of the context within which the moral self defines itself, its values, and its freedom.

Murdoch represents these two lines of thought by means of a contrast between types of moral theory, the Liberal view and the Natural Law view.[6] These serve the purpose of highlighting options for ethical reflection in the manner of ideal types rather than representing actual positions. Murdoch's attempt to defend a view of the individual as situated within some kind of metaphysical framework represents a mediating position between these types. Let me briefly explain this distinction.

The Liberal view, which Murdoch associates chiefly with Kant and with Sartrean existentialism, is characterized by the belief in the autonomy of morals from any kind of metaphysical or theological framework. "From the Liberal point of view," Murdoch writes, "it seems axiomatic that however grandiose the structure may be in terms of which a morality extends itself, the moral agent

6. Murdoch introduces this distinction in her seminal essay "Metaphysics and Ethics" in *The Nature of Metaphysics*, ed. D. F. Pears (London: Macmillan, 1960), esp. 114–17. For further discussion of the Natural Law view see "Vision and Choice in Morality," *Aristotelian Society Supplementary Volume* 30 (1956): 46–47. For a discussion of Murdoch's views on liberalism more generally, see "Against Dryness: A Polemical Sketch," in *Revisions: Changing Perspectives in Moral Philosophy*, ed. Stanley Hauerwas and Alasdair MacIntyre (Notre Dame: University of Notre Dame Press, 1983); "The Sublime and Beautiful Revisited," *Yale Review* 49 (December 1959): 247–71; and *Metaphysics*, esp. chap. 12.

is responsible for endowing this totality with value."[7] This view tends towards solipsism because it pictures the individual and morality as self-contained. Freedom is conceived as a detachment or leap of the will in the face of duty or moral choice, rather than a continuous interaction of the agent with a world that contains value. Value is defined as a function of the choosing will, rather than related to a world that exists prior to and outside of the agent to which the agent must conform. The agent is thus only accidentally related to anything that might be considered a moral world and to other individuals, except insofar as they are considered rational agents like itself.

The Natural Law view, by contrast, counters the Liberal view by picturing the individual as enclosed within a framework which transcends it. Against Kantian and existentialist variants of the Liberal view, Natural Law moralists (among whom Murdoch includes Thomists, Hegelians, and Marxists) insist that the self is not, as she puts it, "a brave naked will surrounded by an easily comprehended empirical world,"[8] but a complex being with dark and not fully rational motives immersed in a reality which always exceeds it. Here there is no "axiom of discontinuity" between the choosing agent and the chosen framework, as there was on the Liberal view; indeed the point is that the framework is not so much chosen, but given antecedently to the self. "The individual's choice is less important [on this view]," Murdoch writes, "and the interest may lie in adoration of the framework rather than in the details of conduct."[9] Instead of a leap of the will, freedom here is closely related to knowledge rather than action and cannot be defined or achieved apart from one's relations to others and to reality.

Although Murdoch endorses much of the Natural Law view's conception of moral identity and its relation to a larger evaluative framework, I believe that she ultimately rejects its contention that "the individual *only* has importance, or even reality, in so far as he belongs to the framework."[10] Against those who want to claim Murdoch as a Natural Law moralist, I argue that she wants to pre-

7. "Metaphysics and Ethics," 116.
8. "Against Dryness," 46.
9. "Metaphysics and Ethics," 117.
10. Ibid., 115, my emphasis.

serve one of the fundamental insights of the Liberal view, namely, that the individual must not be absorbed without remainder by any framework. In effect, then, Murdoch is attempting to chart a middle course between what she sees as the dangers of a type of view in which the self wholly transcends its relation to nature, history, and community by virtue of its freedom and a view which dissolves or assimilates the self into these relations.

The problem that Murdoch is working with can be brought into sharper focus if we briefly consider her relationship to existentialism. Murdoch sees in existentialism a primary example of what she criticizes in the Liberal view of morality, namely, that it separates the individual from any sort of moral framework which is independent of what its will creates. Yet I believe it is important to see beyond Murdoch's strong disavowals of existentialism to what she minimally shares with existentialism. For although she clearly rejects its voluntarist anthropology and what she judges to be its extreme beliefs about freedom, she does not thereby jettison its concern for the integrity of the self as a unique center of value and significance.[11] Indeed, Murdoch argues that this is precisely the danger of "totalizing" philosophies such as those based on the thought of Marx or Hegel: they fail to maintain the integrity and primacy of the individual in the face of the determinism of historical progress, the network of linguistic systems, or the totality of social or class relations. Thus, in spite of her evident dissatisfaction with existentialism, Murdoch wants to preserve one of its fundamental insights, namely, that the individual is irreducible to any totality.

The problem Murdoch takes from her reading of existentialism is how to articulate an adequate defense of the individual that is nevertheless grounded within a larger metaphysical account of the reality of the world and other people as separate and objective sources of value. Yet how does Murdoch accomplish this? The paradox of Murdoch's position is precisely that she attempts to formulate a defense of the individual by producing a metaphysic. This

11. Murdoch argues that this concern for the individual is central to Sartre's moral and political thought in her early monograph, *Sartre, Romantic Rationalist* (London: Bowes & Bowes, 1953).

seems to be an inherently contradictory project: how can one defend the irreducibility of the individual by constructing a large impressive framework? Must not one strip the self of any such framework in order to guarantee its freedom and integrity, as indeed Sartre thought? Murdoch rejects the existentialist account of the self, but I believe that she tries nevertheless to save the individual by picturing it within a "non-systematic non-totalising" framework, that is, within a new conception of metaphysical unity which she presents in *Metaphysics as a Guide to Morals* (364).

Having set up the central problem of Murdoch's thought about the individual, I want to turn now to the problem of picturing the individual as it appears in Murdoch's theory of the novel. I want to show that her attempt to solve this problem in art may provide a clue to her solution in the realm of morals. In doing so I hope to show that there is a fundamental coherence between Murdoch's theory of art and her theory of morals.

III. Form and Contingency in Murdoch's Theory of the Novel

Murdoch describes the problem of form and contingency in several early essays written in the late 1950s and early 1960s which link the fate of the idea of character in the modern novel with the history of liberalism and its defense of the individual. This context is important, because it signals that the question of the portrayal of character in the novel does not merely pose an aesthetic problem for Murdoch, but has moral and political dimensions as well. It *matters*, in literature, morals, and politics, how we portray the human person: a superficial portrayal may signal an impoverishment of thought, a stripping away of our concepts. By the same token, an ability to portray individuals may be connected with the virtues of love, respect, and tolerance. That the human person is "substantial, impenetrable, individual, indefinable, and valuable is after all, the fundamental tenet of Liberalism,"[12] Murdoch writes, and one which literature may help us to rediscover.

From Murdoch's perspective, the fundamental question that

---

12. "Against Dryness," 50.

twentieth-century philosophy and literature have failed adequately to answer is: "Wherein does the reality of a person reside and in what way can one, or should one, display that reality?"[13] In attempting to answer this question, Murdoch uses the novel as an instrument of diagnosis, treating "recent changes in the portrayal of characters in novels as symptoms of some more general change of consciousness."[14] Thus she begins in these essays with a diagnosis of how contemporary thought conceives the individual and then analyzes how this problem is manifest in literature.

Any attempt to conceptualize the person or individual may be menaced from either of two directions, in Murdoch's view. Either we fail to see the individual because we are enclosed in a solipsistic fantasy world and neglect the reality and independence of others; or we fail to see the individual "because we are ourselves sunk in a social whole which we allow uncritically to determine our reactions, or because we see each other exclusively as so determined."[15] The first danger Murdoch calls "neurosis"—the tendency to fabricate self-absorbed myths or fantasies that obscure the reality of others; the second she calls "convention"—the loss of the individual other in the face of a larger social totality. These represent the two dangers that Murdoch believes any adequate theory of the individual must avoid, and the philosopher no less than the novelist may fall victim to either tendency. "The enemies of art and of morals, the enemies that is of love, are the same: social convention and neurosis,"[16] she writes. "And how difficult it is in the modern world to escape from one without invoking the help of the other."[17]

Murdoch traces both dangers to what she regards as the corrupting influence of Hegel's thought on the original stream of Kantian liberalism. In the case of neurosis, the reality and value of the self is inflated to the point where the self becomes a world unto itself, with nothing outside it; Murdoch associates this danger with

13. Murdoch, "The Sublime and the Beautiful Revisited," 247.
14. Ibid.
15. Iris Murdoch, "The Sublime and the Good," *Chicago Review* 13 (Autumn 1959): 52.
16. Ibid.
17. "The Sublime and the Beautiful Revisited," 254.

the Romantic cult of the individual and later with existentialism. In the case of convention, by contrast, the reality and value of the self is diminished in relation to a larger authoritative whole; Murdoch associates this danger especially with the loss of the individual in Hegel's totality. These two failures can thus be regarded as two different sides of the same coin. In either case what is lacking is a portrayal of "the real impenetrable human person,"[18] pictured among other such persons against the background of a rich and receding reality.

Murdoch believes that the novel in the twentieth century succumbs to one or the other of these dangers. It is either a kind of self-enclosed object dominated by the myth-like plight or fantasy of a central character who is frequently a projection of the author's own fantasy; or it is more like "a piece of informative prose"[19] in which thin conventional characters are used chiefly to comment on current institutions or a particular historical matter, rather than being developed in depth for their own sake.[20] Faced with the choice between the two types, we are left in a dilemma in which the novel is conceived either as a kind of "crystalline" object or a more diffuse "journalistic" social epic, to use Murdoch's terminology; neither type of novel offers an adequate portrayal of character: "We are offered things or truths. What we have lost is persons."[21]

The failure embodied by these two kinds of novel represents the dilemma which every novelist faces when attempting to create a literary work: how to reconcile one's own powerful creative myth or fantasy with the realist demand to describe a reality other than oneself? How to balance the need to create a work of art that has

18. "Against Dryness," 50.
19. "The Sublime and the Beautiful Revisited," 264.
20. "So we have on the one hand a novel like *The Mandarins* [by Simone de Beauvoir], which is enormous, formless, topical, and often close to being brilliant journalism and, on the other hand, a novel like *The Stranger* of Camus, which is a small, compact, crystalline, self-contained myth about the human condition, as economical, resonant, and thing-like as it is possible to make any piece of imaginative prose writing to be." Murdoch's examples reflect the fact that she was formulating this analysis in the 1950s. See ibid., 265.
21. Ibid.

a recognizable dramatic shape with the need for realistic, complex characters who have a life of their own? This is precisely the dilemma which is thematized in the distinction between form and contingency. Murdoch describes this distinction as follows: "There is a temptation for any novelist, and one to which if I am right modern novelists yield too readily, to imagine that the problem of a novel is solved and the difficulties overcome as soon as a form in the sense of a satisfactory myth has been evolved. But that is only the beginning. There is then the much more difficult battle to prevent that form from becoming rigid, by the free expansion against it of the individual characters. Here above all the contingency of the characters must be respected . . . for it is the essence of personality."[22] These two forces make up the elements of the two-way movement which I have alluded to as the fundamental structure of Murdoch's thought as a whole. Form represents the novelist's desire to unify, to impose a general order or plan on the random materials that she is working with; contingency represents precisely those forces of disunity and disorder which are essential to a realistic portrayal of human life and personality.

The problem of writing a realistic novel consists in the fact that it requires both of these elements, which tend to pull the work in opposite directions. Every work of art has to be a "closed object" with a very strong internal structure or form.[23] "Without some kind of strong form there isn't an art object present."[24] At the same time, however, Murdoch describes the novel as the kind of form where "within this closed structure you can picture free beings."[25] The ideal novel would attempt to hold form and contingency in tension—the closed structure of the work constantly being opened up by the independent force of the characters; and the fate of the characters held in place by the creative pattern of the work. Such a novel would have enough formal structure to be a coherent work

---

22. Ibid., 271.
23. Iris Murdoch, interviewed by Christopher Bigsby, in *The Radical Imagination and the Liberal Tradition: Interviews with English and American Novelists,* eds. Heide Ziegler and Christopher Bigsby (London: Junction Books, 1982), 214.
24. Ibid., 228.
25. Ibid., 214.

of art, without robbing the characters of their autonomy and essential contingency.

Yet in attempting to balance these elements, the novelist faces formidable obstacles connected with the paradoxical nature of art itself. Of the two elements of the tension it is form rather than contingency which poses the greater threat to the success of the novel, because of the way in which the pleasing forms of art gratify the human ego with consolation rather than truth. Art presents the novelist with the temptation to create a work that is a projection of her own fantasy or ego, rather than suppressing ego for the sake of illuminating an independent reality which may compel our respect. The paradox of art, in Murdoch's view, is that the very form which is necessary to art as a truth-telling medium "partly has the effect of concealing what it attempts to reveal."[26] Yet form in art may also contain its own privileged access to truth, since, by introducing a veil of "protective symbolism"[27] between us and reality, art may be able to show us things that we might not otherwise be able to see. "Art is a special discerning exercise of intelligence in relation to the real," Murdoch writes; "and although aesthetic form has essential elements of trickery and magic, yet form in art, as form in philosophy, is designed to communicate and reveal."[28]

This double-edged status of aesthetic form presents the artist with a moral dilemma: how can images be used to illuminate rather than to falsify the truth? Form is the great temptation of art, because it threatens to become an end or stopping-point in itself, rather than serving to illuminate that reality which always exceeds our descriptions of it. "[T]he satisfaction of the form is such that it can stop one from going more deeply into the contradictions or paradoxes or more painful aspects of the subject matter."[29] In art or life, form may be an attempt to "cheat" contingency by imposing a consoling order or unity on a reality which in fact has neither

26. Iris Murdoch, "Existentialists and Mystics: A Note on the Novel in the New Utilitarian Age," in *Essays & Poems Presented to Lord David Cecil*, ed. W. W. Robson (London: Constable, 1970), 169.
27. Ibid.
28. *The Fire and the Sun*, 78.
29. *The House of Fiction*, 63.

order nor unity. Our sense of form may in fact endanger our ability to apprehend reality truthfully,[30] because it may provide us with a false sense of unity or closure. In this respect, form preserves us from the ambiguity and senselessness of the world by allowing us "to round off a situation, to sum up a character,"[31] rather than to preserve the chancy and incomplete nature of human life and personality. Murdoch argues that this urge for unity or consolation is one of the driving forces of artistic creativity: "A deep motive for making literature or art of any sort," she writes, "is the desire to defeat the formlessness of the world and cheer oneself up by constructing forms out of what might otherwise be a mass of senseless rubble."[32]

The most important testing-ground of the novelist's ability to use form truthfully is the ability to portray the reality of individual characters. In the realm of the novel, Murdoch says, "the most important thing to be . . . revealed, not necessarily the only thing, but incomparably the most important thing, is that other people exist."[33] The virtue required by the novelist to overcome the egoism of her own fantasy is the same as that required by the ordinary person: what is required of both of them is love. This is the basis of that convergence between art and morality which is one of the characteristic features of Murdoch's thought. "Art and morals are, with certain provisos, . . . one. . . . The essence of both of them is love. Love is the perception of individuals. Love is the extremely difficult realisation that something other than oneself is real. Love, and so art and morals, is the discovery of reality."[34] The great nineteenth-century novelists (Murdoch mentions Tolstoy, George Eliot, and Jane Austen) displayed this kind of loving tolerance towards their characters, a value which Murdoch believes connects literature with the liberal tradition of respect for diverse individuals. The greatest novels display "a real apprehension of persons other than the author as having a right to exist and to have a sepa-

30. "Against Dryness," 50.
31. "The Sublime and the Beautiful Revisited," 271.
32. Iris Murdoch, interviewed by Bryan Magee, in *Men of Ideas*, ed. Bryan Magee (New York: Viking Press, 1978), 267.
33. "The Sublime and the Beautiful Revisited," 267.
34. "The Sublime and the Good," 51.

rate mode of being which is important and interesting to themselves."[35]

The novel at its best is that art form par excellence which is able to grasp the individual by combining a careful use of form with a respect for contingent reality.[36] "However sad and awful the things it narrates," Murdoch says, the novel is a comic art form, which "belongs to an open world, a world of absurdity and loose ends and ignorance."[37] In contrast to the tightly condensed form of poetry or tragic drama, the novel form is a loose-textured art form which is particularly suited to the kind of truth it wants to tell—that "reality is not a given whole,"[38] that even the most painful or solemn episodes of a human life contain elements of absurdity and humor, that we are mortal creatures, subject to death and chance. The novel embraces "the invincible variety, contingency and scarcely communicable frightfulness of life" (*Metaphysics*, 96). "What it loses in hard-edged formal impact, it gains in its grasp of detail, its freedom of tempo, its ability to be irrelevant, to reflect without haste upon persons and situations and in general to pursue what is contingent and incomplete" (p. 93). The successful realistic novel enacts in its very form that balance of form and contingency which Murdoch holds up as an ideal standard. In spite of "the novelist's movements towards closing the object and making it into a limited whole" (p. 97), the novel, in Murdoch's striking image, remains a "cracked" or "pierced object," whose very awareness of contingency and the mixed sad-comic aspect of most human doings block the possibility of an aesthetically complete presentation.

Thus, Murdoch conceives the individual in art as an irreducible force that can only be captured by a broken or "porous" object. The aesthetic unity of the novel is constantly broken by—or breaks against—the reality of the individual, which resists formal unity and remains endlessly there to be explained, as persons in life do also. In the domain of both art and morals this means that

35. "The Sublime and the Beautiful Revisited," 257.
36. Ibid., 271.
37. "An Interview with Iris Murdoch," by Michael O. Bellamy, *Contemporary Literature* 18, 2 (Spring 1977): 132.
38. "Against Dryness," 50.

the demand of love remains infinite and unconditional, and that any achieved unity registers an awareness of its own provisional status. The truth captured by art remains a broken truth; the novel remains a provisional art form, aware of its own consolations. "[T]he nature of the novel is somehow that a sort of wind blows through it and there are holes in it and the meaning of it partly seeps away into life."[39]

I contend that Murdoch's treatment of the tension between form and contingency in the novel provides a clue to the kind of unity that she is seeking to articulate in her latest work on metaphysics. Her notion of the ideal novel combines the two conflicting forces of form and contingency in a complex aesthetic unity which is able to portray individuals within an ordered artistic whole. In a similar way, as I will show, Murdoch is attempting to mediate the tension between metaphysics and empiricism in her theory of morals by articulating a complex notion of metaphysical unity which allows room for the idea of the contingent individual and the individual's ordinary moral struggle.

IV. Metaphysics and Empiricism in Murdoch's Theory of Morals

Let me pause briefly to review the argument so far. I have been arguing that Murdoch's theory of art and her theory of morals are structured by parallel tensions: the tension between form and contingency, in the novel; and the tension between metaphysics and empiricism, in moral theory. The problem posed by these two contrasts revolves around the question of how far the concepts, images, and formal strategies of our discourse are able to capture the reality of individuals. In the case of the novel, as we have seen, the question is how far the literary form can adequately portray the reality of the characters without forcing them exclusively into the pattern of the author's fantasy. In the case of morals, the question is how far metaphysical theorizing may obscure the contingent detail of the moral life; and how a desire for systematic unity may obscure the day-to-day lived struggle of individual moral agents.

---

39. "An Interview with Iris Murdoch," Bellamy, 132.

As I have indicated, these parallel tensions reflect what Murdoch calls the necessary "two-way movement in philosophy." It is not a matter of doing away with one or another pole of the tension, but rather finding a way to encompass both elements in a certain kind of unity. A truthful apprehension of reality, in philosophy, art, or life, Murdoch says, requires a "double revelation of both random detail and intuited unity."[40]

It may seem odd, at first glance, to use Murdoch's theory of the novel to illuminate her moral philosophy: what, one might ask, does art have to do with philosophy or metaphysics? Murdoch has often said that art is "the great clue" to morals;[41] nevertheless, the relation or analogy between art and metaphysics in Murdoch's thought perhaps requires some brief preliminary explanation.

Murdoch believes that the elimination of metaphysics from ethics in the modern period has meant the impoverishment of a richly creative area of human thought. Moral theory requires an area of conceptual exploration which involves the creation of complicated heuristic images of human life. Murdoch seeks to retrieve the activities of theorizing and imaginative reflection as an essential part of ethics. In connecting metaphysics with the creation of such images, Murdoch rejects the attempt to render ethics scientifically neutral and brings ethics into closer relation with art. Indeed, Murdoch has always connected metaphysics with the attempt by human beings to "picture" themselves and the world. In a classic early essay titled "Metaphysics and Ethics," for example, she described the human being as a creature who "makes pictures of himself and then comes to resemble the picture."[42] Moral philosophy should attempt to describe and analyze this process, she argues, by making "models and pictures of what different kinds of men are like,"[43] rather than searching for universal formula. Such a description, she says, would be a kind of metaphysics. In *The Sovereignty of Good*, she suggested a further connection between art and metaphysics in her remark that philosophy depends in part

40. *The Sovereignty of Good*, 96.
41. Iris Murdoch, "The Darkness of Practical Reason," *Encounter* 27 (July 1966): 50.
42. "Metaphysics and Ethics," 122.
43. Ibid., 121.

on the use of metaphors, not merely as "peripheral decorations" to thought, but rather as "fundamental forms of our awareness of our condition."[44] The great metaphysical systems consist of such image-play, she writes, which is intended to clarify our understanding of ourselves and our relation to the world. And in her latest work, *Metaphysics as a Guide to Morals,* Murdoch associates art and metaphysics as "one-making" endeavors that attempt to bring a consoling formal (aesthetic or conceptual) unity to a contingent, formless world.

What distinguishes metaphysics from other sorts of philosophical analysis is its drive toward unity, its desire to find the basis of everything, as Murdoch puts it, or to identify the deep structure which cannot be "thought away" from human life. What has traditionally motivated philosophers to erect metaphysical structures, Murdoch argues, is "[t]he urge to prove that where we intuit unity there really is unity" (*Metaphysics,* 1). This is in fact "a deep emotional motive to philosophy, to art, to thinking itself. Intellect is naturally one-making.... We fear plurality, diffusion, senseless accident, chaos, we want to transform what we cannot dominate or understand into something reassuring and familiar, into ordinary being, into history, art, religion, science" (pp. 1–2). Metaphysics is a fundamentally "one-making" endeavor which seeks to impose unity on a mass of detailed perceptions about human life in order to provide a guide to moral reflection. Great metaphysicians are thinkers who have the sheer *nerve,* as Murdoch puts it, to erect large conceptual structures which attempt to put everything in order and to highlight certain unconditional features of human life. Like the artist, the metaphysician is concerned with using formal patterns in order to communicate something true about the nature of reality.

In contrast to this image of metaphysics as the construction of large conceptual edifices, which one finds for example in the work of Kant, there is another kind of reflection, equally important, "which consists of constructing a huge hall of reflection full of light and space and fresh air, in which ideas and intuitions can be un-

---

44. *The Sovereignty of Good,* 77.

systematically nurtured" (p. 422). If the one-making impulse of human thought is paradigmatically what metaphysics is concerned with, then an unsystematic attention to varied ideas and perceptions signals the opposite pole, that of empiricism, which Murdoch believes is just as essential. "In general," Murdoch writes, "empiricism is one essential aspect of good philosophy, just as utilitarianism is one essential aspect of good moral philosophy. It represents what must not be ignored. It remembers the contingent" (p. 236). As much as we may strive for a systematic unity among our moral concepts, or for a single supreme principle of morals, moral philosophy must also discriminate among different aspects of morality, and constantly return to immediate moral instincts which may resist formulation into abstract principles (p. 300).

Primary among these instincts is a recognition that the moral life is lived not at the level of grand theoretical systems, but by ordinary individuals engaged in the ambiguity of day-to-day moral struggle. If the question Murdoch posed for the theory of the novel was "Wherein does the reality of a person reside and in what way can one, or should one, display that reality?" an analogous question for moral philosophy may be posed as "What is the fate of the individual within a metaphysical system?" or "How does metaphysics conceptualize the contingent detail of the moral life?" "The notion of the fundamental existence and value of the individual should not be, need not be, and ultimately cannot be obliterated.... There are barriers of principle which are not reducible to system; and this irreducibility confronts political systems, and theoretical and metaphysical systems of any sort, including religious ones" (p. 365). What is ultimately at stake, in Murdoch's theory of morals as in her theory of the novel, is an ability to articulate and to defend the value of the contingently existing individual, a defense which she believes requires no further justification than this: "Human beings are valuable ... because they are human beings" (ibid.). From this perspective, the entire argument of *Metaphysics as a Guide to Morals* may be read as an argument in defense of "a conception of the idiosyncratic individual as valuable *per se*" in the context of a metaphysical position which remains, somehow, non-systematic and non-totalizing (p. 364). In what follows I discuss Murdoch's conception of the individual first and then turn in the final section of the paper to how she pictures the individual within the metaphysical framework of her theory.

Murdoch centers her defense of the individual in this book on recovering a description of the mind or consciousness as a bearer of value or moral being and not merely a rational surveyor of the facts. In the face of contemporary philosophies which appear "to render problematic the commonsense conception of the individual self as moral centre or substance,"[45] Murdoch hopes to retrieve the inner region of consciousness as a moral domain which is essential to our conception of the individual. "Consciousness or self-being [is] the fundamental mode or form of moral being," she writes (p. 171). This emphasis on consciousness is crucial, because it represents an implicit challenge to two other views of moral subjectivity. First, it challenges those positions which tend to reduce moral subjectivity to a unitary faculty such as reason or the will, the operations of which become the exclusive focus of ethics; and second, it challenges those positions which tend to reduce the being of the self to a mere cipher in a larger network or totality (whether linguistic or social) which is considered the authoritative source of reality and value. Both views, Murdoch might say, fail to picture individuals. That is, they constrict the area of our moral being to something less than the complex of consciousness, which includes a range of states of mind which bear on both will and reason and serve to distinguish selves from one another. As the distinct mode of human selfhood and individuality, consciousness is a complex whole whose unity cannot adequately be represented by reason or will and whose particularity cannot be diminished to being a mere function in a larger network. How then does Murdoch describe the structure of consciousness as the mode of moral being?

Consciousness has two fundamental aspects which embody at the level of the individual the problem of form and contingency

---

45. *Metaphysics*, 153. See especially her critique of structuralism and poststructuralism in chap. 7 and of Wittgensteinian philosophy of language in chap. 9.

I have been discussing. First, consciousness is naturally one-making: it creates unities, it intuits wholes from fragmentary truths, it seeks order among random detail, and is a continuous unified stream that is part of our total fabric of being. This aspect of consciousness is correlative to the first important aspect of the moral life Murdoch is concerned with in this book, the metaphysical attempt to impose unity or order on our moral existence. This is not something that some human beings just happen to do; it is, rather, a constitutive feature of consciousness itself. This analysis of the one-making aspect of consciousness shows the deep influence of one of Murdoch's two great mentors in this book, Immanuel Kant; for Kant, too, treated human beings' "metaphysical craving" as a natural and structural feature of the mind, the excesses of which can be curbed by a certain form of critique, but never entirely expurgated.

The second aspect of consciousness which Murdoch analyzes is that it is truth-seeking, oriented by a fundamental directedness toward the real. In contrast to the first aspect of consciousness, this activity of consciousness particularizes rather than unifies, because it perceives phenomena in terms of gradations of value, which may alter as our knowledge progresses. Consciousness is thus not a neutral mental activity, but is rather structured by qualitative distinctions between good and bad, better and worse; it makes constant discriminations of value in relation to what it judges to be true or false. The truth-seeking aspect of consciousness correlates to the second important aspect of morality which Murdoch is concerned with in this book, namely, the moral life as a pilgrimage from appearance to reality which is guided by an idea of perfection and a desire for spiritual improvement or change. The idea of consciousness as a truth-seeking pilgrimage shows the unmistakable influence of Murdoch's other great mentor, Plato. For Plato's work constitutes a sustained inquiry into the image of human life as a journey or ascent which takes place through a progressive movement of consciousness from relatively false images to the real.

Murdoch's analysis of consciousness as the fundamental mode of our moral being gives rise to a tension within morality itself, a tension which is played out in the constant dialogue between Kant and Plato in Murdoch's text.[46] In other words, the two aspects of consciousness are correlative to two kinds of moral thinking. The one-making aspect of consciousness is reflected in morality as obligation or duty, which tends to reduce the diverse phenomena of morality to abstract principles or rules regarding conduct; the pilgrimage aspect of consciousness is reflected in a morality of spiritual change or perfection, which relies more heavily on vision rather than will and concerns itself with the inner life of emotions, desires, and attachments. This contrast between two kinds of morality repeats the basic contrast between form and contingency I have been tracing: morality, like consciousness, both unifies and discriminates. In one of its aspects it seeks to produce a stable pattern or order among moral rules guiding conduct; yet in its other aspect it particularizes the claims of morality and relates them to specific instances and contexts. The question is, How does Murdoch conceive the relation between these two aspects of morality, both within human life and within the unity of her moral theory as a whole?

In other writings, notably in *The Sovereignty of Good*, Murdoch appears to give priority to the second aspect of morality over the first, that is, to a morality of perfection and change over a morality of duty or obligation. On the whole, she suggests, human beings would rather search for the relative clarity and order of a system of moral rules over the messier task of continually clarifying our vision, seeking greater particularity and detail in our response to specific persons and situations. It may in fact be rather consoling to think that "morality is essentially rules," since this may serve to "secure us against the ambiguity of the world."[47] For these reasons, the one-making nature of our consciousness frequently overwhelms or eclipses its discriminating aspect, just as the desire for form in art may prevent a proper attention to individual realities. In order to counter the strong force of our one-making

46. Murdoch quotes Schopenhauer's maxim that "'Western philosophy is a dialogue between Plato and Kant'. I see the deepest aspects of moral philosophy as contained in this dialogue"; *Metaphysics*, 298; see also 57. Comparisons between Kant and Plato are omnipresent in this work.
47. "Vision and Choice in Morality," 50.

impulse, then, Murdoch has argued explicitly that an account of moral-spiritual change is the most important part of any system of ethics.[48] In keeping with this claim, she has persistently criticized Kantian forms of ethics which neglect the morally eccentric and particular aspects of human life in order to produce a set of general rules or principles. And she has also maintained a relentless attack on those forms of ethics (e.g., existentialism and linguistic behaviorism) which restrict the domain of morality to discrete choices or rule-governed actions rather than conceiving morality as our total response to a complex and ambiguous moral world.

However, in her latest work, it is clear that Murdoch wants to balance the two aspects of morality more evenly. "One might say that morality divides between moral obligation and spiritual change," she writes (*Metaphysics*, 53). In keeping with her general effort in this work to integrate disparate conceptual polarities into a more unified framework, Murdoch finds a place for the notion of duty *within* the more comprehensive notion of the moral life as a pilgrimage. "Duty is not to be absorbed into, or dissolved in, the vast complexities of moral feeling and sensibility. . . . [T]he concept of duty as moral rules of a certain degree of generality should stay in place" (p. 302). In this respect Murdoch attempts to give the one-making impulse of morality its due: the concept of duty or obligation is indispensable because it provides "a formal way of asserting both the orderly pattern-like nature of morality, and its unique absolute demand" (p. 303). Yet she insists that duty must be thought of against the more general background of our changing quality of consciousness. If a morality of duty is not contextualized in this way, what may be obscured is the omnipresent, continuous, and frequently chaotic nature of individual moral struggle—the sense that morality is carried on in the moment-to-moment consciousness of individual moral agents which goes on in *between* the intermittent call of duty and between periods of overt moral choice or action.

Thus Murdoch attempts to defend the individual by offering

---

48. *The Fire and the Sun*, 81. See also Iris Murdoch, "Above the Gods: A Dialogue about Religion," in *Acastos* (New York: Viking Penguin, 1987), esp. 99.

an account of morality as dependent on the evaluative activity of a thinking consciousness which thinks in two aspects: a unifying aspect and a discriminating aspect. The two aspects are interdependent, since for Murdoch general moral principles are apprehended within an inner moral landscape which is constantly being built up by the continuous truth-seeking activity of consciousness as it perceives particulars.[49] Both aspects of consciousness are necessary to present an adequate account of morality as encompassing an unconditional element of duty or obligation as well as particular, fallible judgments about specific courses of action. It remains to be shown how Murdoch conceives the fundamental norm of morality within her system and to inquire whether the pattern I have been tracing in her thought is operative in her theory of the Good. Does Murdoch identify a single principle of morality, and how does she relate this to her understanding of the complex unity of consciousness in its two aspects?

Murdoch presents two arguments for the concept of the Good, one transcendental and the other empirical, which are correlative to the two aspects of consciousness. By affirming such a correlation, Murdoch is claiming that consciousness itself is internally structured by a notion of value or the Good—a claim that cuts sharply against modern assumptions that moral rationality is essentially "value-neutral." In its transcendental aspect Murdoch repeatedly describes the Good using Plato's image of the sun: Human life is lived "under the aspect" of the Good, or in its light. The Good does not represent any particular being or value, but is rather the ground or source of all being and value; it is not a thing we see directly, but rather that which makes seeing possible; it is not an object of knowledge, but the condition of the possibility for knowledge. Murdoch expresses this aspect of the Good by saying that "there is something about moral value" which "adheres essentially to the conception of being human, and cannot be detached; and we may express this by saying that it is not accidental, does not exist contingently, is above being" (*Metaphysics*, 426).

---

49. Summing up this point, Murdoch writes: "The sharp call of an unwelcome duty seems to come from elsewhere; but it descends upon a countryside which already has its vegetation and its contours"; *Metaphysics*, 241.

Murdoch relates this transcendental argument for the Good to the one-making aspect of human consciousness. "The unity and fundamental reality of goodness is an image and support of the unity and fundamental reality of the individual" which is rooted in consciousness as the bearer of our moral being (p. 427). As a transcendental notion, the Good represents a formal notion of value which is the background condition for every act of cognition, perception, or evaluation. In the one-making light of the Good, all of human experience is morally "colored." In this respect, the transcendental aspect of the Good is directly related to Murdoch's emphasis on moral vision. In her view, human beings do not *impose* value on a morally neutral world of facts by an act of will; rather, the world is already constituted as a moral world through our perception, which is a function of the ordinary operation of consciousness. In the light of the transcendental Good, therefore, all perception is moral perception. Murdoch's transcendental aspect of the Good thus unifies the whole of human life and perception under the sovereign concept of goodness.

The second aspect of Murdoch's theory of the Good is an empirical argument about how the concept of Good operates in our cognitive truth-seeking activities. The argument appeals to our experience of gradations or degrees of value through which we gradually come to apprehend the idea of the most perfect as the ideal end-point in a series. We learn about the Good through "reflection upon our ordinary perceptions of what is valuable, what it is like to seek what is true or just in intellectual or personal situations, or to scrutinize and direct our affections" (p. 398). This empirical argument coheres with Murdoch's analysis of the progressive, truth-seeking nature of consciousness as possessed of rankings or qualitative distinctions of value. Murdoch's claim is that perception is not only carried out against a transcendental background of value, but also is progressive in its attempt to make discriminations of value in relation to an implicit ideal of perfection. This pilgrimage from appearance to reality is carried on in every serious exercise of understanding. In intellectual studies, work, art, and human relations, we learn to distinguish gradations of value in relation to the real. In this respect, the whole of our cognitive experience furnishes us with evidence of the idea of perfection. "[T]he unique and special and all-important knowledge of good and evil is learnt in every kind of human activity. The question of *truth*, which we are indeed *forced* to attend to in all our doings, appears here as an aspect of the *unavoidable* nature of morality" (p. 418).

Murdoch thus portrays the moral life as combining the idea of a unique, absolute, one-making Good which places our whole life under a moral demand, with a concomitant recognition that moral progress and failure are measured in the piecemeal but ongoing pursuit of the Good at particular moments along the pilgrimage. This view of the moral life reflects her understanding of the self as a complex being whose individuality resides in the idiosyncratic nature of its moral pilgrimage in the light of the Good. This idiosyncratic character of consciousness cannot be reduced to the operations of reason or will nor effaced in some larger whole of language or society. Using terms introduced earlier, one might say that by emphasizing consciousness as the mode of moral being, Murdoch avoids both neurosis and convention in her conception of the individual.

The question now is, How does Murdoch construct a metaphysic that can accommodate this complex portrait of the individual consciousness and encompass both aspects of the moral life? I attempt to answer these questions by engaging in a brief analysis of the structure of *Metaphysics as Guide to Morals*. I contend that the structure of the book may provide a clue as to where Murdoch finally stands on metaphysics and the human impulse to unify at the expense of the individual particular.

V. Conclusion

I suggested earlier that there might be a relation between how Murdoch treats the tension between form and contingency in the novel and the way she treats the tension between metaphysics and empiricism in her moral theory. In each case, my contention has been that Murdoch is attempting to articulate a complex notion of formal unity which allows room for the concept of the individual. I want to conclude by arguing that *Metaphysics as Guide to Morals* enacts the tension between the themes of one-making and pilgrimage in its very structure, attempting to combine these within the bounds of a single theory of morals.

The first thing to be noted is that this tension is apparent in the actual experience of reading the book. One is confronted not so much with a systematic metaphysical treatise as with a transcript of a brilliant thinker's stream of consciousness, full of detailed reflection and analysis, but also dense with seemingly random associations, humorous asides, and profound insights. The impression that the book gives of being a kind of extended monologue is reinforced by the fact that paragraphs frequently run on for pages, rarely sticking to one topic, but pursuing connections to other thinkers and ideas as they occur and then abandoning them abruptly. Even the chapter divisions, which in the table of contents seem orderly and distinct, are found to be more arbitrary in the actual reading; the topics and themes under discussion in one chapter seem to burst their boundaries and run into the next. In this respect, the narrative flow of the book might be said to resemble the pilgrimage aspect of consciousness, wherein thoughts, images, and perceptions strive for clarity in an endless stream of reflection, sometimes progressing, sometimes falling short.

On the other hand, it must quickly be noted, all is not random in this book. There is a definite structure and formal pattern to the whole which runs beneath the constant stream of analysis, observation, and comment. A systematizing intent is represented, first, in the book's attempt to give a comprehensive account of the most important aspects of morality and how they relate to one another. The book treats the relations between persons and their conduct toward one another (in terms of categories like love, respect, duty, attention, and freedom); the question of the inner life or personal good of individual moral agents (especially in the analysis of illusion as the bane of the moral life, and of realism as the goal of moral vision); and a normative account of human reality in a theory of the Good. Second, the book manifests the impulse to unity in the organization of its subject matter according to three main topics which serve as the fundamental unifying themes of the book: art, which occupies roughly the first five chapters; moral selfhood or consciousness, which is the central theme of chapters 6–12; and religion, roughly occupying chapters 13–18.[50] Finally, the narrative as a whole displays a complex unity in the recurrence of the most prominent themes and motifs throughout each chapter, so that the effect of the insights is cumulative and attains its fullest force only at the end.

Reading the book in its entirety thus requires a sustained effort of attention during which one may lose the overall pattern; yet if one searches only for the underlying pattern and strives to make the book into a system, one loses the extraordinary detail, the insights which may be hidden in a parenthesis, but which illuminate the whole work. In a word, the book's structure amounts to what Murdoch sees as an alternative to the architectonic form of some traditional metaphysical systems: it contains precisely those elements of light, space, and fresh air which open up the structure of the book and allow for an unsystematic reflection on human life. If metaphysics usually "founders on the funny," as Murdoch says, I believe she has produced a kind of metaphysics which, not unlike a novel, incorporates some of the accidental, aimless, and humorous character of human life within an essentially loose-textured but coherent form.

What are we to make of this peculiar metaphysical structure? Are form and contingency held in tension in the book, or does one pole of the tension gain the upper hand finally? I believe that ultimately, the unifying impulse of the book is placed under a negation by another deep formal pattern which emerges from the narrative flow and which works as a countervailing impulse to unity. This pattern is revealed in the progression of themes from the first chapter, called "Conceptions of Unity. Art," to the penultimate chapter, titled "Void." This progression suggests that the narrative movement of the book thematizes a pilgrimage from appearance to reality, from art to void, from the production of images to their dissolution or negation. The terminus of the book in void brings out the essential paradox of metaphysics as a means of *picturing* human existence. For as Murdoch has continually shown, metaphysics faces the problem of every effort of human communication to

50. I am indebted to William Schweiker for these insights into the structure of the book.

capture the nature of the real (i.e., the individual particular) in language, concept, or symbol: the very attempt may also falsify, obscure, or end in nothing.

By ending with "Void," Murdoch's book on metaphysics embraces some of the open-endedness and incompleteness of art. The refusal of closure in her theory points also to a deferral of closure on human moral struggle in the light of the Good. The struggle continues, guided by theory but also continually testing theory against ordinary moral experience. What finally has the last word in Murdoch's metaphysics, I believe, is the theme of pilgrimage, not the theme of one-making, and a final refusal to imagine the end of the journey. In this respect, the one-making impulse of human life is corrected, as it were, by the theme of pilgrimage, which drives us from our false resting places and spurious unities toward greater truthfulness to contingent reality. The individual's day-to-day and moment-to-moment moral struggle cannot be effaced by the unities of theory, and this is perhaps, in its own way, a consolation for which we can be grateful.

6
THE GREEN KNIGHT AND OTHER VAGARIES OF THE SPIRIT; OR, TRICKS AND IMAGES FOR THE HUMAN SOUL; OR, THE USES OF IMAGINATIVE LITERATURE

Elizabeth Dipple

I

I must first address the question of the crazed title of this paper, especially in the light of its apparently overblown alternatives and repetitions. Simply put, it has to do with both the nature of literary studies at this time and the techniques Iris Murdoch uses to maximize the primary functions of literature as a useful genre. In her practice of the tough art of novel writing, she persistently displays a subtle sense of fictional construction at a very sophisticated level, while at the same time she uses novels to address deep human issues. These are connected to the quality of moral action both in the realm of the quotidian world, where most of her characters fail in myriad small and large ways, and in the religious sphere, where she describes the soul's persistent yearning for a perfection that, as her most spiritually advanced characters repeatedly say, only a saint could achieve. Murdoch is at once well aware of the limitations of all too many contemporary novels, and of the ways in which imaginative literature can wrongfully feed the human desire for spectacular displays of magical supernaturalism.

Let me first put Murdoch's work into the context of contemporary literary studies. The critical climate in which literature could flourish has changed qualitatively over the last several years in a way that renders the central concerns of this conference on the work of Iris Murdoch of limited interest to the majority of professional literary critical practitioners, for whom the text itself is secondary to sets of theory generated before the advent of fictional intervention. I look at this decline of interest in the ethical, aesthetic, spiritual, and personal on the part of my colleagues in literature departments warily and often sadly. The prevailing atmosphere among most professional literary critics gives real urgency to the practice of an alternative criticism that stretches the moral and aesthetic imagination dwelling within the human subject, and calls for the practice of a continuous patience while the dominant materialist movements wear themselves out, as they inevitably must. Fortunately for the fate of the study of literature, various kinds of beneficial criticism do exist—in the Bakhtinian studies of Caryl Emerson and Saul Morson, for example, in the ethos of Martha Nussbaum's philosophical literary criticism, in the rigorous, formal, aesthetically oriented work of some practicing poets like Robert Pinsky and Mary Kinzie or fictionists like J. M. Coetzee, and in the efforts of an increasingly large number of workers in the literary vineyards who wish to infuse reading with an apprehension of the path through experience, to a knowledge of the radical insufficiency of material existence, and hence to the divine. I am not myself comfortable with much of the work of the latter group, however, in that the pressure of traditional religions can lead too often to a simplistic misuse of literary texts as a corollary of settled belief. This practice can easily become a dogged essentializing of broad elements that are present in the text but are easily distorted by the heavy hand of dogmatic conviction or religious fantasy. Because of the nature of Murdoch's fiction, with its religious suggestiveness, this issue must early be cleared away as irrelevant to a just and accurate reading of her texts.

In her novels, Murdoch, through specific characters and extended thematics, again and again warns against the dangers of fantasy and illusion in the face of the apparently supernatural, especially because of the human tendency to find miracles and quasi-divine comforts everywhere. In her recent book, *Metaphysics as a Guide to Morals*,[1] she urges the uses of a discriminating and

---

1. Iris Murdoch, *Metaphysics as a Guide to Morals* (New York: Allen Lane/Penguin Press, 1993); hereafter referred to as *Metaphysics*.

disciplined imagination. Through the following quotation I focus attention on only a small portion of her extended discussion in order to stress the potential power of religious infusion in the literary and its severe limitations as fantasy or dogma:

> High imagination is passionately creative. . . . The spiritual life is a long disciplined destruction of false images and false goods until (in some sense which we cannot understand) the imagining mind achieves an end of images and shadows (*ex umbris et imaginibus in veritatem*), the final *demythologisation* of the religious passion. . . . I want to see the contrast [between fantasy and imagination] . . . positively in terms of two active faculties, one somewhat mechanically generating narrowly banal false pictures (the ego as all-powerful), and the other freely and creatively exploring the world, moving toward the expression and elucidation (and in art celebration) of what is true and deep. . . . 'Truth' is something we recognize in good art when we are led to a juster, clearer, more detailed, more refined understanding. Good art 'explains' truth itself, by *manifesting* deep conceptual connections. Truth is clarification, justice, compassion. (*Metaphysics*, 319–21)

A serious reader of literature, as opposed to an ideologue, recognizes that the function of the imagination in any of its definitions is opposed to a wholesale acceptance of the strong concept of cultural or social constructivism—the idea that human beings are more or less passively shaped by the dominant discourses and ideologies of their culture. This constructivist theory, however, is now in firm control in many fields of academic inquiry and is seldom questioned. Central concepts of constructivism itself are not primarily negative, of course, and indeed can offer help in such fields as the anthropology of literature—a movement that cries out for new thought instead of the kind of ideological borrowing that is now too often going on. A philosopher of science, Arthur Fine, rescues the field. He points out that our ideas are indeed socially formed, arranged and rearranged in subtle ways as two or more (indeed, multiple) minds work through local conversations, reading, discussions of other topics, or human discourse of any sort, toward shifts and changes in our individual apprehension of the world. This continuous, ongoing process keeps us within the world, using our local experience and solving problems within that experience. In terms of Fine's principle of the Natural Ontological Attitude—NOA (pronounced Noah)—this sort of subtle constructivism does not trap us in a socially determined mode, but rather allows us to open the doors to ethical and aesthetic considerations, as well as to a renewed critique of social and scientific constructivism. One important thing that Fine's NOA work teaches a literary critic is that the rigidity of theory or the tight, Marxist/Feminist political-cultural nexus of current ideology lacks the fluidity of mind and strong attention necessary for real analysis or a sensitive listening to the work at hand. As Fine puts his case in another context: "NOA . . . is an open, particularist and nonessentialist attitude to science. It promotes a no-theory attitude [of letting the ontological chips fall where they may] toward truth, and thus avoids the metaphysics of [scientific] realism or metaphysical constructivism."[2]

For Murdoch, as for a thinker as unlike her as Fine, all human problems are indeed local in very specific ways. Given her carefully enforced novelistic repetitions, the reader of Murdoch's fiction is always aware of the need to work slowly through the dense and often contingent material that crowds each novel. Although central ideas—such as her complex concept of the good, the muddle of contingency in the experienced universe, or the fallacy of comforting unitive thought—may be passed on from novel to novel, their context is always skewed, renewed and reworked by the freshly conceived structure in which they appear.

As Murdoch's novelistic production advances through time, there is a consistent increase in compositional strength and a progressive refinement in her metaphoric reach. About a dozen years ago I wrote a book on Murdoch's fiction, feeling at that time that *The Black Prince* (1973) was her best novel. I argued moreover that the earlier novels, although of great interest, lack the density of the later work. Another way of putting this was to use Henry James's vocabulary, as Murdoch herself has done, thus opening the door for most of her critics endlessly to reiterate her opinion as

---

2. Arthur Fine. "Science Made Up: Constructivist Sociology of Scientific Knowledge," in *The Disunity of Science: Boundaries, Contexts, and Power*, eds. P. Galison and D. Stump (Stanford: Stanford University Press, 1995).

I do here: She moved steadily from her tendency toward tightly controlled plots and form to the "big baggy monsters." She became more like James, more like the nineteenth-century novelists and particularly the Russians. In reading individual Murdoch novels, one feels that occasionally Tolstoy and almost always Dostoevsky is tapping on one's shoulder. And behind the whole oeuvre is the encompassing, disruptive spirit of Shakespeare.

This particular intertextual insight does not get the reader very far, however. It can lead too easily to generalized readings of the novels, to a misprision of the particular which Murdoch has labored intensively to create. Imaginative literature dies under the hammer blows of a priori theories: If one considers the task of author and reader as somehow shared within certain areas of cognition, then each participates in the tension of constructivism, of the making of the text within usable mental boundaries. This shared responsibility is not frivolous, nor is it a property of simplistic first readings.

After the publication of her twenty-fourth novel, *The Message to the Planet* (1989), I became convinced that it and the previous work, *The Book and the Brotherhood* (1987), could productively be seen as paired novels and that each indicated a stride forward from her already impressive record in the most recent previous books. Not only was she consistently and relentlessly driving her standard of fiction forward from the early novels to the high achievements of the 1970s and early 1980s, but she was also working more freely and successfully within strong structural and metaphorical areas that set these novels both qualitatively and narratologically apart from those that preceded them. Having decided this, but feeling nevertheless that this attitude might be a temporary disaffection based on current enthusiasms, I went back and carefully reread *The Good Apprentice* (1986), which is individuated and surprising in its own right. It was not until the publication in Britain of *The Green Knight* in the summer of 1993, however, that my overly tidy pattern of response was bent if not entirely broken. Murdoch's sudden entry into the Arthurian world as one of her intertexts led to a myth-ridden area which both she and her novelistic characters, standing in for her authorial viewpoint, had always forsworn, passionately preferring the open, particularized sphere of Shakespeare's plays. For Murdoch's fiction, the implied magic, the fantasy-ridden mythology, and the potential trumpery of that romance tradition had previously appeared to be too distractive for such a serious writer. Indeed, they have too often tempted modern writers and readers easily with an illusionary/visionary world like that of Charles Williams or like John Cowper Powys's *A Glastonbury Romance,* a Modernist quasi-Arthurian saga that one of the characters is languidly reading through much of Murdoch's *The Green Knight.* I therefore began this novel armed with suspicion. However, I rapidly came to the conclusion that it is one of her most compelling books and one that develops ideas suggested in her earlier work but which are here taken into new dimensions.

The strength of the novels seems to me to grow progressively through a ceaseless rethinking of thematics within the new framework of each book. In other words, although many of Murdoch's critics, particularly the journalistic ones, have claimed to be unable to distinguish one novel from the other and to feel that once you are in the phenomenology of Murdoch's world you know all the rules, the opposite is more often true. Her novels constantly surprise because repetitive patterns lull the inattentive and generalizing reader into a kind of mental softness, from which one is suddenly awakened by an often infuriating series of reversals that, on first reading, meet strong reader resistance. When the Russian Formalist Victor Shklovsky came up with the term *ostrannenie,* "defamiliarization," Mikhail Bakhtin attributed it to that quality of Tolstoy's writing that makes the reader reperceive the world as somehow adequately, mimetically represented in the fiction, but also made strange and "other." This insight can be taken a small step further in Murdoch's case: As novel readers, we both recognize and rethink the two structures involved—our perception of the experienced world represented by fiction and, held in tension against this, the structure of the fictional representation that we thought we could master.

Fiction has an important task, that of disarming and alienating its readers from their sense of security in the world they perceive in habitual ways. Within Murdoch's particular agenda, the slippery presentation of narrators, of characters, of action reversing logical expectation, robs the reader of interpretative certainty. I find again and again in teaching Murdoch's novels to students, who too often and willingly attach themselves to brutally singular meanings, that I must answer their queries by saying that I simply do not know why such-and-so happens, or why a certain character says a particular something. I can, however, present a series of possibilities (although even in presenting that series I feel that a better reader might come up with a better list). Because the novels are so crowded with myriad details, all significant from one point of view or another, any reading feels small and eccentric in the face of the crowded, resonant text. The multiple interpretations called out by Murdoch's work defy the single reading, or the smug sureness of the theoretician.

Although Murdoch does not in any general or straightforward way reflect the thought patterns of the postmodernist novelists who have appropriated several of the ideas of the American "pragmatist" C. S. Peirce, her novels can be seen as participating in a version of realism the reading of which demands a *mise-en-abyme* structure. In terms of the multiplicity of adequate readings of her fiction, then, it is helpful to look at Peirce's stripteasing explanation of the problem of representation within a context that chimes with the ambitions of any one of Murdoch's recent novels: "The meaning of a representation can be nothing but a representation. In fact, it is nothing but the representation itself conceived as stripped of irrelevant clothing. But this clothing never can be completely stripped off; it is only changed for something more diaphanous. So there is an infinite regression here. Finally, the interpretant is nothing but another representation to which the torch of truth is handed along; and as representation, it has its interpretant again. Lo, another infinite series."[3]

In a very real sense, Murdoch's mimetic representation of a flimsy world of infinite interpretational regress is hermeneutically analogous to her apprehension of the spiritual questing of the religious soul. As a case in point, one can refer to *Henry and Cato* (1976), where the Catholic priest Brendan Craddock tries to call Cato back to the rigors of the church: "The point is, one will never

---

3. C. S. Peirce. *Collected Papers*, vol. 1, ed. Charles Hartshorne and Paul Weiss (Cambridge: Harvard University Press, 1960), sec. 339.

get to the end of it, never get to the bottom of it, never, never, never. And that never, never, never is what you must take for your hope and your shield and your most glorious promise" (p. 339). In an increasingly secular world, one central use of literature as practiced by Iris Murdoch is to detach us from the illusion of determinate meaning, in both fiction and the spiritual life.

II

The toughness, the flex and play of Murdoch's dense fiction can be approached through her Ovidian instincts, a possibility I put forward in order to focus on the particular achievements of her most recent novels. The hellenistic idea of the "continuing song" of literature, put forth and practiced by Callimachus (third century B.C.), is part of the complex intertwining of Ovid's *Metamorphoses* (A.D. 7–8), a long narrative poem in fifteen books thematically linked by ideas of transmutation. Here the structuralist intuition of the endlessly relational aspect of literary knowledge (and for Murdoch one would have to add art historical and religious knowledge as well) is useful. Jonathan Bate, who in his excellent recent book *Shakespeare and Ovid* gives the best radical critique of Ovid that I have read, is aware that Ovid is par excellence a poet of Derridean *différance*—of differentiation and endless deferral.[4]

Murdoch, who has studied and heavily criticized the excesses and traps of the various structuralisms in *Metaphysics as a Guide to Morals*, however, is also a fastidious reader of Shakespeare, whose plots, characters, and themes she incorporates obliquely and iconoclastically into her own fiction. Shakespeare's grasp of the contingent, the tragic, and the performed life alters her understanding of Ovid, whom I suspect sets her route. In major respects, Murdoch's art lives in a milieu of oblique commentary on Shakespeare's techniques as well as on those she has learned from her enormous interest in the Venetian Ovidian painters of the cinquecento, particularly Titian. Again and again she evokes those mythological paintings, derived from Ovid and transmuted into the spiritual allegories of the Italian Renaissance, particularly the im-

---

4. Jonathan Bate, *Shakespeare and Ovid* (Oxford: Clarendon Press, 1993).

age of Titian's *Flaying of Marsyas*, of *Actaeon and Diana*, and *Perseus and Andromeda*, to mention only the major ekphrases of the Ovidian Venetian connection. The lens of Titian's representations turns continuously into transmuted visions—Diana hunting actively in the foreground while Actaeon is roughly torn by the hounds in the misted background, Marsyas overturned in body as well as mind by a torturing, flaying Apollo. The transmutation of the myth is everything to Ovid, and his freedom before the idea of metamorphosis is seized on by Murdoch's own sense of literary, intertextual inversion.

It would, however, be a serious disservice to Murdoch's fiction to say that she is wholly or even largely dependent on an Ovidian frame of reference. What I imply when I say that her style is Ovidian has to do much more with methodology, with a sense of succession in novel after novel, as a long continuing song unfolds discretely and freshly with each new presentation. Living as her fiction does very much within the real world of the late twentieth century, Murdoch's method of imagistic and metaphoric presentation goes widely beyond the strictures of classical mythology. The purpose of the central part of my study is to illustrate how her imagery, metaphors, and allusions work, as one senses that within every one of her fictions books endlessly talk to books within the minds of the narrator, the characters, and the readers, who share in the process of constructing a world in which the images and stories of the past beget story after story in the present. This endlessly generative process ties every reader to a large referential frame from western literary and art historical culture, from Judeo-Christian texts, Buddhism, Hinduism—in short, the whole panoply of cultural armor that a privileged, educated audience wears and wishes to embellish.

Herein, I might add almost parenthetically, lies a problem that Murdoch's fiction neither engages in nor attempts to apologize for. The social doctrines now endemic in cultural criticism bounded by narrowly doctrinaire Marxism, the strictures of multiculturalism, and radicalized feminism make most culturally elitist art of any sort (the buzzword is "museum art") blameworthy. The blame is doubled when the issues also involve ethical or spiritual examinations beyond the materialist expositions of politicized issues like race, class, and gender. Murdoch uses these issues when they are useful to the larger designs of her fiction or of her ethical thought, but she sturdily refuses to reduce the learned world that our hard-won education presents us with. (For which Allah be praised.) Even a critic like Nicholas Spice, whose occasional reviews of Murdoch's novels in *The London Review of Books* are among the most insightful work to be done in short measure on the books under review, felt obliged—no doubt under the pressure of the materialist concentration of thought in current Britain—to chastise her mildly for presenting the moral action of *The Green Knight* against a background with no socioeconomic or historical depth. It is essentially outside the boundaries of this paper to defend Murdoch on this front, or to concentrate attention on her no doubt elitist but strong conviction that education, through a broad reconception of its function and content, is necessary for us as a society to retain any kind of access to virtue. I will simply say that in *The Green Knight,* Sefton, one of the three sisters who are almost enchanted princesses, lives in a glorious haze of passionate book learning (her field is history) which feeds and enriches her imagination. Sefton is, to my mind, a mythical representation not only of the wisdom that her real name, Sophia, allegorically points to, but also of the high progressive feeling of liberation and clarification that a genuine, disciplined search for manifold, not merely politicized, knowledge can give us.

III

In carrying out even a brief analysis of Murdoch's recent fiction, it seems clear, at least to me, that two points are imperative: (1) It is essential not to clog the investigation with theory. An overtheorized approach stops the fluidity and multidirectional aspect of the novels at the same time as it calls attention to itself rather than to the more challenging job of trying to gather some of the salient aspects of these broadly beckoning artifacts. (2) A fruitful reading should be aware of but significantly separated from heavy reliance on Murdoch's recent philosophical work, *Metaphysics as a Guide to Morals*. This generically different product has been broadly touted as the primary guide to the fiction, as it is to her interpretations of the moral and spiritual life. The close intertwining of literature, art, ethics, and religion present in that volume is of extraordinary interest, but if misused it can also be seen as a sort of unfriendly takeover of the experience of reading, of thinking about fictional writing, of being in the old Lutheran sense one's own priest. Reading the novels side by side with this capacious inquiry is too much like relying on the pre-theorized aspects of *The Golden Bough* in all Modernist anthropological studies. I believe that Murdoch wants readers to have a go on their own, helped but untrammeled by her own powerful interpretative, authorial hand. I am not simply raising spectres of the Barthesian idea of the absence, which he called "death" of the author; but it is clear to me that the novels must also make their own way within the responsiveness of the individual reader.

I will begin by examining specific but brief scenes in *The Book and the Brotherhood* and outlining the broad contours of *The Message to the Planet*, as a preparation for engaging in a study of some central metaphors in Murdoch's next novel, *The Green Knight*. A few small episodes from *The Message to the Planet* illuminate something important about Murdoch's mastery over technique. At one crazed point in his obsessive, Kafkaesque experience, Alfred Ludens, whose surname evokes the image of *homo ludens* and is ultimately connected to the idea of play and interpretation, comes upon a shed full of muddled up, injured bicycles. Their presence on the estate is carefully heralded by a posted sign. Ludens, marred to a satiric degree by his reliance on book culture and its accompanying semiotic confusions, instantly begins to interpret what seems to be the locutionary force of this sign: "FREE BICYCLES. Ludens contemplated the notice which was prominently set up inside the gates on the side of the gravel drive. Free bicycles? Unwanted bicycles offered gratis? Bicycles released to wander like free-range hens? Or a protest: unjust to bicycles, bicycles lib?" (p. 67). The exact genesis and status of these bicycles are never given, but Ludens, in this essentially charming scene, comically stands in for the reader faced with a text and a feeling of compulsion toward its interpretation. Like every other image in this densely written book, however, the bicycles are part of a larger pattern that passes incrementally through the plot. First, there is the description of Ludens's potential fiancée, Irina, on her bicycle going for a ride with him and then her final appearance with her preferred lover where they are also on bikes. Second, we are told that the current area of Ludens's historical scholarship is a study of Leonardo who, inter alia, was the inventor or conceiver of the bicycle. Finally, compellingly, the novel takes us into a dream sequence that strikes at the heart of the novel:

> He dreamt that he was in a large empty room, lit from above by grey daylight, rather like one of the studios of the art college, only larger. He was alone, standing in the middle of the room, frightened, expecting some person or some happening. A door opened at the far end and Leonardo came in. Leonardo was tall, young, with long pale flowing hair and brilliant luminous eyes. He was dressed in a long white smock or shirt which might have been a painter's overall, but which Ludens realised was the garb of a priest. He felt at that moment a wave of delicious and terrible emotion. . . . [Leonardo] said to Ludens in a peremptory tone, 'You must go on your bicycle and take this message to Milan.' He handed the piece of paper to Ludens. Ludens said, 'B-b-but, sir, I haven't got a b-b-b-bicycle.' Leonardo, pointing to the paper, said, 'There's your bicycle!' Ludens looked down and saw the drawing of the bicycle which he had shown to Irina. He cried, 'But, sir, this is not a bicycle, this is a drawing of a bicycle.' Leonardo said, 'You can ride it if you try hard enough.' As he turned to go Ludens called after him, 'What about the message?' The reply was, 'That is the message.' (pp. 281–82)

In keeping with the narrator's slippery feeling for aporia or connotative dead-endedness, this dream is left without comment and the text abruptly turns to the more frivolous preoccupations of the novel's characters. The resonance of Ludens's quasi-nightmare is both comical and profound, but it is clear that Murdoch as implied authorial voice intends readers to do their own work. The novel's commitment to exploring the nuances and snares of the spiritual life infuses even an apparently secular dream, for Leonardo appears as a priest (of meaning and interpretation perhaps). Ludens's stammer, which occurs only when he is neurotically upset, is in evidence and indicates that even his subconscious responds through his physical disability. The art historical reference to the Surrealist movement in painting is particularly important, in that it reminds the reader that, within Murdoch's subtle revisions of realism, art—and by extension her novels as well—is significantly surreal, anti-real, in touch with the irrational and contingent. Ludens's objection that a drawing of a bicycle can't be ridden to Milan like a real bicycle evokes the most famous painting of the genre, Magritte's *pictorial* representation of a pipe labelled *Ceci n'est pas une pipe*, which reminds the viewer that the various forms of mimesis are not equivalent to the *Ding an sich* of the phenomenal world. A painting of a pipe is not a pipe. A picture of a bicycle is a representation whose empirical function is automatically symbolic.

Most crucially for this novel, the idea of message is forefronted in the dream and throughout the fiction, for Ludens is convinced that Marcus Vallar, with what Ludens perceives as his nearly supernatural power, can write out and *publish* a salvational message to the violent, damaged, post-holocaust planet. At the point of reunion with Ludens after a long, mysterious absence, Marcus had indicated that he did indeed have a message, or perhaps *was* in himself a message. In the light of such illusionary power, he had dubbed Ludens his messenger, vaguely and rather incoherently following the pattern of John the Baptist's role during Jesus' preparation for his ministry. As the novel demonstrates, the vehicle of human desire for a sublime coherence is not a practical reality but an artifact, a picture, something made from individual human genius and yearning, something that doesn't exist in the phenomenal world but that we can somehow learn to ride intelligently when we know its and our limitations and capacities. The message of the novel is that there is *no* message to the planet beyond the rubble out of and through which we ride as well as we can, hoping not to be intruded upon by fantasy and the unreality of ecstatic solutions, keeping on the road to a symbolic Milan.

The length of my discussion of one image, touching on the profundity of these two scenes' most obvious connotations will, I hope, serve to indicate how endless the task of literary criticism is when one thinks about this complex, image-spinning novel. It might be possible to shorten the task, but not without failing in the critic's only genuine contract—that between the work of art and our power to interpret its function in human lives, as cognition darts through the conscious and unconscious minds, aided by the constant pressure and tension put upon us by the narration itself.

There is a significant duality in any reader's reception of a work of art: on the one hand, the reader/viewer undergoes a sense of "extasis," of standing outside the boundaries of our lived quotidian life; on the other hand, the work of art causes us to reflect steadily on our own broken, disjointed, experienced world. This intermingling of two realms constitutes the primary nature of our reception of art, and in this sense it is unlike our apprehension of any other human experience. It also means that each reader/critic has a specific and difficult responsibility to develop and ponder the to-and-fro movement of the work's inter-suggestive detail. Readers interpret not only the broad outline of the characters and action, but also the local line-by-line, word-by-word detail. As I said previously, leaning on Fine's theory of NOA, all problems are local, all tasks immediate, all attention total.

Of her three most recent novels, *The Book and the Brotherhood* can perhaps most simply and directly be used as a methodological paradigm for key elements in Murdoch's work. Applying such an argument to this atypical novel requires a reasoned explanation. I will begin by going back to *Nuns and Soldiers* (1980), where Anne Cavidge, a nun who has left the convent after 15 years to rejoin the secular world, picks up on novel-reading, a frivolous pastime that she had forsworn during her period of religious vocation: "She inspected them with amazement. There was so much heterogeneous *stuff* in a novel. She had been interested in pictures once.... One day she walked along the river as far as the Tate Gallery and looked at the Bonnards. They affected her rather as the novels did, marvellous, but too much.... Anne had been reading *Little Dorrit*, it was amazing, it was so crammed and chaotic, and yet so touching, a kind of miracle, a strangely naked display of feeling, and full of profound ideas, yet one felt it was all true!" (pp. 53–54). *The Book and the Brotherhood* is like conventional novels of the sort described by Anne Cavidge's reaction in its being crammed with heterogeneous stuff, and brimming with complex episodes that can at first look chaotic. In addition to this sense of repleteness or plenitude, it also includes ironic parodies of the traditional novel—comedic closure in marriage, for example, and the overly fortuitous tying up of the futures and destinies of all of the characters. There is an ostensibly omniscient narrator, a strong antagonist and a doubtful protagonist, and a careful alignment of characters over a broad range of points of view. Its putative slogan is enunciated by Jenkin Riderhood, who is perhaps the novel's most admirable character: "The brotherhood of western intellectuals versus the book of history." This tidy way of dealing with *The Book and the Brotherhood*, however, doesn't correspond to the puzzling experience of reading the book, although Charles Newman, reviewing it in *The New York Times Review of Books*, exuberantly reacted to it as an amazing, crowded, multiply complex novel that was everything an extended fiction should and can be, in addition to being brilliantly political without mentioning or being bogged down by the specific details of politics.

Why, then, does the experience of reading this novel with care work so strongly against such straightforward exuberance and generalization? I have always found it impossible to imagine Murdoch's actual process of writing. I know, of course, about the fountain pen, the time conscientiously set aside, the extraordinary fecundity of her plot-spinning imagination, her careful planning and subsequent conviction of authorial control over and knowledge of what she is doing. But I cannot conjecture where and how and through what constructive thought processes her manifold affects are produced. Habitual novel readers always begin their analysis with the narrator, and certainly the apparently omniscient narrators of the novels are difficult to pin down. In *The Book and the Brotherhood*, one can perceive the choices being made about which minds to enter and in what order. In offering an analytic presentation of individual characters, the narrator is capacious, generous, amusing, and often heartbreakingly direct. There is, nevertheless, a strong sense of constriction and limitation: This narrator strains against limitations and must be described in Bakhtinian terms as a third-person restricted narrator. The voice is one of restrained skepticism and careful silences. The shifting uncertainty of the narration obliquely demonstrates the difficulty inherent in the formation of meaning—a difficulty that the characters also have in committing themselves to action. The novel has been constructed so that the characters and reader alike experience the unfathomable and even infuriating difficulty of locating meaning in a text. Frequently, long conversations occur without adequate identification of the speaker, so that the reader sometimes has to count back to see who is saying what, an old habit of Murdoch who, like Henry James, has a spirited interest in the dramatic functions of all fictions.

Most significantly, this restricted narrator cannot enter directly into the minds of the novel's two most dubious (perhaps wicked) characters, Violet Hernshaw and the massively negative but occluded David Crimond. Added to these peculiarities is the sense of absence: The narrator is present for reportage but for nothing else. There is a notable absence of judgment, or didactic function, or self-revelation—and, above all, of location. The reader is stymied by the absence of a sense of where this narrator might stand: From where does one view the scene? What is the perspective? Clearly this narrator is friendly but alien from us and is not connected to the characters. Perhaps this is what Thomas Nagel called the view from nowhere? One driving force behind the construction of a narrator is that one must get the technical job done: hence, in this novel, the arrangements of action and the parody of closure. In an earlier novel, *The Philosopher's Pupil* (1983), the narrator actually became part of the action—a gamesome trick much used in one way or another by contemporary novelists like Martin Amis or John Fowles. But in *The Philosopher's Pupil,* the game is unusually and elaborately witty and parodic: The narrator N creates N's town or Ennistone, in which he tries to manipulate intractable characters, thereby demonstrating the impossibility of interpreting the sequence of action he puts into play. As in *The Book and the Brotherhood,* he forces closure and then smugly, cleverly reflects on his job:

> The end of any tale is arbitrarily determined. As I now end this one, somebody may say: but how on earth do you know all these things about all these people? Well, where does one person end and another person begin? It is my role in life to listen to stories. I also had the assistance of a certain lady.
>
> THE END (p. 576)

Where does a character begin? Where does a narrator? Where a novelist?

Unsettling as the narrator's mystery is in *The Book and the Brotherhood,* the presentation of character and event is equally slippery—or perhaps the trickiness of the narrator fundamentally alters the potential securities of the novel. Certainly there is an interestingly evocative structure based on plausible triads: first, there are the flower women, Rose, Lily and Violet, who like Milton's flower lady, Eve, are unable to concentrate on very much beyond their own passional nature. The more absorbing triad of men compellingly falls into the symbolic Hindu pattern suggested at the beginning of the book when Crimond's intense, grim, concentrated Highland dancing reminds Jenkin of Shiva. The association of the women with flowers indicates something deeply old-fashioned if not entirely Miltonic and hence genuinely satiric: Lily, and, particularly, Rose define themselves only in terms of the men, living and dead, on whom their dull lives are built. Violet's dangerously neurotic self-pity and destructive mothering of Tamar, the only novelistically well-developed example of the younger generation, also appear to spring from the fact that she cannot have a life or the will to live without the accompaniment of a man or his money. Because no adequate man appears on the scene until Gideon takes over the situation late in the book, Tamar must take on the male role, bury her academic hopes, quit Oxford, and support the catastrophic Violet. Jean Cambus too defines her life in terms of men, and escapes the trilogy only because she is a pawn between the two major male antagonists, Crimond and Gerard Hernshaw, while her husband Duncan, like Jean, holds a fully human—active, but nonsymbolic—role in the novel. If Crimond is Shiva the destroyer god, then Gerard, with his languid allegiance to the classics of western culture, can be read as Vishnu the preserver. Holding the balance is the third figure in the trinity—Brahma the creator, who in the development of Hinduism diminished as Vishnu and Shiva shared power over the universe. Jenkin Riderhood ambiguously plays the role of a doomed Brahma.

This schematized, structural reading is ingenious, and may be one of the tricks built almost casually into the formal aspect of the novel. It certainly in no way corresponds to the reader's discontent. Putting aside Crimond momentarily, as well as the renewed Tamar who is set to become an ominous power figure at the end, we are left with characters who are limp, helpless, almost effete. The central characters are in their fifties and are mostly idle. Only

Jenkin really works for a living, while Crimond toils on, unabashedly financed by the brotherhood who are now his enemies, for an unconscionable number of years on his great book. The arrogant, younger character, Gulliver Ashe, is too conceited to submit to a menial job; everybody else either retires early or sits helplessly around, contemplating a long gone golden youth when Sinclair—Rose's brother and Gerard's lover—was still alive. His accidental death seems to have frozen their developmental capacities decades ago, and although we can perhaps follow their lives with sympathy, their claustrophobic stalling diminishes them.

Indeed, there is something decidedly surreal about these characters, as though they are frozen pictures emerging from the subconscious. Plausible to an uncanny degree, they also feel like tricks of the spirit, or like the uncommitted moral flotsam and jetsam that makes them an easy target for the evil impersonated by Crimond. Their separation from the opaqueness of a continuously sought after, almost inconceivable good is palpable and is part of the overriding feeling of absence in this novel. Their paralysis appears to come from something profound, a failure to commit themselves to the present, and to a sense of energized meaning that might force them into purposeful action. Sinclair, dead, unwillingly governs them, and even the belligerent spirit of the old professor, Levquist, at the Tolstoyan opening of the novel, is unable to goad their central representative, Gerard, into useful activity. They live in a state of nostalgic reminiscence of their younger lives and of the culture they learned in university. Levquist makes it clear that Gerard has frittered away his life and that it is too late now to write the book on Plotinus. With no capacity for self-evaluation, Gerard assumes his superiority to Jenkin Riderhood in front of their old teacher, only to be caught up short by Levquist's acerbic tongue: "A pity he's let his Greek slip so. He knows several modern languages. As for 'getting anywhere', ridiculous phrase, he's teaching isn't he? Riderhood doesn't need to get anywhere, he walks the path, he exists where he is. Whereas you . . . were always dissolving yourself into righteous discontent, thrilled in your bowels by the idea of some high thing elsewhere. So it has gone on" (p. 24). It is starkly and depressingly true that Gerard is stalled by his languid desire for mountaintops and philosophical spiritual summits. He lives falsely and egotistically within a mind-dependent image of himself on some spiritual and moral high ground. At the same time he, like so many other characters in the book, is unable to commit himself to the quotidian world, to seeing and acting in order to create, if not meaning, at least the necessity of commitment within his present milieu.

Setting himself up against the destructive power of Crimond, Gerard waxes briefly but wanes rapidly. At the end of the novel, when he declares that he will study and work toward a definitive, crushing book that will serve as an antidote to the impressive tome Crimond has finally finished, one cannot believe him. The only acceptable interpretation I can see is that Gerard's plans fit into the parodic design of the novel's closure. In this respect, his ambition is equivalent to Jean and Duncan Cambus's second reclamation of their marriage, as they head, both keeping their lies and secrets to themselves, into a life of idle, unproductive "happiness" in France. In other words, Gerard moves from forefront to background, and the reader is left with the sense that he is at best an uncertain antagonist to Crimond. Murdoch devises the structure so that readers are left to work out their own interpretation of the ending to the novel, and indeed that final resolution is subjective or mind-dependent to an extraordinary degree.

It is important to note too that as the reader becomes committed to *The Book and the Brotherhood,* there is an accompanying commitment to certain ideas of anti-realism which can be profitable within the mimetic practice of fiction. The sense that these characters live in a crowded, locatable phenomenal world where people act and stories happen is undercut by their surreal aspect. This frozen unreality battles against the narrator's sympathy for them and entrance into their hearts and minds. If the narrator were more reliable, more perspectively situated, this novel would be more in line with conventional realism. In other words, the taut anti-realist and anti-foundational functioning of the novel, so crucial to its place in experimental modes, would evaporate. Murdoch's task is notably large and exacting, because, within the performative direction of this fiction, she opens up technical paths that occlude traditional realism and strike out toward a world where the mind does its own choosing.

The Book and the Brotherhood can thus be read as a sour commentary on the difficulties human beings confront when they try to work through the formation of meaning to the point of commitment and action.

Embedded in the fiction, however, is another important struggle that alters the contours of the novel and reduces the interpretation I have been at pains to adumbrate. This struggle centers on Jenkin Riderhood, the only character at home in the world and all its smallest particularities. Humble and unpretentious, he is neither bound to the past nor dismissive of the two would-be antagonists, Crimond and Gerard. When Levquist says that he walks the path, that he just is what he is, we rapidly identify him as one of Murdoch's characters of the good. He is the only character among the brotherhood who tries for genuine perspective and wishes to locate himself within meaning and significance: He says, "Well, where is my battle? I'd like to be somewhere out at the edge of things. But where is the edge?" (p. 16), and later Gerard mentally acknowledges his power: "Gerard had always recognised his friend as being, in some radical even metaphysical sense, more solid than himself, more dense, more real, more contingently existent, more full of being. . . . It was also paradoxical (or was it not?) that Jenkin seemed to lack any strong sense of individuality and was generally unable to 'give much of an account of himself'. Whereas Gerard, who was so much more intellectually collected and coherent, felt sparse, extended, abstract by contrast" (pp. 122–23).

Jenkin says that he just wants to know what is happening on the planet, but he keeps the book he is reading on liberation theology a secret from Gerard, almost as though he were shielding his frailer friend from reality. His sudden death shocks even the immovable Crimond, whose activities and interferences are the principal agents of that death, to tears. Jenkin's extinction leads to a series of narcissistic internal narratives, in which central characters among the book's inhabitants egotistically warp the tale in order to make themselves its guilty center. The characters' unreliability, their need to interpret through the lens of their own being, is an illustration *in parva* of the generative fecundity of experimentation within this novel.

Jenkin is a hint in the fiction of a better world of acting, doing, living within workable meaning. He has no narcissistic image of himself at the center of things and is satisfied with the fringe. When Gerard "proposes" to him, Jenkin breaks into a *fou rire*, while at the same time he is sensitive to what it is in Gerard that would lead to such a proposal. In like vein, and unlike Gerard, Rose, and Gull, he alone declines to deride and belittle Crimond's Marxist project; instead, he cuts through to the heart of the matter: "Look, David, it won't do.... There's a large lie in it somewhere" (p. 341). Brief, trenchant, without bitterness or jealousy, Jenkin's statement has the ring of truth—and oddly enough the reader believes this very brief critique, although the contents and central argument of Crimond's great book are never revealed to us. In other words, we sense truth, because we see someone acting on it. At the heart of the novel, then, the real antagonists are Crimond and Jenkin, potential evil versus potential good. Jenkin lives in the novel to extend a temporary, limited, but just estimation of the plight of others, rather than as an agent of antagonism. His violent removal from the plot leaves Crimond withdrawn and in some perhaps minor way defeated.

On the other hand, Crimond as character forms a significant link between this secular novel and the intensely complex, doubly plotted next novel, *The Message to the Planet*. As part of an entirely secular novel, Crimond can be perceived as a magical source of power, whose primary attribute is a misuse of others. He exudes a conviction that the very concept of the soul in a bourgeois, Marxist-leaning, self-absorbed world is pointless: "What's the use of a soul, that gilded idol of selfishness! I've sold it and I'm going to *do something* with the power I've got in exchange.... You all idolise your souls, that is yourselves" (p. 340). Mysterious and fascinating, Crimond is grim within the many realms of his destructive power. But he also wishes to create, like Shiva, whose metaphor is simultaneous destruction and creation. With Gerard/Vishnu weakened, and without the balancing power of Brahma, he represents the materialist, technologically driven, intellectually rarefied anti-soul of a terrifying new world order.

IV

Crimond's spiritual/mystical counterpart in *The Message to the Planet* is Marcus Vallar, a tormented man whose dubious powers begin with the Christlike restoration of the almost dead Patrick to life. Patrick is a poet, who lyrically eulogizes his savior, and becomes, as another character puts it, a "resurrection bore." (I lack the space to balance the morally horrific secular plot, seen through the consciousness of Franca, against the hermeneutical one, interpreted by Ludens; I will concentrate briefly only on the latter.) Ludens jealously attaches himself to Marcus, assured that he can become the effective agent of Marcus's great book which, in Ludens's obsessed view, will send a necessary and absolute message to the planet. It is oddly interesting that Ludens, a secular, Kafkaesque Jew, should adore (even idolize) Marcus—but technically he is necessary to highlight the ambiguous problem of meaning within the novel. Again, that meaning is entirely mind-dependent, because Ludens, playing with his interpretations, creates an idea of Marcus that the action and diverse thought patterns of the novel are calculated to deny. Ludens's view of events is manically book-oriented, and never during Marcus's lifetime does Ludens give up on the idea that the written word is utterly central. He buys pens and notebooks for Marcus, he cajoles him, he tries himself to take notes on the contradictory and shifting intellectual fumblings that Marcus gropes through. Hopelessly dismayed by Marcus's sudden access to mystical power, not only over New Age travelers but over virtually everyone else, Ludens is particularly unnerved by the startling authority Marcus, during his "showings," has over the skeptical and truth-telling Gildas.

Marcus is a remarkable human and novelistic phenomenon, a creation at once readable as an evil, power-seeking charlatan and equally interpretable as a positive phenomenon, particularly in his brooding over the unspeakable pain of the Holocaust and during his powerful manifestations of himself to the crowds on the porch of his cottage at the private mental hospital where, according to his cynical daughter Irina, he richly deserves to be. Ludens's fiction-making, mind-dependent anti-realism misinterprets Marcus at every turn, a factor which helps to hide him in plain view. At the same time, Marcus seems to be an exemplification of Murdoch's view of the ontological proof: His spirituality and divine message are created by the perceiver out of some magnetic energy that he possesses. Thus, little Fanny looks at him entranced and enchanted, Gildas kneels, and even Ludens, who finally reluctantly stands at some distance before him, looks and finds his own interpretation—not of the holy, but of the horrors of the spiritual world: "With a slight effort, [he] managed to focus his attention on the face. . . . It was as if Marcus's head, leaving his body and very much enlarged, had advanced towards him, hanging in space at a point half-way from the yew wall and the Stone. The face that he saw was contorted with grief . . . and the most dreadful fear" (p. 428). Consumed with anguish over the Holocaust, seeing himself as does Rozanov in *The Philosopher's Pupil* as beyond good and evil (and hence evil, as Gildas emphatically states), Marcus is also a wounded monster, a new Minotaur, a human reflection of mythic horror. Ludens has heard Marcus describe himself, and no doubt this information feeds Ludens's image of him: "It was as if some evil being came to me and overthrew everything and accused me of everything and made me see myself as something terrible, something loathsome, a monster" (p. 378). The brilliant but unreadable psychiatrist, Marzillian, sees him as someone headed inexorably for death, but even he cannot unravel his mystery or decode the mysterious language he records from Marcus's bedroom shortly before his death. Marcus finally represents something wholly other, mysterious, beyond psychiatry, a spiritual being whose local habitation and name are insufficient to the humbler tasks of reality. He is an image or a series of images and metaphors, but as Gildas says in another context: "One must beware of images, they console and are made to be destroyed" (p. 416). In the stringency of Murdoch's novels, this statement indicates why Marcus must take leave of life and of the novel.

V

While Marcus Vallar is a compellingly mysterious image larger than the human subject's capacity to understand, the Green Knight of the next novel is even more so. This is not merely because he is necessarily the more interesting character, but because he derives his very existence from the heart of literature, not only through his intertextual rubbing against the fourteenth-century poem, *Sir Gawain and the Green Knight,* written in the West Midland dialect, but because he is so self-consciously a construction outside the arena of rational discourse. In a sense one can argue that Crimond, Marcus Vallar, and Peter Mir (the Green Knight) are all out of the range of our perception, except through the surfaces of their actions and words. Each of them is veiled from us by the narrator and as such kept beyond our interpretative range.

The only other novel that departs from Murdoch's normative but unusual rendition of realism so boldly is *A Fairly Honourable Defeat* (1970), where she worked out an atypical allegory of the eternal combat between Christ and Satan, good and evil, for the human soul. The Trinity is bizarrely represented as a moribund family, where only Tallis, the Christ figure, will be able to endure in a world where the great angels have been set free to abuse their moral intelligence. Julius King, the Satan figure, bears some relation to Lucas Graffe of *The Green Knight,* but nothing in the analogy really holds up to serious analysis. Murdoch's vocabulary when talking about her work is infectious, and ever since her first novel, *Under the Net* (1954), critics have written endlessly about her opposing the artist with the saint. The creation of metaphoric (or allegorical) characters in *The Green Knight,* however, is quite separate from and qualitatively different than any novel that precedes it. Although it is clear that the Green Knight (Peter Mir) and Lucas Graffe are in opposition as two powerful magicians, one possibly good and the other evil, the focus of the novel is on Peter Mir.

Rivaled only by Dickens in her name-play, Murdoch here outdoes herself, calling attention by having Peter Mir translate his surname from Russian as meaning both "world" and "peace." No one needs to be told that Peter is the rock on which the Christian church was founded. This latter identification leads us into an allusive tangle, because Moy, of whom more later, lives amid collected rocks and stones, which she endows with spirit, moving them through her adolescent psychokinetic power. The name game does not end there, of course, and can drive one into a veritable tizzy of association. After Peter Mir, however, the naming of the three teen-aged Anderson sisters by their now dead father as Alethea, Sophia, and Moira—Truth, Wisdom, Destiny—is most significant. In depicting these three, Murdoch takes on her biggest challenge in the book—to give them both allegorical and "real" existence. The three have long since taken matters into their own hands, labeling themselves Aleph, Sefton, and Moy, but the problem persists and is, indeed, elaborately expanded: Aleph as the first letter of the Hebrew alphabet is fraught with symbolism, Sefton evokes connotations, among others, of awe and high regard, and Moy, is just *moi*, "myself." The novel begins by placing them outside of the experiential world through Joan's mocking quotation of the dormouse's tale from *Alice in Wonderland:* "Once upon a time there were three little girls. . . . And they lived at the bottom of a well." They exist as a trilogy of fairy princesses, of ripe young women about to be plucked by life. A great deal of energy goes into an account of this plucking, or their emergence from the well or Romance tradition.

By the end of the book, they have all been transposed from the magical world of "milk"—the protective aura of the house in Hammersmith, which they inhabit as their castle of allegory. All of them, even sixteen-year-old Moy, have entered another realm, as the time of change and metamorphosis, heralded by the appearance of Peter Mir, the great shapeshifter and catalyst, and instituted by his magical symbolic being. Peter Mir's very presence scatters metaphors through the novel in a trail as lush and connotative as any tangle of weeds.

For those readers who do not know *Sir Gawain and the Green Knight,* Clement gives a vague run-through of the plot late in the novel. This poem, which is one of the glories of late medieval times, has deep resonance within this fiction, not least because Peter Mir self-consciously fashions himself as a contemporary parody of the mighty giant who disturbs the Christmas celebrations at Arthur's court by insisting on a game of death. Peter hides out in a pub called The Castle, an ironic reference to Bercilak's castle. He carries a green umbrella which is also a knife. He always wears something green, as though to present himself not as a person but as a self-contrived image. A green girdle, linked with Bercilak's lady in the poem, is picked up by Moy as she leads the Minotaur-Mir to her birthday party. As he is taken away by the demonic psychiatrist, Fonsett, ultimately to die, Peter leaves behind his last green garment, a cravat, which is taken up and carried off by Sefton.

There are, however, other important connotations in the medieval poem that I would like to call attention to. It is, above all, a poem about courage and fear, justice and mercy. Courage and justice should, in a virtuous sphere, win; in a world where the knights are not magical but human, Gawain fails not in chastity but in fear, accepting the lady's green girdle on the third day at Bercilak's court, because he is assured by the lady temptress that it will save him from the beheading he has accepted as part of the Green Knight's challenge. He expects justice, but hopes—even cheats—for mercy. The Green Knight who is also Bercilak gives him both, only nicking him on the third stroke of the axe, because he succumbed in fear to the temptation of the lady's girdle. In Murdoch's novel, Lucas receives only a small cut between the ribs (causing Clement/Mercy to faint). Lucas is no Gawain, although he is much admired as an historian and revered by most of the characters. He never acknowledges guilt, shame, or awareness of the moral intensity of the situation. It is, however, marvelous to watch Peter Mir's performance of mercy after he has followed an almost Shylock-like path of revenge. His insistence on reenacting in the park the original scene which "killed" him leads to a flashing light and a total metamorphosis, during which he discovers what he had lost through his death and recovery: God, and an attendant mercy that transforms his murderous, justice-ridden intention. This metamorphosis within Peter Mir leads to a steady rippling of metamorphoses throughout the characters of the novel, as one era ends and another begins.

Another important point stemming from the original Gawain poem has to do with two important details left out by Clement in his rough summary of the story. The gigantic Green Knight with his green horse carries a sprig of holly in his hand. His real castle is a burial mound. He is at a remove from the potential source material for the poem, in that he is a sort of nature god, lord of the living in nature and the dead. Elderly Welsh folk still talk about childhoods where Christmas had no Dylan Thomas sentimentality but involved taking birds and holly through the woods to propitiate the malign spirits of nature. In Murdoch's novel, Peter's magnetic power seems to be connected with nature: The technicians of modern medicine are at a loss over the wound of the Philoctetes figure, Harvey, but Peter Mir lays on his hands and the foot instantly responds. Moy, the rock-, spider-, animal-loving animist, as a character recognizes and "knows" Peter as he does her. On his death and the completion of everyone else's metamorphoses, she enters the sea in a pagan baptism among the seals where, like the Green Knight, she fearlessly sees death. This new Moy feels that she, like Peter Mir, must leave the world as she's known it, perhaps to go to India where the spiritual life might be more available.

The manuscript containing the original Gawain poem (Mus. Brit. Cotton Nero A, x) precedes that poem with the long didactic poem *Cleannesse,* which has always been seen as ideologically tied to *Gawain.* The connotation of cleanness as virtue in all its connotations is present in the doubly plotted tale of the Gawain poet, and the temptation to its opposite, uncleanness, is evoked in both plots as well—in its challenge to the moral purity of the Arthurian court and in the denotation of uncleanness as unchaste or defiled. The sexual underlay of Murdoch's novel is strong, with Lucas's smoldering sexuality hinted at through connections with Joan, his secret proposal to Louise long ago, and his rapacious theft of Aleph. The same is true, but somehow not as salacious, in the case of Peter Mir, who is suspected of being after Aleph, calling her the Princess Alethea and giving her, not the lovely stone necklaces that he gives to her sisters, but a diamond V-shaped collar—V for Veritas or the Virtue in his own family insignia, *Virtuti Paret Robur.* Murdoch's novels always crackle with erotic energy, about which not enough has been written or said, and in this one there is a passionate sense of hidden Eros.

Peter Mir's primary identification for most readers is, no doubt, his Christlike identification through his death and resurrection. Dogged realists will continue to fault Murdoch for this "death," which is, like Desdemona's, medically lax. Slammed on the head with a weighted baseball bat (for Americans, this sounds odd, but I assume it is a short leaded rounders bat, not the three-foot-plus thing swung by American players in their national sport), Peter Mir apparently dies but is revived magically and secretly by a team of Aesculapian doctors of whom Fonsett is the demonic representative. By superhuman strength, Peter maintains an aura of normal humanity during a brief period before he is reclaimed by the doctors and relapses to the world of the dead. Like the Old Testament God, he is justice itself until metamorphosed into the mercy of Christ. I myself do not put much stress on this interpretation, finding it not as interesting as his related identifications, especially those associated with his role as scapegoat and his possible apocalyptic function.

For a partial reading of his performance as scapegoat, I turn briefly to the work of René Girard, in his book of that title.[5] Girard's theory of mimetic desire, in which one person's love object is claimed or mimetically desired by another, is played out by Lucas Graffe's interpretation of his brother Clement's love for their mother. Lucas's resulting hatred leads to a determination to kill his brother, Cain-like, for that mother's preferring Clement over him. As Girard sees it, mimetic violence, when it arises, can only be stopped by claiming an innocent victim and putting him to death as an embodiment of the obstacle to all desires. Thus, there is constant potentiality for mimetic violence between twinned antagonists. Within this rigid scheme, Peter Mir can be seen as the innocent victim—as was Christ, as was the Minotaur, in whom Murdoch is also deeply interested in this novel and in *The Message to the Planet*. I mentioned earlier in this paper that theory fails as a response to the fluidity of Murdoch's fiction, and I therefore want to cut against the grain of Girard's idea by referring to the idea of the apocalyptic which is also strong in *The Green Knight*.

Peter Mir, during his premetamorphic manifestation as Justice, quotes an image that, as Lucas points out, is used both in Isaiah and Revelation: "The heavens shall be rolled together—as a scroll—" (p. 253). In the Apocalypse, this occurs after the opening of the sixth seal and indicates the end of life in the universe. The two brothers engage in a fascinating conversation about Pe-

---

5. René Girard, *The Scapegoat*, trans. Yvonne Freccero (Baltimore: Johns Hopkins University Press, 1982).

ter's possible existence in an after-death state—in a *bardo* (like Charles Arrowby in *The Sea, The Sea*), or the Christian limbo, or Hades, or, as Lucas puts it, "the brain may continue to operate in some twilight way, ticking on like a machine" (p. 254). In apocalyptic thinking, men appear from the skies or from nowhere, rather than being violently killed and hence excluded from society. An apocalyptic arrival can be seen in the person of Peter Mir (or the Green Knight in the medieval poem) as an abrupt and unstoppable inclusion of a concealed person or spirit whose authority is imposed on the world. Peter Mir demands that he be allowed into the tight coterie of the novel's characters, having no friends or connections of his own except for the jaunty Australian publican at The Castle. His entrance leads to a metaphoric millennium conceived through the idea of metamorphosis. At the end of the book, all is changed, and the apocalyptic being exits of his own free will. As he says to Bellamy, "Now I can go straight on *through* it all" (p. 354).

Peter Mir exists at the extreme boundaries of real life and the spiritual world, through both of which we wander as we read, following now this lead, now that, now this myth, now that. As a liminal figure, he participates in both worlds but cannot be clearly located. His places fade, and we are left remembering his transfiguration, his magnetism, his total commitment to enacting a metaphorically constructed emblem, trying to make his way in the experiential world. As a thinker, Iris Murdoch is committed to agency and action within the material world, whereas Peter Mir is pledged to hearkening in this limbo to a different spiritual sphere. His temporary "life" within a literary work is insubstantial and the contradictory literary self he presents throughout the novel is not important to his ultimate function. He does *not* fit in the assemblage of characters; apparently, he does not want to—his will is other-oriented, and what he perceives in people is their moral, spiritual, or allegorical being. Of course he loves truth, and so Alethea; he recognizes wisdom and book-learning and admires Sefton; he *knows* who Moy is. In order to "go through it all" as an apocalyptic figure, he goes from death to resurrection and life in the world and back to death. He has begun the new era, and like Christ, the original apocalyptic figure in western culture, he departs, leaving it behind.

Who is the Moy he knows and who knows him? Who is this late adolescent girl who lives her life in an experienced present and ponders a difficult future? She is what Peter Mir was in a sense, but whereas he is made of images, she, perhaps, is the only anti-metaphorical anti-mythical character in the book. She sees the details, the suffering, she is at home in the natural world and full of imaginative creativity, of yearning love for all beings. She is also a creature of loss, of suffering, of a world that she chooses not to mess up with book learning. Her loss of the beloved dog Anax breaks her heart even more than the fact that she can never have Harvey, her heart's desire. Like a sprite, she embodies human spiritual yearning, committed to the world to which the reader is condemned.

The final character I want to look at briefly is Bellamy James, who is oddly emblematic of the strength as well as the folly of humankind. I think he stands for the vagaries of the human spirit—and in his weaknesses and inchoate love he, like the feckless Frances in *The Black Prince*, stands in for us. Comically afflicted by fantasies about angels, and especially the warrior archangel Michael, he is absurdly greedy for romanticized religious experience. He wants visions, the dark night of the soul, and all the tempting images of religious consolation. Finally, and above all, he wants to serve Peter Mir, who unwillingly becomes his Christ. Drolly chided by his priest for his vaguely gnostic fancies, he nevertheless is a bel-ami (as Percival called himself in Chrétien's romance), someone who crosses all boundaries and is loved or tolerated by everyone in the book. Emil seizes him and the wonderful Anax at the end of the novel and returns him to life in the world, although he remains full of spiritual longings. He loves both the evil Lucas and the metamorphic Peter Mir and is a figure of two worlds—the metaphoric and the real. His stumbling presence ties the novel more firmly to the "real" than anything else in the book. His double participation represents the human valence of Murdoch's artistic endeavor. The reader, like Bellamy, tends to want a world energized by spirit and has to settle for considerably less. The English painter and mystic, Cecil Collins, expresses what Bellamy wants through art and the spiritual life: "Art is a point of interpenetration between worlds, as a marriage of the known with the unknown, for it is the unknown that freshens our life. In Art we can converse with that abundant life whose energy glows through the sad terrestrial curtain of time."[6]

Iris Murdoch's novels, on the other hand, strive to exist at the crossroads adumbrated by Peter Mir and Marcus Vallar and even the brittle, mysterious Crimond. Whereas her earlier novels tended to set up a dichotomy between saint and artist, she now works toward another configuration, in which a single complex character carries an enormous weight of metaphoric power beyond the boundaries of the possible. It is this sense of stretch that makes the most recent novels so ambitious from both a spiritual and literary point of view. It also makes them tough, experimental, tenuous, unabsorbable. Murdoch, who has never read the work of Mikhail Bakhtin, operates fully within his definition of the "unfinalizability" of the literary work—that sense that the last word about our lives cannot be written nor the final analysis achieved.

6. Cecil Collins. *A Retrospective Exhibition* (London: Tate Gallery, 1989), 37.

PART THREE

MORALITY, METAPHYSICS, AND RELIGION

7
On the Loss of Theism

Franklin I. Gamwell

Iris Murdoch is a reserved friend of theistic religion. She is obviously reserved, because she is not herself a theist. In the contemporary philosophical setting, however, those who do affirm the reality of God might well be tempted to feature her friendship in a manner that neglects the circumspection with which it is offered. At the close of a century that has been, on the whole, decidedly unfriendly to metaphysics and, especially, has massively denied that moral theory depends on it, her affirmation of "metaphysics as a guide to morals" is, at least for philosophical theists, a welcome exception, and they should be the more grateful by virtue of the comprehensive scope, argumentative force, and insight into the human condition with which her proposal is advanced. When one adds her insistence that morality is necessarily related to religion and, further, her reassertion of fundamental importance in the ontological argument, the fact that Murdoch herself is not a theist is of little or no consequence with respect to the most widely accepted alternatives in which philosophical theism is currently discredited. But just because they have the best of reasons to appreciate and admire her achievement, theists cannot ignore her considered refusal to affirm a divine reality. In this paper, then, I will pursue an understanding and assessment of her reservation.

I. Emphatic Moral Realism

Given that our century has been, at least in moral philosophy, so decidedly unfriendly to metaphysics, it is useful to identify what

I take Murdoch to mean by metaphysical thinking. It is clearly something other than empirical science and, moreover, something other than empirical thought generally, where the latter means any thought about the variable conditions of human life and the world of which it is a part. In contrast, metaphysics seeks "to promote understanding of very general features of our lives" (p. 212).[1] We may understand this to mean the *most* general or abiding features of the human condition, because she also says that metaphysical systems offer "huge general *pictures* of what 'must be the case' for human being to be as it is" (p. 259). For this reason, she insists that there is a certain circular character to metaphysical argument. It attends to what is "essential" and, therefore, what "must be built into the explanation at the start" (p. 55), and, for this reason also, metaphysics seeks to show us "the internal relations between concepts of great generality" (p. 434).

Because "good metaphysical arguments" (p. 395) seek, in this sense, "to make models of the *deep* aspects of our lives" (p. 55), they "are successful appeals to experience" (p. 395). The enterprise is possible, in other words, because "levels and modes of understanding are (somehow) levels and modes of existence. My general being coexists with my particular being" (p. 146), so that metaphysics "sets up a picture which it then offers as an appeal to us all to see if we cannot find just this in our deepest experience" (p. 507). Thus, Murdoch can also say that metaphysical thought is circular because it is "determined to *argue* for something which it already *knows*" (p. 435). We might even say that, for Murdoch, metaphysics "leaves everything as it is"—except ignorance of self or self-deception.

Simply to say this, however, permits misunderstanding, because the same might be said of Kant. At least if his "prolegomena to any future metaphysics" means that the most general features of our lives are solely features of subjectivity, theoretical and practical, he too, in his own way, seeks to identify the essential character of human being. Notwithstanding other respects in which Kant is important to her, Murdoch is in this respect Platonic rather than

---

1. Iris Murdoch, *Metaphysics as a Guide to Morals* (New York: Allen Lane/Penguin Press, 1993), hereafter referred to as *Metaphysics*.

Kantian. Adequate concepts of the greatest generality are not solely about the human subject, much less solely about our language or about our historically specific form of life. They also picture or express the deep or fundamental character of reality, because what our deepest experience already knows is its encounter with a real world that transcends us, in distinction from what merely appears. It has been said that the metaphysical task is self-differentiating because it includes both a broad and a strict sense of the term. On the former, one seeks to display the conditions of the possibility of human being or existence and, on the latter, the conditions of the possibility of all reality. Subtleties aside, I judge that Murdoch reaffirms this understanding.

Whatever else she offers in her picture of the deep character of reality, surely its most important aspect is what she calls "the ubiquity of value" (p. 250) or "the omnipresence of value" (p. 259). With Plato, she holds that "goodness is connected with reality" in the profound sense that she implies in saying that "the supremely good is the supremely real" (p. 398). This does not mean, of course, that all reality is good, at least not in the sense that all real things are equally good. Rather, the ubiquity of value is the omnipresence of "an opposition between good and bad" (p. 259) in the world we encounter. One might even say that the reality to which we are related *is* its value—good or evil, better or worse—and, for this reason, Murdoch's project includes a persisting and powerful critique of all philosophical proposals that assert in some form or other the separation of fact and value. She is, on my reading, in full accord with Whitehead's affirmation: "Our enjoyment of actuality is a sense of worth, good or bad. . . . Its basic expression is—Have a care, here is something that matters!"[2]

Alasdair MacIntyre has written that the separation of fact and value is "the epitaph" of the Kantian or Enlightenment project and, he holds, the modern dissolution of moral theory derives from the dominance of this separation in thinking subsequent to Kant.[3] On my reading, MacIntyre is not the metaphysician that Murdoch

---

2. *Science and the Modern World* (New York: Mentor Books/Macmillan, 1925), 159.
3. *After Virtue*, 2d ed. (Notre Dame: University of Notre Dame Press, 1984), 56.

is, and, for this reason, she finds far more to affirm in Kant's critique of practical reason, especially in the religious character of the categorical imperative. But she also agrees that "most recent [moral] philosophers" are "neo-Kantian" because they sever the connection between goodness and reality and do so for reasons that may be traced to Kant's critique of theoretical reason and, thereby, his separation of knowledge and morality (*Metaphysics*, 46). In resistance to this dominating picture of our cognition, she reaffirms that consciousness as such "is a form of moral activity" (p. 167). "Value, valuing is not a specialized activity of the will, but an apprehension of the world, an aspect of cognition, that is everywhere" (p. 265). Or, again: "It is certainly often worth saying: Look at the facts! . . . But what we look at, and attempt to clarify and know, are matters in which value already inheres. . . . Value goes right down to the bottom of the cognitive situation" (p. 384). Because reality is its value, apprehension or cognition must be an evaluation, and this view is so far from a fact/value separation that she can say: "Perception itself is a mode of evaluation" (p. 315).

It follows that the good life should be inclusively understood as a quest to apprehend or be conscious of reality—or, if we may speak redundantly, to apprehend reality truly. Morality is identified in terms of reality; "the good man perceives the real world, a true and just seeing of people and human institutions" (p. 475); and we might characterize her position by saying that Murdoch is a moral realist in an emphatic sense of the term. Not only are moral values real in a sense that transcends our explicit interpretation or construction of them, but also all of reality as the object or possible object of human attention is good or bad in a morally relevant sense. With Plato, then, we should understand human life as "a spiritual pilgrimage from appearance to reality" (p. 10), a metaphysical fact given unsurpassed expression in his myth of the cave. "Life is a spiritual pilgrimage inspired by the disturbing magnetism of *truth*, involving *ipso facto* a purification of energy and desire in the light of a vision of what is *good*" (p. 14).

Cognition or apprehension as a moral goal is something for which we must quest because human consciousness is prone to distort the world egoistically and, thereby, to see the world through prejudices, illusions, and fantasies that accord with our own unrealistic evaluations of ourselves. "The human mind is naturally largely given to fantasy" (p. 322), and our energy is "naturally selfish."[4] I am inclined to think that Murdoch would not object to the claim that human illusions can take the form of debasement as well as aggrandizement of the self, as, for instance, in the possibility that victims of racism internalize the prejudice of their victimizers and, insofar, see the world with the same debasement of themselves. In any event, "the world is not given to us 'on a plate,' it is given to us as a creative task" (p. 215). What we require or what is required of us, then, is a "progressive redemption of desire," a movement that is "patiently and continually a change of one's whole being in all of its contingent detail," that is, the detail of its cognition or consciousness, "through a world of appearance toward a world of reality" (p. 25). Moral advance *is* the movement toward reality.

This pervasive connection between cognition and morality is not an ethic that elevates the *vita contemplativa* over the *vita activa*, as Plato's thought has sometimes been accused of doing (see, e.g., p. 39; cf. Hannah Arendt). Truthful cognition is internally related to or expressed in good action. "The whole of morality involves the discipline of desire that leads to instinctive good action" (p. 384). Another way to make the point is to underscore that the moral pilgrimage is incurably individual, and "belief in this person is an assertion of contingency, of the irreducible existence and importance of the contingent" (p. 349). A contemplative understanding of human life in some sense that depreciates action cannot consistently affirm the importance of particularity. In contrast, Murdoch's moral realism affirms the significance of this world in "all of its contingent detail."

II. Good without God

Enough has already been said to confirm that Murdoch is, at least in the contemporary philosophical setting, a friend to theistic religion. If moral realism in the emphatic sense departs from the dom-

---

4. *The Sovereignty of Good* (London and New York: Routledge, 1970), 54, hereafter referred to as *Sovereignty*.

inant consensus of post-Kantian moral theory, it is also a conviction to which theists, at least those who have sought metaphysical formulations, have traditionally adhered. "Goodness and being," says Thomas Aquinas, "are really the same, and differ only in idea."[5] But the concert between Murdoch and the theistic tradition is the more profound because she too insists that emphatic moral realism implies an idea of something real that is beyond us and all else, an idea of perfection.

"We *know* of perfection as we look upon what is imperfect" (*Metaphysics,* 427), above all the imperfection of people and human institutions. Human life as a moral pilgrimage implies an ideal of *the* Good, "a distant moral goal, like a temple at the end of the pilgrimage, . . . glimpsed but never reached" (p. 304), to which or by which this quest is oriented. This implication may also be expressed through the recognition that contingency is "irreducible incompleteness." Given "the essential contingency of human life" (p. 490) and its world, the connection of goodness and the things in our experience is always more or less incomplete, so that we also experience "both the reality of perfection and its distance away" (p. 508), an absolute or complete good through which incompleteness is identified. Moreover, "the idea of the perfect object is one with its reality" (p. 400), because the moral character of reality "is not one empirical phenomenon among others. . . . [It] cannot be 'thought away' out of human life" (p. 412), and this is the abiding significance of the ontological argument or, to use Charles Hartshorne's phrase, of "Anselm's discovery."[6] We experience, in Paul Tillich's words, the "unconditional element in the structure of reason and reality" (*Metaphysics,* 432).

Just this unconditional element of morality makes it essentially religious, because religion is concerned with "the absolute in a specifically moral way" (p. 140). Religion "is a mode of belief in the unique sovereign place of goodness in human life" (p. 426), "the *attachment* to an ultimate . . . demand," indeed, "the *love* of that demand" (p. 146). Morality is religious because the essence

---

5. *Introduction to St. Thomas Aquinas,* ed. Anton C. Pegis (New York: Modern Library, 1948), 34.
6. *Anselm's Discovery: A Re-examination of the Ontological Argument for God's Existence* (La Salle, Ill.: Open Court, 1965).

of the former is orientation or attraction to the unconditioned Good that "exerts a magnetism which runs through the whole contingent world" and the response to which "is love" (p. 343). Of this religious reality also, unsurpassed expression occurs in Plato's myth of the cave. The idea of perfection or Form of the Good is the sun to which all consciousness is attracted because in its light alone do we see what is real, and, in this respect, Murdoch repeats in her own way the characteristic theistic claim that we see "everywhere in the world" the One who is beyond or above all of the world (p. 398; see also p. 474).

But the Good is not God. Murdoch's metaphysics moves "from 'God' to 'Good,' taking 'religion' along too" (p. 426). This is the central respect in which her proposal occupies common ground with those who pursue a demythologized theology, and she can say that "the 'demythologisation' of religion is something absolutely necessary in this age" (p. 460). Notwithstanding that some may "extend the meaning of our word 'God' to cover *any* conception of a spiritual reality," including the idea of perfection, in truth "'God' is the name of a supernatural person" (p. 419; see also p. 425), and the difference between God and the Good is that the latter may be loved but is not loving, while the former means a supreme person or Thou who is responsive to us. "God is love" is, perhaps, the identifying conviction of theistic religion (see pp. 342–43).

We need a "theology that can continue without God" (p. 511) not simply because the picture of a loving, supernatural Thou is increasingly inaccessible to or unpersuasive within modern modes of thought. The concept of God is also problematic for more profound metaphysical reasons. A supreme person must be a supreme individual. But a supreme being, if it is not totalizing in a sense that implicitly denies all differences, "becomes one more contingent thing among others, even if the grandest one" and, therefore, cannot be the "'unconditional element' in the structure of reason and reality" (p. 432), the perfection beyond all else that our moral pilgrimage includes or implies. As *a* being, the ultimate could not be ultimate, and, for this reason, Murdoch holds that the ontological argument itself clarifies "the reasons for rejecting [the concept of] God" (p. 425). "That than which nothing greater can be conceived" is not a sensible combination of words if it refers to a contingent individual and, therefore, God is impossible.

But "we can lose God" without losing Good (p. 473). The idea of perfection is not a being or "a Person, it is *sui generis*. It is a 'reality principle' whereby we find our way about in the world" of beings (p. 474). Here again, we recur best to Plato, although, in this respect, he and Kant, the other singular participant in the dialogue that underlies all of western philosophy (see p. 57), speak with one voice (see p. 407). To identify the Form of the Good with a metaphysical individual or supernatural deity "would be absolutely un-Platonic," because Plato recognized that Good is "above being" (p. 342) or "above the level of the gods or God" (p. 475). So Murdoch also appreciates Paul Tillich, who spoke of the "God above God," even if she probably does not think that this is the happiest formulation.[7] Our experience of the "light in which the whole world is revealed" (*Metaphysics*, 39) "leads us to place our idea of it outside the world of existent being as something of a different unique and special sort" (p. 508).

It is just because this something is outside the world of existent being that Murdoch, for all her critique of philosophical separations of fact and value, can also write: "A proper separation of fact and value, as a defence of morality, lies in the contention that moral value cannot be *derived* from fact" (p. 26). To that claim, a metaphysical theist is bound to take exception. If the idea of perfection is the idea of God, then a claim about the character of God entails a claim about the character of the good. Moreover, her insistence that the Good is beyond beings explains why Murdoch departs from "philosophers [who] have sought a single principle upon which morality may be seen to depend" and, in that sense, to reduce the moral life "to a unity" (p. 492). She certainly affirms that "good as absolute, above courage and generosity and all the plural virtues," is a "pure source, . . . which creatively relates the virtues to each other in our moral lives" (p. 507). But, as she wrote in *The Sovereignty of Good*, "'all is one' is a dangerous falsehood at any level except the highest; and can that be discerned at all?" (p. 56).

---

7. *The Courage To Be* (New Haven: Yale University Press, 1952), 186.

It cannot because it is in all respects unique, and it can because all of our consciousness occurs in its light. "The One who alone is wise does not want and does want to be called by the name of Zeus" (Heraclitus, cited in *Metaphysics*, 465). The essential religious affirmation, then, means that the demythologization of religion must be succeeded by a remythologization. Because metaphysics as a guide to morals must include reference to something real beyond existence, an adequate moral theory cannot finally escape formulations that are pictorial or figurative in character, just as Tillich insisted that all positive statements about the "God above God" are symbolic, and these pictures are offered "to see if we cannot find just this in our deepest experience" (p. 507).

III. The Loss of Worth

If the foregoing will serve as a relevant summary of Murdoch's emphatic moral realism, then I am now in a position to discuss the reservation in her friendship to theistic religion. Often "when a general philosophical viewpoint loses its charm," she observes in another context, "something is lost" (p. 221). If I understand rightly, she means that the viewpoint included, however inadequately, some metaphysical insight that is neglected when philosophy turns generally in another direction. With the loss of theism, I now wish to argue, something in this significant sense is lost.

We may approach what is at stake by making explicit what has been at least implicit above, namely, that Murdoch so connects goodness and the real that either may be defined in terms of the other. If moral advance is identified as the movement of consciousness from appearance to reality, reality is identified as the object or possible object of moral advance. More precisely, reality is that the apprehension of which, in distinction from ignorance or misapprehension, makes an individual better, and this definition simply repeats that the real world is that which we see in the light of the Good. The two definitions are convertible because they are both metaphysical; each concept identifies a condition of the possibility of human existence, what "'must be the case' for human being to be as it is" (p. 259), and, therefore, the two concepts are internally related.

Assuming that we do so with care, we may also formulate the point as follows: If Murdoch is morally an emphatic realist, she is metaphysically a pragmatist. On this usage, a pragmatist holds that cognition of the truth about ourselves and the world of which we are a part insofar makes us better, and this is simply to repeat that the apprehension of reality is never cognition of mere fact, independent of our orientation to perfection. Care is here required because Murdoch is clearly not an empirical pragmatist, in the sense often associated with the thought of John Dewey and in accord with which the method of empirical science is *the* method of intelligence; much less is she a neopragmatist, in the sense often associated with the thought of Richard Rorty and in accord with which true understandings are those that "pay their way" in relation to our historically specific interests. We can protect against these misunderstandings and underscore the distinctive character of her proposal by saying that she is, however irregular the term may seem, a Platonic pragmatist. If I understand rightly, she thinks that finally Plato was one too.

The pertinence of this point is that it implies a criterion for the validity of claims about reality. No such claim can be true unless believing it makes us better. This, of course, is not to say that all true claims are about good things, as if this were the best of all possible worlds. The point is, rather, that a claim about reality cannot be true unless it involves an "opposition between good and bad" (p. 259), so that believing it orients us to the good. To be sure, it may appear that this criterion is useless in the absence of some norm or principle of the good, and pragmatists are often accused of begging the question because they simply posit or define persuasively the putative character of the good life. But the pragmatic test, I judge, does serve us in this respect: No valid metaphysical claim can be completely negative.

With the term "completely negative claim," I mean a negation that has no positive content, the assertion of absence that is not by implication the assertion of some presence. "The rose is not red" is, we may say, only partially negative, because it implies the positive claim that a rose exhibiting some color other than red is present. In contrast, the Kantian claim that things in themselves are unknowable is, I believe, a complete negation, devoid of positive content. To say that this negation is also positive because it implies that all knowable things are only phenomena in distinction from noumena simply repeats the point, because noumena can be identified only as not-phenomena and, therefore, phenomena are said to be distinguished from only complete negation.

Notwithstanding her considerable appreciation of Kant, Murdoch rejects his distinction between phenomena and noumena because, as I have mentioned, she rejects his separation of theoretical and practical reason. That she is, in this respect, Platonic rather than Kantian is, I now suggest, an expression of her pragmatism. Completely negative metaphysical claims could never be true because believing them adds nothing to our orientation and, therefore, cannot orient us to the good. It is the same to say that such a claim could be true only if it identified a sheer fact, separated from or independent of value. Whatever else pragmatism means, then, it is the conviction that all apprehension of reality is at least partially positive. We do not apprehend absence without apprehending some presence, and we know what is absent only because it is incompatible with what is present. In the light of the Good, sheer nothing cannot be seen.[8]

Now, I believe that Murdoch's denial of theism is in truth a completely negative metaphysical claim, because it is equivalent to the claim that our moral pilgrimage makes no difference beyond itself. In saying this, I do not mean that she denies the difference, for better or worse, each of us makes to ourselves and other human individuals, including succeeding individuals, and to the subhuman world that sustains and enriches us. What the denial of theism denies is that the leading of our lives makes an unconditional or everlasting difference, so that something about strictly all of the

---

8. The argument, it may be objected, has concerned itself with completely negative *metaphysical* claims rather than all claims about reality, so that the conclusion about all claims is unwarranted. But any putative claim about reality that is completely negative implies a completely negative metaphysical claim, because metaphysical conditions are the conditions of possibility. If all valid metaphysical claims are at least partially positive, then, since metaphysical conditions always obtain, no valid claim about reality can be completely negative.

future is at stake in what we do. An unconditional difference requires an unconditional or everlasting reality to which the difference is made. If "God is love" is the identifying conviction of theistic religion, its central affirmation is that we ought to love God because all of our lives in all of their detail make an abiding difference to the divine reality. In contrast, the Good, as an Idea rather than an individual, is always to be loved but is never loving.

Precisely because her pragmatism is Platonic rather than theistic, then, Murdoch could write in *The Sovereignty of Good:* "I can see no evidence to suggest that human life is not something self-contained" or "self-enclosed" and, therefore, has no "external point or *telos*" (p. 79). It is also in this context that we should understand her saying that "the only genuine way to be good is to be good 'for nothing.'" The Good, because it is not God, "excludes the idea of [external or ultimate] purpose" (*Sovereignty,* 71; see *Metaphysics,* 312). "If there is any kind of sense or unity in human life, and the dream of this does not cease to haunt us, it is of some other kind and must be sought within a human experience which has nothing outside it" (*Sovereignty,* 79).

But, we may ask, what is the positive implication or content of the claim that human life is self-contained or self-enclosed, or, to rephrase the question, what presence could we possibly apprehend that would confirm the absence of any ultimate difference and orient us to the good? Some may respond that the absence of an everlasting difference implies the presence of a temporary difference, and it is this temporary difference that is better or worse. But this response has missed the question. We have assumed, with the pragmatists, that all we do makes a difference and, therefore, our lives are worth leading. At issue is the claim that this assumed difference is *only* temporary or *not* permanent, and the question is: What presence does this negation imply? Absent some positive content to this claim, it must be inconsistent with the pragmatic affirmation of our significance.

We may now be told that the indifference of our lives within their largest context is what makes them dear or gives to them their importance while we lead them. So far as I can see, this is a non sequitur. The claim that what we do here will be in the long run neither good nor bad neither implies nor is implied by the claim that what we do here is in the short run significant. On the contrary, to say that value is constituted by its own eventual nullity is a confusion similar to the thought that responsibility is constituted by the absence of any transcending or real norm of the good. The absence of a real norm means only that there is nothing to be responsible to, and the absence of something ultimate at stake means only that ultimately there is nothing at stake in how we lead our lives. To the best of my reasoning, the claim that human life is "good 'for nothing'" is, at least if the term "everlasting" makes any sense, a thought with which we can do literally nothing and, therefore, purports to identify a condition of our lives the apprehension of which could not possibly make us better or be seen in the light of the Good. For a pragmatist, it could never be valid, because it is completely negative and, therefore, could only be a valueless fact.

Good metaphysical arguments, Murdoch rightly insists, successfully appeal "to us all to see if we cannot find just . . . [their conclusions] in our deepest experience" (*Metaphysics*, 507). So far from the conclusion that we have no external purpose or telos, I suggest, our deepest experience and, therefore, all of our cognition includes the irrevocable affirmation or conviction that our lives are unconditionally significant. To assert the contradictory can only be a pragmatic self-contradiction, and to believe it could be insofar only moral immobility. "No matter what the content of our choices may be," writes Schubert Ogden, "we can make them at all only because of our invincible faith that they somehow make a difference which no turn of events in the future has the power to annul."[9] What in truth does not cease to haunt us is, in the words of Whitehead, "that the immediate facts of present action pass into permanent significance for the universe. The insistent notions of Right and Wrong, Achievement and Failure, depend upon this background. Otherwise, every activity is merely a passing whiff of insignificance."[10]

9. *The Reality of God* (New York: Harper & Row, 1966), 36.
10. "Immortality," in *The Philosophy of Alfred North Whitehead*, ed. Paul A. Schlipp (Evanston, Ill.: Northwestern University Press, 1941), 698.

Franklin I. Gamwell

IV. THE NECESSITY OF GOD

isional conclusion is that Murdoch's religion without God is inconsistent with her emphatic moral realism because that philosophical proposal is also a pragmatism. On her own terms, the loss of theism is the loss of a deep aspect of human life. But this conclusion must be provisional because it cannot be sustained without a return to the ontological argument. Murdoch offers reasons to think that Anselm proved in fact, even if contrary to his intent, the necessary nonexistence of God. If she is correct in this assessment, then her claim that human life is "good 'for nothing'" is not the assertion of a completely negative fact but simply a denial of the impossible. If she is right about Anselm, in other words, then either pragmatism does not imply theism or something is altogether amiss with metaphysics as a guide to morals.

On her accounting, the proof proves that God is impossible because an individual, even the best one, "becomes one more contingent thing among others" and, therefore, cannot be perfect. Anselm insisted that perfection, "that than which nothing greater can be conceived," cannot be conceived not to exist and, therefore, must exist necessarily. This conclusion is implied, Anselm argued, because necessary existence is greater than contingent existence, a premise that is less than clear in the widely-criticized second chapter of the *Proslogium* but unmistakable in chapter three and the reply to Gaunilo. On this premise, which Charles Hartshorne has called "Anselm's principle," it is not existence but, rather, mode of existence that is said to be a property and necessary existence that is said to be a perfection, and Murdoch credits the claim that to this premise Kant's objection, "'existence' is not a predicate," is a begging of the question (see *Metaphysics*, 408–10).[11] But, as Leibniz and, perhaps, Gaunilo before him pointed out, the argument is not sound unless the idea of a greatest conceivable thing can itself be conceived, is a sensible or non-self-contradictory concept.

Murdoch holds that this is not a genuine concept if it is taken

---

11. See Charles Hartshorne, *The Logic of Perfection and Other Essays in Neoclassical Metaphysics* (La Salle, Ill.: Open Court, 1962).

to identify an individual, precisely because such an individual would exist necessarily, and all individuals are contingent. Still, as we have seen, perfection is a genuine concept if it is understood to mean an Idea or Form of the Good "outside the world of existent being" (p. 508), because the pervasive moral character of our cognition implies it. For this reason, Murdoch cites Tillich's contention that the ontological argument successfully displays the question of the unconditioned, even while it obviously fails as a proof of God's existence.

It is, then, the logical choice between perfection as one contingent thing among others and perfection as an Idea or Form beyond existent being that precludes a theistic pragmatism. But I suggest that these alternatives are in truth logical contraries rather than contradictories; although both cannot be true, both may be false. There is, in other words, a third option that is something like a common contradictory of the other two: Perfection identifies an individual that is universal or coextensive with all other reality and, therefore, not simply one contingent thing among others, and this individual includes an Idea of the Good as its own essential or constitutive purpose.

It may be objected that the concept of a universal individual implies a totalizing metaphysical system, and, as Murdoch says, with Hegel's *Phenomenology of Mind* in view: "What makes metaphysical ('totalising') coherence theories unacceptable is the way in which they in effect 'disappear' what is individual and contingent by equating reality with integration in a system, and degrees of reality with degrees of integration," so that "'ultimately' or 'really' there is only one system" (p. 196). But this objection also fails to consider all of our options, because Hartshorne's achievement is principally directed to the formulation and defense of a nontotalizing concept of the divine individual. Definitive of his account is his distinction between the divine existence and the divine actuality, in accord with which only the former is necessary and means that strictly universal coextension is always actualized somehow. In contrast, the divine actualizations are contingent, because they consist in completely adequate relativity to whatever else is in fact real, and contingency is everywhere else in evidence. This concept is nontotalizing, in other words, because temporality is a necessary characteristic of the divine existence. At every time, the divine individual is perfectly related to all other actuality and to all possibility; it now includes all that has occurred, and succeeding divine actualities will include all that will occur.[12] God is the light in which all is seen because God sees all of reality and reality alone.

On this account, then, perfection identifies an individual that cannot be rivaled in its relations to reality or goodness and an individual that is also self-surpassing because its relations to goodness increase without end insofar as any good is achieved by others. Its own everlasting telos, namely, that maximal good should be achieved by others in order to maximize what God includes, is the Form of the Good, the condition of the possibility of our own moral pilgrimage because the divine purpose is the constitutive telos of reality as such. Conversely, just because the moral good consists in so leading our lives as to maximize our contribution to the divine good, the choices we make "pass into permanent significance for the universe."[13] What we do in response to the "magnetic" force of this telos makes an everlasting difference, for better or worse, and it is because we have our being in God's sight that we live and move with an irrevocable confidence in the unconditional worth of our adventure.

As an alternative to Murdoch's Idea of the Good, Hartshorne's concept of the perfect individual implies, I believe, an important qualification to the claim that metaphysics cannot escape pictorial or figurative formulations. I do not deny that symbolic language is inseparable from religious expression, because I take the function of religion to be the representation of perfection in a manner that cultivates or evokes our pilgrimage from appearance to reality. But Murdoch, if I understand rightly, holds to the necessity of pictorial representation even in critical metaphysics because, as Tillich also believed, the unconditioned is beyond beings. Since it is in that sense unique, perfection cannot be identified literally by concepts that refer literally to existing things. Insofar as the claim about metaphysical formulation depends on this

---

12. See Charles Hartshorne, *The Divine Relativity: A Social Conception of God* (New Haven: Yale University Press, 1948).
13. Whitehead, "Immortality," 698.

putative uniqueness of the unconditioned, we may expect that a differing concept of perfection will have consequences with respect to philosophical expression.

I am inclined to think that the long tradition in philosophical theology for which all positive statements about the divine reality are symbolic or analogical is critically unacceptable, because this tradition asserts that there is a reality about which, literally speaking, we can say nothing. Whitehead said that philosophy has insofar failed when it has paid "metaphysical compliments"[14] to God because it has "exempted [God] from all the metaphysical categories which applied to the individual things in this temporal world."[15] I am persuaded that the concept of self-surpassing perfection pays no such compliment. To be sure, the divine reality is unique in the sense that only one individual can be coextensive with all else. But it is not unique in the sense that its difference from all others cannot be identified literally. On the contrary, the difference between some and all is a literal distinction implied by the term "some." If we can speak literally of human and other nondivine individuals as imperfect because they are related merely to some other reality and, thereby, capable of only some good, then we can also speak literally of the divine as related to all actuality and possibility and, thereby, perfect.

In any event, I hope that this account of perfection is sufficiently clear to confirm that it merits attention as a third alternative to perfection as simply another contingent thing, on the one hand, and perfection as solely an Idea or Form of the Good, on the other—and, therefore, another alternative for what the ontological proof proves. Even if that is so, however, my summary characterization can hardly suffice to establish that this theistic account is valid. In the end, no metaphysical concept can be fully redeemed without a more or less comprehensive metaphysical proposal on the order that Murdoch has pursued and that Hartshorne also has sought to formulate and defend. Moreover, we should, I believe, agree with her that the final appeal is to what we already know in our deepest experience because it "'must be the case' for human

---

14. *Science and the Modern World*, 161.
15. *Adventures of Ideas* (New York: Free Press, 1961), 169.

being to be as it is" (*Metaphysics*, 259). Properly speaking, I hold, theists believe that the place of theistic arguments in our cognitive and moral life is precisely that which Murdoch attributes to the metaphysical enterprise. Successful proofs for the divine existence are not meant to create an experience of God where one is not already present and, in that sense, to argue us into religious faith. On the contrary, their purpose is critically to clarify the inescapable relation to perfection that constitutes our every thought and action. In that sense, they too leave everything as it is.

Some who concede that Hartshorne's concept of divine perfection is a self-consistent one still insist that it does not redeem the ontological argument but warrants only the conclusion: *If* God exists, God exists necessarily. On this reading, metaphysical necessity must be distinguished from logical necessity. Those who are persuaded to side with Kant against Plato in the matters that fundamentally divide the two will, I judge, insist on this distinction. Since reality as such is unknowable, no existential denial is logically impossible. Thus, a divine individual, if it exists, is metaphysically necessary or coextensive with all other reality, but whether or not God exists remains logically contingent.

As I have suggested, this reading requires, against the pragmatic view, the logical possibility of valueless facts, because the claim that a perfect individual is possible but does not exist is a completely negative metaphysical claim or has no positive implication. It is solely the negation of any unconditional worth in what we do with the possibilities given to us. Precisely because a universal individual is one to which literally everything can and does make an everlasting difference, its existence must be strictly noncompetitive or consistent with anything else that could conceivably be present. Accordingly, there is no presence we could apprehend that would imply its absence, and, conversely, its absence would have no implication about what is present.

I am inclined to think that there are convincing arguments against the logical possibility of any completely negative existential claim, but I have not pursued them here and, therefore, have not sought here to defend the soundness of the ontological argument. In other words, I have not offered a defense of pragmatism. Although I find convincing Murdoch's sustained argument for the "ubiquity of value" (p. 250), I have assumed her Platonic view in this respect. The burden of my reflections, then, has been to suggest that her emphatic moral realism, because it denies the validity of all complete negations, is a reaffirmation of metaphysics that implies theism. Thereby, I have sought to recommend that her friendship with theistic religion need not be reserved and in truth may become an embrace.

8

Murdochian Muddles: Can We Get Through Them If God Does Not Exist?

Stanley Hauerwas

I. On Stealing from Murdoch

"I can only choose within the world I can *see*, in the moral sense of 'see' which implies that clear vision is a result of moral imagination and moral effort."[1] How I love that sentence from Iris Murdoch's *The Sovereignty of Good*. Actually, that is to put the matter in a misleading fashion. I do not just love that sentence, I have made a career out of that sentence. Indeed, I sometimes wonder if I have ever said anything of importance that was not stolen from Iris Murdoch. That I have stolen much from her is without question, but the question I wish to investigate in this essay is whether I have, as a Christian theologian, been wise in having done so.

The issue can be nicely put by reading a review by Professor Mermon Bourke of my book, *Vision and Virtue: Essays in Christian Ethical Reflection*.[2] The review is but a paragraph long and I cite the whole so you can get its full flavor:

I am indebted to Dr. Jim Fodor, Dr. Reinhardt Hütter, and Mr. Scott Saye for their good criticism of the initial draft of this paper.

1. Iris Murdoch, *The Sovereignty of Good* (New York: Routledge & Kegan Paul, 1970), 37, hereafter referred to as *Sovereignty*. I will refer to Murdoch's *Metaphysics as a Guide to Morals* (New York: Allen Lane/Penguin Press, 1993) as *Metaphysics*.
2. *Vision and Virtue* was originally published in 1974 by Tides Press of Notre Dame, Indiana. The University of Notre Dame Press edition was published in 1981. The book contains my essay "The Significance of Vision: Toward an Esthetic Ethic," in which I discuss Murdoch's work. Lawrence Blum has more recently shown the continuing power of Murdoch's account of morality in his

> The articles gathered here have been published before in various theological journals. Hauerwas studied at Southwestern University and is now director of graduate studies in theology at Notre Dame. His point of view seems to be non-denominationally Christian: when he speaks of 'the church,' he means all of Christendom. Ranging over a broad field, the essays pay some attention to the general character of a truly Christian ethics but show most interest in specific problems such as abortion, euthanasia, treatment of the retarded, and pacifism. On these issues Hauerwas displays wide reading (chiefly in liberal Protestant and left-wing Catholic moralists) and an open mind. Indeed his mind is so open that his own views are rarely apparent. On abortion, for instance, he criticizes Callahan, Ramsey, and Grisez, says the conceptus may be viewed as human, but then concludes that other accounts are possible. There is a latent anti-intellectualism running throughout. Hauerwas is not convinced that human understanding can solve the difficult moral problems. The 'vision' mentioned in the title and at various points owes a good deal to Iris Murdoch's estheticism. How an avowed atheist, like Miss Murdoch, can contribute to Christian ethics is an enigma.[3]

I confess that when I read this review, now almost twenty years ago, I thought this guy had to be crazy. Of course a Christian theologian can use an atheist[4]—particularly one as subtle as Iris Murdoch. Bourke had obviously never read Murdoch and therefore had no appreciation for her intriguing account of the ontological argument. After all, Aquinas had used Aristotle in his work. There is good precedent for theologians using atheists in their work.

I thought the differences between Murdoch and myself had little to do with her atheism. Rather, I thought my disagreements with

---

Moral Perception and Particularity (Cambridge: Cambridge University Press, 1994).

3. Professor Bourke's review appeared in *Review for Religious* 34, 2 (1975): 328.

4. "Atheism," of course, is as ambiguous as "theism." I am simply accepting Iris Murdoch's self-description, but I thereby do not mean to imply that her "atheism" is the same as Aristotle's. More important, I am not sure that it is appropriate to describe Aristotle as an atheist though he obviously took a critical attitude toward aspects of Greek theology. Murdoch's atheism is obviously more interesting for the Christian since she believes she is denying the God Christians worship. I am not sure, however, she in fact is denying the God we Christians know as trinity since she seems to think that God's existence and transcendence, what she identifies as supernaturalism, is more basic than God being trinity. That she does so is the result of distortions in Christian practice and thought.

her, if in fact they existed, had much more to do with her Platonism and my attraction to Aristotle. I confess I was not anxious then or later to explore that difference, but I suspected it had something to do with her attraction to and my dislike of mysticism. I thought the difference was as simple as her claim that "we develop language in the context of looking," whereas I was convinced (and I thought I had learned this from Wittgenstein) that I can only see what I have been trained to see through learning to say (*Sovereignty*, 33).[5]

Yet even in that respect I was not sure how different our views might be, since she emphasized that truthful seeing, that is, seeing that is able to combine "just modes of judgment and the ability to connect with an increased perception of detail," comes to those formed by the virtue of honesty (*Sovereignty*, 96). No doubt, as Murdoch so ably depicts in many of her novels, such honest seeing often must be forced on us, sunk as we are in our fantasies. Nonetheless, a training in any skill has the potential to transform our imagination so that we can see more truthfully. To be sure, Murdoch's virtues never seem as "habitual" as we Aristotelians think they need to be, but that seems like a minor matter.[6]

Yet now, after twenty years of stealing Iris Murdoch, I am not as convinced as I once was that Bourke's "enigma" may not deserve closer scrutiny. When I first read Murdoch I was so impressed that her enemies were my enemies I may have failed to see

5. Murdoch's views on the relation between thought and language are most developed in her early article "Thinking and Language," *Proceedings of the Aristotelian Society*, supp. vol. 25 (1951): 25–34. I believe she has continued to assume the views set forth there that in effect argue that language and thought are not coextensive. Although I am sympathetic with her critique of the crude behaviorism that was the target of her argument, I do not think her views about language and thought presented there are nearly complex enough. I associate her views about language with her "mysticism" insofar as the former may be necessary to sustain her account of the ineffability of certain types of experience.

6. One of the troubling features of Murdoch's appeal to the virtues is the lack of a moral psychology in which they might be rooted. As a result, we have little idea how she might justify why she treats the virtues as she does, that is, how the virtues are individuated, nor does she tell us how they are interrelated. One suspects she may, like Plato, assume the unity, if not the "oneness," of the virtues. Accordingly, we have little sense from her work how the virtues are acquired through habit.

that common enemies do not necessarily make us friends. For example, she observes quite rightly in *The Sovereignty of Good* that Hume and Kant, each in his own way, abhor history (p. 26). I took that to be an opening for Christian theological discourse, but I am not so sure now if I was right. As I will try to show, because we Christians are convinced we are creatures, we are more "historical" than Murdoch believes is wise.[7] The redemption we think God has offered is not a "mystical" possibility, but that made possible through the Jews.

I confess that I realized I would have to interrogate my adherence to Murdoch's work when I reached the next to last page of *Metaphysics as a Guide to Morals*. What bothered me was not her suggestion that "we need a theology which can continue without God" (p. 511). For those familiar with her work that was no surprise. Rather, what bothered me there as well as earlier in the book was her positive appreciation of Paul Tillich's work. Her friend Tillich is my sworn enemy—thus the necessity to investigate the "enigma."

I wish to be clear about how I am approaching this task. It is not my primary purpose to criticize Murdoch. Rather, I want to explore her account of why we can no longer believe in the Christian God in order to test the extent to which her rich insights can be appropriated by those of us who work as Christian theologians. I hope this will be a particularly useful exercise for me, as I am normally willing to expose my own metaphysical and ontological claims only under severe duress.[8] I begin, then, by affirming Mur-

---

7. The issue can be put more strongly. Murdoch at times seems to suggest we are "saved" just to the extent we are free of history—a "solution" that she equally displays, particularly in her novels, as impossible. I cannot work out here, or probably anywhere, the relation between the Christian understanding of creation and history, but it at least involves the claim that given that existence is created, we should not be surprised that we only know ourselves as creatures through a narrative. For an attempt to develop these suggestions see my, *The Peaceable Kingdom: A Primer in Christian Ethics* (Notre Dame: University of Notre Dame Press, 1983), 24–34.

8. My reticence about metaphysics is a correlate of my attempt to resist reductionistic accounts of theological claims so common in modern theology. Obviously, Christian conviction entails metaphysical claims—such as all that is is finite—but one does not first get metaphysics straight and then go to theology. Rather, metaphysical claims are best exhibited not only in Christian theology

doch's claim that "metaphysical systems have consequences" (*Metaphysics*, 197). Indeed, showing how her metaphysics and ethics are interrelated is, I believe, a helpful way of underlining the difference the Christian account of creation ex nihilo should have for the Christian moral life.

I do not wish to keep you in suspense, so I will state my argument baldly. I will suggest that Murdoch's account of the moral life cannot be appropriated uncritically by Christian theologians for the simple reason that her account of the "muddles" that constitute our lives is correlative to a metaphysics we cannot accept. Christians believe that our lives are at once more captured by sin and yet sustained by a hope that cannot help but appear false given Murdoch's account of the world.[9] A Christian understanding of sin and hope is, moreover, correlative to an account of creation that sustains a teleological account of the world and our place in it.[10] Accordingly, Christians as such ask more of ourselves and our world than, I think, Murdoch can believe is warranted.

The problem with this comparative procedure, of course, is there is no news in it. Murdoch has always been admirably candid that she has little use for religious myths and, in particular, those associated with Christian theology. She has always been, with some qualification, on the side of those intent on demythologizing Christian discourse. So it will not be news to her that she does not believe that the Jews are God's promised people or that Christ's resurrection inaugurates the end time. Yet I hope to show that we are not simply left with "So you believe this and I believe that." Instead, we are left with the very character of our lives which, I

---

but in any endeavor as imbedded in our behaviors, not as the "background" of our behaviors.

9. One could make a fascinating study of how the lives of Murdoch's characters only make sense insofar as they are sustained by hope. Philosophically, she at least seems closer to stoicism than Christianity on the matters of hope; yet at least imaginatively, living as we do at the end of fading Christian practices, hope is hard to give up even for Murdoch.

10. These issues are not unrelated to the issues raised above about habituation since sin is not a "natural" category but rather an achievement. One must be trained to be a sinner which means one must have one's life embedded in a narrative through which one's sins can be named. I develop these suggestions in *After Christendom* (Nashville: Abingdon Press, 1991), 93–111.

would argue, gives us a basis for thinking that we might be creatures with purposes that we did not create.

II. Murdoch on Christianity and God

Murdoch's reflections on Christianity are complex and, I believe, interrelated in a complex manner. I, therefore, need to display her views about Christianity in the hope of making sure I am not misrepresenting her. Murdoch simply begins with the observation that in our age the influence of what might be called orthodox Christianity is waning rapidly (*Sovereignty*, 75). She offers us no extended account of why this may be, but calls our attention to Don Cupitt's observation that humankind is just now emerging from its "mythological childhood." Accordingly, religion must come to terms with autonomy (*Metaphysics*, 452).[11]

Her account, in this respect, is not unlike that of Charles Taylor in *Sources of the Self*.[12] What Taylor helps us see is that most people simply do not decide no longer to believe in God as Trinity or in creation ex nihilo. Rather they gradually or suddenly realize that the "sources" that made such beliefs intelligible are no longer in place. One may still believe such things but it simply does not matter any more. Indeed, exactly because it does not matter, some insist on the importance of holding such beliefs as beliefs, particularly if they are held sincerely or enthusiastically.

I think this kind of atheism is what Murdoch is suggesting when she asks rhetorically, "Do not a large number of those who go to church *already think* in a new non-literal way without bothering about theology and metaphysics?" (*Metaphysics*, 458–59). The answer is obviously, "Yes," but the interesting question is "Why?" Murdoch does not provide thick accounts of how this came about, although she does offer the following observation: "The Cartesian era is coming to an end. Wittgenstein said that he was ending it. In moral philosophy it may appear that the Kantian era is coming to an end. Theology not only reflects these problems

---

11. I find it surprising Murdoch underwrites Cupitt's account of autonomy since she is so critical of Kant elsewhere in her work.
12. Charles Taylor, *Sources of the Self: The Making of Modern Identity* (Cambridge: Harvard University Press, 1989).

but is forced to struggle with them in ways which bring it closer to philosophy now than it has been for some time. This is so in spite of, and partly in reaction to, the fact that in a materialistic technological society, theology might be expected to be increasingly isolated from general trends of thought" (*Metaphysics*, 38–39).

The story of how theological claims are made to bear the burden of proof in light of certain social and intellectual developments is obviously complex, but I think the broad outlines of Murdoch's position are clear. What is particularly interesting is that the very developments that have made traditional Christian theological claims unintelligible are also implicated in legitimation of precisely those accounts of the moral life Murdoch finds so disastrous. That is, the peculiar combination of behaviorist, existentialist, and utilitarian accounts of the moral life Murdoch so trenchantly criticizes in *The Sovereignty of Good* (pp. 4–15) is produced by exactly the same forces that have made Christianity unintelligible to itself.

Therefore, Murdoch's case against Christianity is not just that people no longer believe, or, perhaps more accurately, that even if they wanted to be Christian they would have no idea what that would mean. Her position is considerably stronger than that. She wants to replace Christianity because she has a better alternative. Murdoch thinks her alternative is friendly to Christianity, and she even describes herself as a "neo-Christian or Buddhist Christian or Christian fellow traveller," who believes "Christianity can continue without a personal God or a risen Christ, without beliefs in supernatural places and happenings, such as heaven and life after death, but retaining the mystical figure of Christ occupying a place analogous to that of Buddha, a Christ who can console and save, but who is to be found as a living force within each human soul and not in some supernatural elsewhere. Such a continuity would preserve and renew the Christian tradition as it has always hitherto, somehow or other, been preserved and renewed. It has always changed itself into something that can be generally believed" (*Metaphysics*, 419).[13]

---

13. Even though Murdoch suggests elsewhere that which consoles cannot be true, she also recognizes the need for consolation. It remains unclear to me how she understands the way someone might negotiate these contrary positions. I sometimes suspect that she, like some other Platonists, assumes that some must

I have, of course, been spending my life trying to make Christianity hard to be "generally believed." Therefore, when Murdoch offers to help Christians redescribe their convictions in a "naturalistic" fashion, I am less than convinced. For example, she notes that "the idea of another's suffering as redemptive is certainly intelligible. Christians may tend to connect it with Christ and see lesser human efforts as an *imitatio Christi*, but redemption can exist without God" (*Metaphysics*, 131). I have no doubt that such a redemption does exist, but I also think that redemption so understood has little to do with the redemption found in Christ's cross and resurrection. Such a counter assertion, of course, requires spelling out but I make it at this point only to suggest that Murdoch's attempt to "save" Christianity involves a substitution of one religion for another. What is worrisome about Murdoch is not that she is an atheist, but that she is too religious.

For Murdoch religion is about "the change of being attendant upon our deepest and highest concern with morality" (*Metaphysics*, 183). She suggests, for example, that we cannot live without the exercise of prayer. "But, someone may say, what can we do now that there is no God? This does not affect what is mystical. The loss of prayer, through the loss of belief in God, is a great loss. However, a *general* answer is a practice of meditation: a withdrawal, through some disciplined quietness, into the great chamber of the soul. Just sitting quiet will help. Teach it to children" (*Metaphysics*, 73). Or perhaps better, learn it from children who have the extraordinary capacity to see this single blade of grass or this rock in all of its particularity. Such is the attitude of prayer (*Sovereignty*, 55).[14]

---

bear the philosophical burden of refusing to be consoled in order that most people can be contented with stories that are less than true.

14. Children often play a crucial role in Murdoch's novels as they seem to have an "innocent seeing" she equates with the mystical. Children do not need to unlearn the connections we adults impose on the world, the "necessities," that domesticate the contingent. To be able to see the sheer givenness of this rock or tree in its givenness is to be on the way to being good. Murdoch seems to think such goodness is lost through our growing up. We lose our ability to see the contingent because of our desire to control the world.

Prayer is an attention to God which is a form of love. "God was (or is) a single perfect transcendent non-representable and necessarily real object of attention." It is the task of moral philosophy to retain such a central concept, that is, the good, without that concept offering us false consolation of a premature unity. For the great enemy of the moral life is "personal fantasy: the tissue of self-aggrandizing and consoling wishes and dreams which prevents one from seeing what is there outside one" (*Sovereignty*, 59). That is why art is so crucial. For by experiencing the transcendence of the beautiful, we are called out of our fantasies (*Sovereignty*, 60). Art can be the occasion for training us to see this or that rock or this or that person free from the fantasies of who they should be for "us."

Our muddles are the result of our self-absorption. Those that people Murdoch's novels always seem to love the wrong person or get caught in nets of illusion. That they, and we, are so caught reflects our condition, a condition rightly described by Freud (though Murdoch says she is no Freudian) and equivalent to the doctrine of original sin. The psyche is but "an egocentric system of quasi-mechanical energy, largely determined by its own individual history, whose natural attachments are sexual, ambiguous, and hard for the subject to understand or control. Introspection reveals only the deep tissue of ambivalent motive, and fantasy is a stronger force than reason. Objectivity and unselfishness are not natural to human beings" (*Sovereignty*, 51).

It does no good, as most of modern moral philosophy presumes, to try to will our way out of our illusions, for such willing simply mires us deeper in fantasies of freedom. What is needed is a violent jolting, which can come from a near drowning in a sea cave or from the presence of an avatar whose mysteriousness cannot be explained. The trick, of course, is to accept without explanation the gift of dislocation provided by the avatar. To be able so to live is to begin to live virtuously.

This all too brief summary of Murdoch's understanding of morality helps locate her greatest objection to Christianity. The problem with Christianity is not the mythological character of its belief, but its tendency, like other totalizing metaphysical theories, to destroy the contingent. By "equating reality with integration in system, and degrees of reality with degrees of integration, and by implying that 'ultimately' or 'really' there is only one system," the contingent character of the particular, which is also the source as well as the necessity of mysticism, is lost (*Metaphysics*, 196).

The purification of virtue, characteristic of the mystic, derives from the mystic's refusal to be consoled. What must be acknowledged, in other words, is that morality has no point. Kant rightly insisted on the purposiveness of art without purpose, finality without end. "The 'true saint' believes in 'God' but not as a super-person who satisfies all our ordinary desires 'in the end'. (There is no end, there is no reward.) This has also to do with time, how we live it. It is a religious position where the concept of God is in place, indeed, in a fundamental sense, defined. A proper understanding of contingency apprehends chance and its horrors, not as fate, but as an aspect of death, of the frailty and unreality of the ego and the emptiness of worldly desires. So, our evil part is condemned 'not to suffering but to death'. (I expressed this once in an aphorism: the false god punishes, the true god slays.)" (*Metaphysics*, 106–7).

The problem with much art and religious myth is that they have the effect, and it is an intended effect, of concealing the fact of death and the absolute contingency of existence which is a correlative of death (*Metaphysics*, 139). Even tragedy can console, but only if, while drawing on death, it breaks the ego and thus destroys the illusory whole of the unified self (*Metaphysics*, 104). "Almost anything that consoles us is a fake" (*Sovereignty*, 59), including the presumption that we are consoled by the knowledge that anything that consoles us is a fake.

Murdoch is admirably clear that her morality is a metaphysics, though she might prefer to say that metaphysics is a guide to her morality. Just as the mystics have understood that God cannot be pictured, that in the end everything, including God, must be given up, neither can the good be depicted. She employs the language of the ontological argument to argue that God (the good) cannot simply be one thing among others, but exists of necessity (*Metaphysics*, 470). The ontological argument, therefore, becomes the metaphysical expression of the pointless character of morality.

Such a "proof" cannot be exactly a proof, but rather is a

"clear assertion of faith" which can be made on the basis of a certain kind of experience. Such an experience is the "authority of the Good (which) seems to us something necessary because the realism (ability to perceive reality) required for goodness is a kind of intellectual ability to perceive what is true, which is automatically at the same time a suppression of self. *The necessity of the good is then an aspect of the kind of necessity involved in any technique for exhibiting fact.* In thus treating realism, whether of artist or of agent, as a moral achievement, there is of course a further assumption to be made in the field of morals: that true vision occasions right conduct. This could be uttered simply as an enlightening tautology: but I think it can in fact be supported by appeals to experience. The more the separateness and differentness of other people is realized, and the fact seen that another man has needs and wishes as demanding as one's own, the harder it becomes to treat a person as a thing. That it is realism which makes great art great remains too as a kind of proof" (*Sovereignty*, 66).

Our experience of the good is not derived from high or general ways of understanding, but from the experience present in its most minute relations and within our perceptions of the minutest things (stones, spoons, leaves, scraps of rubbish, tiny gestures, etc., etc.) and the capacity they create for being deeper, more benevolent, more just (etc., etc.) (*Metaphysics*, 474). The myth that best exhibits the ontology of our experience of the Good is that of the Demiurge. In contrast to accounts of creation ex nihilo, the Demiurge creates the cosmos with love towards the forms. In creating, the Demiurge makes use of necessity to which we must submit, as well as understand and use, if we are to be good as well as happy.

This creation myth, the myth of the Demiurge, "represents in the most elegant way the redemption of all particular things which are, although made of contingent stuff, touched and handled by the divine. The contingent can become spiritually significant, even beautiful, as in art, as in Simone Weil's idea of the beauty of the world as an image of obedience. Plato's myths are the redemption of art. This is an aspect of the return to the Cave, where illusions are not only rejected but understood" (*Metaphysics*, 477). The Demiurge is the paradigmatic artist making beauty out of necessity. The Demiurge teaches us we must finally learn to love our death, or better, to see our death as necessary for us to love.

In the light of this myth of creation we can see better why the ontological argument binds together Murdoch's metaphysics and ethics. The argument displays the necessary non-existence of God. "No existing thing could be what we have meant by God. Any existing God would be less than God. An existent God would be an idol or a demon. (This is near to Kant's thinking.) God does not and cannot exist and is *constantly* experienced and pictured. That is, it is real as an Idea, and is *also* incarnate in knowledge and work and love. This is the true idea of incarnation, and is not something obscure. We *experience* both the reality of perfection and its distance away, and this leads us to place our idea of it outside the world of existent being as something of a different unique and special sort" (*Metaphysics*, 508).

III. Creation Ex Nihilo, Sin, and Hope

That Murdoch rightly, I believe, locates her account of morality as entailing the myth of the Demiurge should give pause to Christians like me who have been influenced by her work. Indeed, I wonder whether we Christians should even refrain from reading her novels, since they so powerfully form our imagination, urging us to see our lives in her terms. She is, after all, quite right. Art has "helped us to *believe*, not only in Christ and the Trinity, but in the Good Samaritan, the Prodigal Son, innumerable saints and a whole cast of famous and well-loved scenes and persons" (*Metaphysics*, 82). Whether or not it is good for the Christian imagination to have that art renarrated in a manner that may make the Christian understanding of creation unintelligible for us is therefore no mere idle issue.[15]

Before such questions can be explored, however, I need at least to try to suggest why Christians rightly embrace the doctrine of creation ex nihilo and what difference it makes for how we un-

---

15. Censorship of art and literature should not be associated, as it often is in liberal cultures, with denying to some the right to see or read certain works of art. Rather the serious issue is *how* these paintings or works are to be read in relation to other works.

derstand our ontological and moral commitments. In trying to make this case it will be apparent that I remain in Murdoch's debt. For without Murdoch's defense of the ontological argument, I suspect I would have never understood the significance of Aquinas's rejection of that argument.

Aquinas's comment on the ontological argument is quite interesting. He begins by noting that not everyone that hears the word "God" understands it to signify that than which nothing greater can be thought. Yet even if everyone so understood the word, "it does not follow that he understands that what the word signifies exists actually, but only that it exists in the intellect. Nor can it be argued that it actually exists, unless it be admitted that there actually exists something than which nothing greater can be thought. And this is what is not admitted by those who hold that God does not exist" (*Summa Theologica*, 1.2.1.1).[16] He then goes on to observe that while it is self-evident that truth in general exists, the existence of a First Truth is not self-evident to us.

Aquinas's objection to the ontological argument is not that existence cannot be a predicate (Kant), but rather that the intellect cannot have a priori knowledge of God's nature. Any Being whose essence is existence cannot be known through the idea of such a being, but rather through arguments from its effects. If God's existence is to be "proved" it must be through an examination of God's effects. I have no intention to explore how Aquinas's "five ways" should be interpreted in the light of this presumption.[17] More interesting for the case I am trying to make is why Aquinas must take this stance given his understanding of the gratuity of God's creation.

In this regard, I am following David Burrell's contention that

---

16. I am using the edition of the *Summa Theologica* translated by the Fathers of the English Dominican Province (1911; rev. ed., London, 1920; reissue, New York: Benziger Bros., 1948; reprint, Westminster, Md.: Christian Classics, 1981). References to the *Summa* in the text are to part, question, article, and, where relevant, objection.
17. For an extraordinary account of Aquinas's understanding of our knowledge of God, see Eugene Rogers, *Thomas Aquinas and Karl Barth: Sacred Doctrine and the Natural Knowledge of God* (Notre Dame: University of Notre Dame Press, 1995).

Aquinas's "proofs" are rightly understood against the background of creation ex nihilo. Burrell argues that creation ex nihilo for Aquinas (and Maimonides) is not in itself derived from a reading of Genesis, but rather "the notion of absolute beginning was a sign of the difference between believers in scripture and neoplatonist advocates of eternal emanation, rather than itself marking that difference. Creation ex nihilo underscored the fact that the very existence of such a dependent universe did not belong to the nature of divinity but represented a free initiative on God's part, for if the universe were without beginning, it would be more natural to think of it as the necessary concomitant of its creator."[18]

Creation ex nihilo is the correlate of the Jewish and Christian view that the existence of all that is, is the result of a free decision of God. Exactly what was at stake was the issue of the necessity with which the universe "emanated from the One," and the consequent necessity characteristic of the universe itself. "It is the freedom of divinity to act, in creating and in revealing, which constitutes the nub of the notion of creator which both Maimonides and Aquinas consider to be the deliverance of the scriptures. And if that freedom means primarily that the act of creating is a spontaneous and gracious one, then the God who so creates is fulfilling no natural need and has nothing to gain thereby."[19]

In a later article in which he reflects on the Trinity, Aquinas observes how useful, indeed how "necessary" such revealed knowledge can be to us "for the right idea of creation: the fact of saying that God made all things by His Word excludes the error of those who say that God produced things by necessity. When we say that in Him there is a procession of love, we show that God produced creatures not because He needed them, nor because of any other extrinsic reason, but on account of the love of His own goodness" (*Summa Theologica*, 1.32.1.3). Aquinas is therefore quite clear that the belief that the world "has not always existed cannot be demonstratively proved" but must be "held by faith alone" (*Summa Theologica*, 1.46.2).

---

18. David Burrell, C.S.C., *Freedom and Creation in Three Traditions* (Notre Dame: University of Notre Dame Press, 1993), 7–8.
19. Ibid., 9.

In the same article Aquinas argues that the world offers no grounds for demonstrating that it was once new. "For the principle for demonstrating an object is its definition. Now the specific nature of each and every object abstracts from the here and now, which is why universals are described as being everywhere and always (Aristotle). Hence it cannot be demonstrated that man, or heaven, or a stone did not always exist" (*Summa Theologica*, 1.46.2). Nor can creation be demonstrated through efficient causation. The will of God can only be investigated through those things God must will of necessity, but what God wills about creatures is not among these. That the world began to exist is therefore an object of faith and not of demonstration or science. The article concludes appropriately with the following warning: "And it is useful to consider this, lest anyone presuming to demonstrate what is of faith, should bring forward reasons that are not cogent, so as to give occasion to unbelievers to laugh, thinking that on such grounds we believe things that are of faith."

Reinhardt Hütter nicely sums up Christian, and I think Aquinas's, thinking on creation by suggesting that "'*ex nihilo*' has to be understood as a graceful, contingent and finite gift of God who was not in need of the world. There is no lack or insufficiency in God that needs the creating of the world to overcome it. Creation is the overflow of God's abundant love as reflected in the inner life of the triune God. '*Ex nihilo*' is a strictly theological predication of God. It secures God's transcendence over against the world."[20]

From the perspective of creation ex nihilo Murdoch's account of necessity and contingency is reversed. The task, therefore, is not to see the particular as necessary, but to see the contingent as just that—contingent—or more accurately in Christian language, as created. For the whole point is that the world, and our existence in the world, does not have to exist, but it and we do. The task is not to see the purposelessness in the sheer existence of the contingent, but rather to see the contingent as "gift" whose purpose is to praise the creator. Such a task does not mean the otherness of the contingent is obliterated by its place in a larger purpose, but

---

20. Reinhard Hütter, "Creation ex Nihilo: Promise of the Gift," *Currents in Theology and Mission* 19, 2 (1992): 92.

that its contingency can be enjoyed because God so enjoys God's creation.[21]

That all God has created praises God as creator does not obliterate the otherness of other creatures, but rather helps us see our own "otherness" in God's other creatures. "The 'others' are other to us inasmuch as we are other to them. Respect of and care for all of God's creatures is the primary means of doxological acknowledgment of God the Creator in creation. The very plurality of cultures, traditions, languages, and species is to be welcomed as the wealth of created otherness. Creation *'ex nihilo'* undercuts uniform secularity, in which consumer subjects and objects are exploited and from which God is utterly absent."[22]

In contrast to Murdoch's account of the absolute pointlessness of existence, Christians believe that God means for all creation to worship God. Such a "purpose," however, does not mean that all that we do is guaranteed to "come out all right." "Purpose" understood doxologically can only be displayed by a narrative that is subject to constant retelling given the contingent character of our existence. We do not know what will happen next, but more importantly we do not even know how we will need to retell "what happened," since the past, no less than the future, must remain

---

21. I confess I find the current enthusiasm for contingency among contemporary philosophers such as Richard Rorty in his *Contingency, Irony and Solidarity* (Cambridge: Cambridge University Press, 1989) puzzling. For example, Rorty suggests "Our language and our culture are as much a contingency, as much a result of thousands of small mutations finding niches (and millions of others finding no niches), as are the orchids and the anthropoids" (p. 16)—that is, contingency is just another word for randomness. Which, of course, is fine but why not simply use "randomness" since contingency invites the question, "Contingent in relation to what?" I am not arguing that the word "contingent" implies a metaphysics that assumes creation or at least the finite character of the world, but rather to suggest that those who use the word often may trade on presumptions they have not adequately defended.

The language of gift requires considerable theological analysis that I cannot provide here. For an example of the kind of display that I think is required, see John Milbank's, "Can a Gift Be Given? Prolegomena to a Future Trinitarian Metaphysic," *Modern Theology* 11, 1 (January 1995): 119–61. For a quite different account, see Jacques Derrida, *The Gift of Death*, trans. David Mills (Chicago: University of Chicago Press, 1995).

22. Hütter, "Creation," 96.

open to renarration. The "purpose" that sustains the Christian is eschatological because we believe that creation names not just a beginning but God's continuing providential care of creation. Creation for us is not only "in the beginning" but continuing.

The telos that characterizes the Christian understanding of morality is not that of a single overriding purpose that violently forces all we do into a preestablished hierarchy. Rather it is a telos of hope that gives us the confidence to believe that we are not fated by our collective or individual pasts. We know that we cannot avoid being creatures of history, but that very way of putting the matter presumes we should desire, if possible, an alternative. Such a desire cannot help but appear to the Christian as a sinful attempt to escape our creatureliness. Our only alternative is not a salvation that mystically frees us from history, from our past, but rather an alternative history made possible by a community of people across time who maintain a memory of God's hope for us and for the world. Given the created character of our existence we cannot hope or wish for more.

We are no doubt possessed and blinded by the "fat relentless ego" so wonderfully depicted by Murdoch. That we are so afflicted, moreover, results in muddles from which we cannot will to be free. The problem with Murdoch's muddles is not simply that we lack the resources to be free of them if God does not exist, but that the full reality of such muddles remains unarticulated in a world without God. For the Christian "sin" names the training we must undergo to discover that our lives are possessed by powers, by narratives, whose purpose it is to hide from us the fact that we are creatures of a gracious God. Such "knowledge" does not come "naturally," but rather from being made part of a community with practices that offer the transformation and reordering of our lives and relationships. Prayer is certainly one of those practices, but at least such prayer by Christians begins with "Our Father" and goes on to seek forgiveness and reconciliation with God and our neighbor. Only through such a reconciliation do we believe we can fully acknowledge our contingency and particularity.

Christian salvation, then, is not "mystical," but comes through the ordinary. Murdoch rightly calls attention to the wisdom of "ordinary people," who know that prayer can induce a better quality of consciousness and provide an energy for good action otherwise unavailable (*Sovereignty*, 83). But the "ordinary people" called Christians know that they must learn to pray together in communities that will teach them to pray rightly. Prayer is not a self-authenticating "spiritual exercise," but rather a practice intelligible only as we have learned to acknowledge our existence as forgiven creatures. Murdoch's world is finally too lonely for those of us called Christian, those who believe that we were created to be friends with God and, consequently, with one another and even ourselves. No doubt the Christian story, like any significant story, can be used and is often used, to offer false consolation. But as Murdoch demonstrates often in her novels, our hedge against false consolation, against self-deception, cannot be found in ourselves. We cannot will our way out of our fantasies but rather any escape comes externally. Christians believe that God has made available to us friendships and practices correctly embodied in a community called church that supplies such "externality." A people who know their salvation and have been secured through Jesus' cross and resurrection are accordingly required to live resisting the false consolations of this world.

IV. Where Does This Leave Us?

All I have done is contrast what I take to be the metaphysical and moral implications of the Christian account of creation with Murdoch's understanding of the purposelessness of our existence. I wish I knew better how to engage her in argument. There are surely metaphysical issues that would be worth pursuing—that is, why necessity is not a characteristic of God; or why goodness is a predicate of God and can only be displayed by analogy.[23] Yet how that is to be or should be done has been made difficult by Murdoch because she rightly, I think, refuses to separate metaphysics and morality. So it is finally not a question of how to characterize "what is" but how "what is" reflects as well is determined by what we

---

23. These matters are, of course, interrelated. Since the contingent characters of our as well as the world's existence is that of creature, we can only "know" God analogically.

are or should be. That she insists on such a close interconnection between metaphysics and morality is at least part of the reason she is such a challenge to those of us who understand ourselves to be Christians.

There are, moreover, as I indicated at the beginning, issues in what might be called moral psychology that would be useful to explore. The "inner" character of our lives is much more dependent on the habituation made possible by a community's practices than Murdoch seems to acknowledge. This can now be seen not simply as a point of moral psychology, but also as a reflection of a much stronger sense of our embeddedness as historic creatures— at least as suggested by the Christian understanding of our status as creatures. Murdoch and Christians alike believe that we must be trained to see, but I suspect the kind of training that distinguishes the two will be quite different.

I think, however, that the deepest difficulty Christians have in knowing what an argument with Murdoch might look like is that we simply lack the imaginative power to do so. Our greatest difficulty as Christians is we have lost the "sources," the practices, that are necessary to sustain our conviction that God is the origination and end of our existence. In such a world Murdoch surely offers, through her novels, a reimagining of our existence that powerfully reflects "the way we live now." Her novels, even more than her philosophy, become a temptation for us, since being trained through them we lose our ability to imagine any other world.

Any response to Iris Murdoch, and it is a response that we rightly owe to her wisdom about such matters, will come from other artists—for example, Walker Percy or Flannery O'Connor—who have the imagination to create a world of hope. Yet such artists, as Murdoch has taught us, depend on quite ordinary people who have learned to live well against the odds. If Christians are to survive or deserve to survive in a world that has no capacity to acknowledge our created status, they will do so only because our communities are still capable of producing and locating those among us whose lives are living prayers.

9
THE SOVEREIGNTY OF GOD'S GOODNESS

William Schweiker

Every ethic seeks to show persons how they ought to live in the face of the suffering and joy, conflicts and possibilities, of personal and social life. Throughout her many works, Iris Murdoch has presented a comprehensive moral philosophy which is indebted to strands of Western thought, especially Platonic philosophy. The good life, according to Murdoch, is a movement towards selfless care for individuals guided by ideas of perfection which are objects of love. Murdoch is unique among moral philosophers because of this focus on the reality of goodness and the individual.

In presenting this moral vision, Murdoch, unlike most contemporary thinkers, does not believe that we ought to expunge religious concerns from ethics. However, she does insist that we can and must replace God with Good as the central concept in ethics. In fact, at the end of *Metaphysics as a Guide to Morals,* Murdoch claims that we "need a theology which can continue without God."[1] And then she asks, "Why not call such a reflection a form of moral philosophy? All right," Murdoch continues, "so long as it treats those matters of 'ultimate concern,' our experience of the unconditioned and our continued sense of what is holy" (pp. 511–12). Yet in presenting the task of moral philosophy in this way, Murdoch is explicit, even insistent, that the Good "is not the old God in disguise, but rather what the old God symbolized" (p. 428).

I want to thank Maria Antonaccio, Lois Malcolm, and James Thompson for helpful comments on this essay.
1. Iris Murdoch, *Metaphysics as a Guide to Morals* (New York: Allen Lane/Penguin Press, 1993), 511; hereafter referred to as *Metaphysics.*

In the following pages I want to explore Murdoch's argument about God and Good. I hope to show that the divine is not exhausted by the idea of Good, and, furthermore, why a theological perspective is needed in ethics if we are to make sense of moral value. My argument requires that I reclaim and also radically rethink some basic theological ideas, especially, as we will see, the moral meaning of theistic discourse and also the idea of conscience. In order to do so, the paper will move in several steps. First, I want to introduce in some detail what will be argued. Second, by drawing on Murdoch's work, I will outline the basic problem which contemporary ethics faces. With this in hand, I turn, third, to Murdoch's work and briefly explore how she pictures the human, her account of the Good, and the way she establishes the reality of the Good. Finally, I will forward a theological ethical response to Murdoch's moral philosophy along these same lines, a response which draws upon, but also transforms, some of her insights.

I. What Will Be Argued

The inquiry of this paper can be seen as another round in the long encounter between Platonism and Christian ethics.[2] This is important to note for several reasons. First, each of these traditions insists on one supreme reality, God or Good, in relation to which human beings and the world are to be valued and understood. These are, in other words, monistic or monotheistic forms of thought and life. Second, these forms of thought are realistic in the sense that they seek to understand a reality not reducible to how we construe the world. The real is not simply what we make or

---

2. I have specified a method for comparative ethics in my essay "The Drama of Interpretation and the Philosophy of Religions: An Essay on Understanding in Comparative Religious Ethics," in *Discourse and Praxis*, ed. Frank E. Reynolds and David Tracy (Albany: State University of New York, 1992), 263–94. Also see Sumner B. Twiss, "Curricular Perspectives in Comparative Religious Ethics: A Critical Examination of Four Paradigms," in *Annual of the Society of Christian Ethics* (Washington, D.C.: Georgetown University Press, 1993), 249–69.

invent even if our interpretations or pictures of the real are human constructions. Morally, this means that we can choose to conform our lives to the real or deny it. In other words, each of these traditions aims at finding some coherence between a view of reality, a metaphysics, and an account of moral goodness, an ethics. What is morally good strikes to the root of things, and, conversely, the way things are is important for how we can and should live. Third, given these claims, Christianity and Platonism in their various expressions are forms of ethical universalism. Thinkers within these traditions grant their particular, fallible, and historical starting points. Mindful of that fact, they seek, nevertheless, to specify the norms and goods which ought to characterize all human life.

These points of agreement between Platonic and Christian ethics are taken by their critics to be a denial of the particular, a stifling, even tyrannous, monism unmindful of the obvious plurality of the world, hankering after some way to escape the travail of history by adopting a God's-eye perspective on life, and a futile search for some way to reduce the anxiety and risk of the moral life. Morality, the critics argue, is not rooted in the way things are but in the power to bring about outcomes, social consensus, or creative imagination. As J. L. Mackie and others have put it: we do not discover morality, we invent it.[3] In this light, Platonic and Christian forms of ethics seem fantastic from the perspective of most current thought. This is because the point of these traditions, as Murdoch has insisted, is to articulate the unconditioned character and depth of morality. There are then good reasons for a Christian theologian to engage Murdoch, who is the most compelling recent advocate of a form of Platonic ethics.

My approach to Murdoch's work is not simply for historical or comparative reasons. The question I want to address about God and Good is nothing less than the question of first principles in ethics and thus how we speak morally about the real. By a first principle I mean the idea, symbol, or root metaphor which gives systematic integrity to an ethics. This idea, symbol, or metaphor is

3. See J. L. Mackie, *Inventing Right and Wrong* (New York: Viking Penguin, 1977).

a principle insofar as it is the source of intelligibility within an ethics; it is first because the principle is irreducible and primary.[4] This way of putting matters ought not to detract us from the real human significance of the question. For what is at stake is how, if at all, one can show the intelligibility of a way of life in which respecting and enhancing things and persons is in fact primary and irreducible in existence.[5] In terms of the title of this paper, the first principle of an ethics is that which is sovereign over all other moral concepts, and, more important, sovereign over our lives. The judgment about which idea, symbol, or metaphor we use in speaking about the first principle of the moral life and how we should live is then of grave importance.

I aim in this paper to specify the first principle of theological ethics through a critical comparison of Christian morality with Murdoch's ethics. The first principle of any ethics, I contend, has to do with the value and direction of power with respect to the value of the world and others. This follows since we live as agents who exercise power, interact and suffer in the world, and also make evaluations about our lives, the world, and others in order to orient our lives in the world. Murdoch seems to agree with this insofar as she sees the problem of the moral life centering on the direction of the energy of the psyche away from selfish fantasy and towards reality. Ethics must show, then, the intelligibility of a way of life in which values other than power, such as the value of other persons and the world, is irreducible and primary. If this is not the case, then the struggles and possibilities which characterize human life cannot be understood or evaluated in any other terms than the

---

4. For a helpful discussion of this point in religious ethics see Albert R. Jonsen, *Responsibility in Modern Religious Ethics* (Washington, D.C.: Corpus Books, 1968).

5. While different ethical positions might agree on practical matters, say that war is in principle wrong or that under certain circumstances a war is justifiable, they might still differ with respect to what integrates the dimensions of reflection on the moral life. To the extent that ethical positions disagree at that basic level, they represent divergent accounts of how we should live. It remains an open question whether or not this means that those moral outlooks are finally incommensurable. Yet one task of any ethics is to show why in fact a particular idea, symbol, or root metaphor ought to be first in our moral thinking and our actual conduct.

quest for power and the fantasies we use to promote our power. I want to isolate the error in the belief that power is the primary value, that it alone is sovereign in our lives because it is what gives value to our lives.

I will be arguing that the transvaluation of power and the ground of value is what the word God symbolizes. This is, admittedly, a constructive claim about how to understand theistic discourse. I do not imagine that philosophers, let alone all theologians, will agree with it. But as I understand it, Christian faith is about sin and redemption; it is about creation and destruction, death and resurrection; it is about radical love and the hunger and thirst that righteousness and mercy should reign in human life. In other words, this faith is about which power or powers one ought to serve in giving meaning and value to life. If this is so, then the question of God is the question of the first principle of morality. Theological discourse, a construal of the divine, symbolizes what must be affirmed in our actions and evaluations if the primacy and irreducibility of morality itself is to be intelligible. In other words, theological ethics critically and constructively uses the symbolic and conceptual resources of the Christian tradition in order to articulate and interpret the intrinsic moral structure of experienced reality. The wager is that its symbolic and conceptual resources will in fact prove their indispensable worth in just this way. And this is of course what I am attempting by engaging Murdoch's theology without God, her moral philosophy.[6]

That said, let me now turn to the problem our situation poses for ethics. The account I will offer draws on Murdoch's work and

---

6. Ethics seeks to articulate the meaning and demonstrate the truth of moral convictions, religious or otherwise, for the sake of understanding life, our existence as agents, and providing guidance for how we ought to live. An ethics is theological only if human beings are understood to exist most basically in relation to God rather than simply natural reality, a social totality, or historical existence. See William Schweiker, "Hermeneutics, Ethics and the Theology of Culture: Concluding Reflections" in *Meanings in Texts and Actions: Questioning Paul Ricoeur*, ed. David E. Klemm and William Schweiker (Charlottesville: University Press of Virginia, 1993), 292–313. This account of theological ethics is indebted to H. Richard Niebuhr and his conception of "Christian moral philosophy." See his *The Responsible Self: An Essay in Christian Moral Philosophy*, intro. James M. Gustafson (New York: Harper & Row, 1963).

then introduces new factors from the perspective of theological ethics. The reason for detailing these points is to see the full extent of the task of ethics in our time.

II. THE PROBLEM OF ETHICS IN OUR MORAL SITUATION

Murdoch has sought to uncover the deep underpinnings of our current situation and the grave challenges this poses to ethics. As she sees it, our situation is the product of the long process of the removal of value as metaphysically basic in an account of the world and with this the loss of the individual into vast non-human systems. The eclipse of God, the secularism of the modern West, is but one historical expression of this basic shift in modern consciousness. Murdoch attempts to show how modern philosophy often merely reflects this deeper shift rather than critically assessing and responding to it.

Murdoch sees in post-structuralist philosophy an interpretation of the world as "a vast system or sign structure whereby meaning is determined by a mutual relationship of signs which transcends the localized talk of individual speakers" (*Metaphysics*, 188). This metaphysics of meaning, like any total system, is one in which individual persons and the complexity of the interior life are forfeited in favor of an analysis of meaning systems and actions. "Meaning, then, is an internally self-related movement or *play* of language" (p. 193). There is nothing outside of the text. This is, furthermore, a linguistic determinism, since individual speakers, subsumed into the linguistic system, are players in the play of language. Insofar as that is the case, there is, Murdoch believes, a loss of value as the metaphysical background of the complexity of individual personal life.

In Murdoch's eyes, existentialists developed a picture of human beings which neatly fits this account of the world. In existentialist thought, the human is described as randomly thrown into a meaningless world condemned to create meaning for himself or herself. The focus of ethics becomes the creative act of the will; the self is manifest in action, sovereign in the moment of choice. As Murdoch notes, morality on this account "resides at the point of action. What I am 'objectively' is not under my control; logic and observers decide that. What I am 'subjectively' is a foot-loose, solitary, substanceless will. Personality dwindles to a point of pure will" (p. 16).[7] Once this picture of human beings is accepted it is hardly surprising that ethics would focus on actions, norms of choice, and the meaning of public moral discourse—important words like "duty," "ought," and "right." The complexity of the interior life, the depth and chaos of personality, and what we love are simply beyond the pale of ethics. The world outside is discontinuous with the world inside, the unfettered will-to-choice. The human person, defined as a will, moves about in an alien world.

Any response to the reigning conception of the world and human beings requires rehabilitating the idea of transcendence, saving the individual, examining the complexity of personality, and combating deterministic as well as voluntarist pictures of human beings. Murdoch undertakes this task by asking us to look closely at ordinary life. When we attend to actual experience do we find the reigning theories of meaning and subjectivity confirmed? As creatures we live in and as our bodies and thus are part of the larger natural world. All of our linguistic and social actions, Murdoch notes, return at some level to actual speaking and acting persons. We regularly have experiences of life saturated with value, experiences of beauty, and moral admiration of others. All our choices are not aimed simply at maximizing self-interest, and human freedom is inherently limited by what we apprehend as good. The sun setting in streams of red, orange, purple over a wood-lined Wisconsin lake as the stars emerge in crystalline points of light evokes more than wonder about the physics of it all and the prospect of a new development project. Its beauty, Murdoch would argue, is a sign of the transcendence of goodness. The embrace of a loved one deeply missed is the sense of what simply *ought* to be. The death of innocents sacrificed for political or religious ideologies evokes our grief and outrage.

It is then incorrect to say that we are contingently thrown into a world devoid of value and left to find our way and to create value. We regularly have experiences of what transcends us and also the

---

7. Iris Murdoch, *The Sovereignty of Good* (London: Routledge, 1970); hereafter referred to as *Sovereignty*.

reality of value not definable in terms of our wants and desires or acts of will.[8] As Murdoch cryptically notes, the "ordinary person does not, unless corrupted by philosophy, believe that he creates values by his choices. He thinks that some things really are better than others and that he is capable of getting it wrong" (*Sovereignty*, 97). She challenges the current outlook by insisting that we cannot eradicate evaluative judgments from human existence. If one thinks away value, one thinks away what it means to be a human being. The Good is the source of intelligibility in life and it is primary and irreducible.

Thus, Murdoch insists that what is at root of our current situation is a loss of vision for the real and our desire for consoling fantasies driven by our natural egoism. Late-modern society is something like the ego writ large; a factory of self-serving illusions to help us escape responsibility. But here we must press some basic questions. Is this flight into illusion all that is going on? More pointedly, I want to ask: What comes to the fore morally when we consider the connection between power and value? Seen from that vantage point, the problem of the loss of vision in late-modern society is rooted not simply in an ego that seeks omnipotence, but, rather, in an equation of power with value. That is, the origin and

---

8. Erazim Kohák has noted that most "Western thought has been consistently personalistic and specifically *naturalistic*, at least in the generic sense of that term, understanding humans as continuous with and at home in nature." To be sure there are good reasons to challenge much traditional Western ethics. The status of being human has too easily been denied some persons, notably women and those in dominated cultures. So too the naturalistic tendency of Western thought, that is, the claim that the human good is to be specified in terms of what respects and enhances the flourishing of life, has been used to delimit the range of human freedom. And this same naturalism and personalism has backed wantonly anthropocentric valuations of the natural world. Still, the picture of the world and ourselves which dominates current Western societies simply cuts against the grain of its own heritage. Ought we to try to eradicate from our view of the world and ourselves a conviction about the primacy of persons and our relation to the natural world? See Erazim Kohák, *The Embers and the Stars: A Philosophical Inquiry into the Moral Sense of Nature* (Chicago: University of Chicago Press, 1984), 7. On this also see Robin W. Lovin, "The Limits of Freedom and the Possibility of Politics: A Christian Realist Account of Political Responsibility" *Journal of Religion* 73, 4 (1993): 559–72.

ground of value, what confers worth on persons or things, is believed to be power. Existentialism is a compelling picture of the self in these societies because we believe our acts of will somehow connect us with value creating power. And contact with power is what gives value to our lives. The only binding constraints upon us are then ourselves. Similarly, the post-structuralist account of meaning is not only about the loss of value; it is the analysis of the productive power of language to create meaning. There is nothing outside the text, because the "text," and not nothingness, is productive of meaning. "Text" is a name for the matrixes of meaning producing power. Finally, the loss of God from our picture of the world simply signifies the shift in the creation of value from God or Nature to the domain of human power. The belief that holds together our current outlook, I contend, is the equation of power and worth. We do not see value in reality because value is a matter of power, and power too easily conceals itself behind its workings—the workings of desire, political institutions, and economic systems.[9]

The problem we face in ethics is then that the ground of value has shifted from being to power, or, more precisely put, being itself, the source of value, is conceived in terms of power. Seeing this shift does not entail jettisoning metaphysical questions from ethics. It is not to champion will over mind, doing over being. But it is to realize that the metaphysical dimension of ethics has also shifted. The modern world no longer sees nature as creation or the human as created in the image of God. We no longer dwell in the classic, mimetic universe wherein persons and things derived

9. I should note that in this respect my argument represents an Augustinian line of moral and theological reflection. That is, St. Augustine, in *The City of God*, understood that the central problematic of the "earthly city" was the grounding of the political and social order in the "love of ruling." The "city of God," conversely, rejects that foundation of the social and political on that principle and affirms the centrality of the love of God. In the terms I am developing, the central issue in ethics and theology is this relation of power and value. This is the case, because that relation formulates the most basic principle of human activity and association. Thus, to consider the relation of power and value is, theologically understood, to reflect upon the human relation to the divine and what persons and communities hold as sacred.

their value from a place in the system of being.[10] The "paradox of the modern condition," as Hans Jonas rightly notes, "is that the reduction of man's stature, the utter humbling of his metaphysical pride [as the image of God], goes hand in hand with his promotion to quasi-God-like privilege and power. The emphasis is on *power.*"[11]

Given this picture of the human and our world, is it any wonder that current societies are characterized by unending conflict over access to the mechanisms of social, economic, cultural, and political power? We see ourselves not as creatures responding to a world of values but as value-creating actors—economic agents, for instance—and linguistic systems, as post-structuralists argue, are themselves productive of meaning. How surprising is it, then, that inner-city youth living amid racial injustice and poverty have developed moral codes based on the principle that respect and self-esteem are grounded in the power to defend oneself, and, if necessary, to exercise lethal force on others. In light of this fact, ethics must ask the question of the value of the power to create value.[12] And it is this question, I insist, that theological ethics has always been concerned with because it symbolizes the real in terms of the relation of power and value, that is, in terms of the reality of God.

10. On this see William Schweiker, *Mimetic Reflections: A Study in Hermeneutics, Theology, and Ethics* (New York: Fordham University Press, 1991).
11. Hans Jonas, *Philosophical Essays: From Ancient Creed to Technological Man* (Englewood Cliffs, N.J.: Prentice-Hall, 1974), 172.
12. Christians have never thought that Platonists could answer this problem. Given their confidence in mind, Platonists could never really understand St. Paul's insistence on the abyss of the will, the frightful contradiction between mind and inclination which infests human existence. They could never see the fact that the political order is too often, maybe always, driven by the thirst for power, as theologians from Augustine to Reinhold Niebuhr have insisted. Even human illusions are not simply consoling fantasies; they are idols, icons of the human power to attempt to create unconditioned value. Finally, in the eyes of Christian thinkers, Platonists could also never understand the importance of creation, that is, that all temporal natural value, the goodness of being, is dependent on a value creating power characterized by righteousness, that the Creator acknowledges the goodness of what is finite (God saw that it was good, as we have it in Genesis), nor, more radically, the moral meaning of incarnation, that God redeems fallen existence.

This enables us to formulate the nub of the problem about first principles in ethics; it is the problem I will be exploring throughout the remainder of this essay. Insofar as we are concerned with a principle in ethics, this principle must specify how and in what way power is to be evaluated and exercised by agents and thus what confers value on things and persons. Two options are possible in trying to isolate the ground of morality. These options explain why Murdoch thinks that the most crucial ethical systems in the West are those of Kant and Plato, and why, finally, she sides with Plato.

First, one can try to show that these constraints on power are internal to the agent, for example, in pure practical reason as Kant argued. Formulating a principle of right action with respect to the well-being of others and acting according to it is itself an act of freedom. The agent is sovereign over herself or himself and yet is also bound to exercise freedom in respect of others; the subjective act of self-legislation is the ground of objectively binding moral norms. Insofar as we recognize this in other persons, they evoke our moral respect. Conversely, we can argue that the principle of right action refers to what is other than the agent, as Platonists and Christians hold. That principle might be given by a divine command, as some theologians have argued; it could be understood in terms of the mind of God, the face of the other, or as the Good beyond being. God or the Good is sovereign; the objective norm is to be subjectively appropriated by the agent in rendering life morally intelligible. These externalist positions, if I may call them that, suspect that any purely internalist answer, like Kant's, never really escapes the self and the drive to maximize its power. Because of this, Platonists and Christians look elsewhere. They seek a good which transcends the self but which nevertheless accords or resonates with the self.[13] In terms I have been using, they seek a norm beyond power—even the desire of love—which can constrain, direct, and even transform the power to act so that it serves good ends.

13. On this see Charles Taylor, *Sources of the Self: The Making of Modern Identity* (Cambridge: Harvard University Press, 1990). Also see William Schweiker, "The Good and Moral Identity: A Theological Ethical Response to Charles Taylor's *Sources of the Self*," *Journal of Religion* 72, 4 (1992): 560–72.

We have returned then to a basic point of agreement between Christian and Platonic ethics, specifically the insistence that morality is basic given the nature of reality. Yet in spite of all of these agreements, we have also hit upon a matter of continuing dispute in the encounter between these moral traditions. The dispute turns on what the norm beyond power is conceived to be, how it is symbolized, how we are to make contact with it, and, thus, the formulation of the first principle of ethics. Put simply, what is at issue is how the real is symbolized since the real is what morality is about; the real is the ground of value. Christian theology claims that we can and must understand God, the divine goodness, as the first principle of ethics; Platonists speak of the Good. In order to clarify the point of dispute and my own argument, I want to turn now to Murdoch's ethics and progress through levels of her argument ending with how she justifies the reality of Good. This will allow me to pose a question about the value of the individual in Murdoch's thought that opens anew the question of God.

III. Murdoch on Persons, Good and God

Murdoch's understanding of what it means for us to be moral creatures is summarized in her claim that self-being or consciousness is the fundamental mode of moral being. "What we really are," Murdoch writes, "seems . . . like an obscure system of energy out of which choices and visible acts of will emerge at intervals in ways which are often unclear and often depend on the condition of the system in between the moments of choice" (*Sovereignty*, 54). Consciousness is the means to organize and direct the chaotic energy of the ego; the direction of energy is what the moral life is all about. Given this construal of the self, a construal indebted to Freud and Plato, Murdoch is interested in exploring the formation of consciousness that gives rise to right action rather than centering her account of agents on our capacity for willing.[14]

14. Some years ago Elizabeth Anscombe wrote an important essay in which she insisted that the idea of moral obligation ought to be jettisoned from ethics. This radical move was necessary because in order to make sense of the experience of obligation one needed a more subtle moral psychology than found in ethics at that time. It also demanded a full recognition of and then escape from the de-

Not surprisingly, Murdoch contests any ethics which defines valuing as epiphenomenal to cognition by reducing it into an act of will and which construes the moral agent as a willing chooser rather than a knowing subject seeking contact with a world different than itself. The self defined by its capacity to will can only picture itself and others as substanceless wills that are self-identical in acts of choosing. If that is indeed the case, then moral discourse refers to nothing in the world; it refers to the worldless act of the will.[15] Murdoch contends that "value, valuing, is not a specialized activity of the will, but an apprehension of the world, an aspect of cognition, which is everywhere" (*Metaphysics*, 265). The problem for Murdoch is that the ego in its quest for omnipotence easily and readily pictures itself in a world of its own making, a world of self-serving fantasy. But in fact, other persons are transcendent to the self and so is the value of their lives. The moral life is about coming to see this fact and living by it. It is about constraining and directing the exercise of freedom by making contact with the reality of others. Perception is thus basic to self-being, to consciousness. Given this, sustained attention, serious contemplative perception, is central to moral betterment, the arduous struggle to see the world and others rightly.

---

pendence of theories of obligation on Jewish and Christian ideas of God as commander, a dependence, she insisted, always present but rarely acknowledged in modern ethics. If I understand Murdoch rightly, her moral philosophy is a complex response to Anscombe's challenge. And by responding to Anscombe, she is also, we might note, responding to our current situation. See G. E. M. Anscombe, "Modern Moral Philosophy," *Philosophy* 33 (1958): 1–19. It is significant that Iris Murdoch dedicates *Metaphysics as a Guide to Morals* to Anscombe.

15. Murdoch's attack on voluntarism runs along several lines. She notes that when ethics focuses on actions and discrete acts of will, one does not need an elaborate moral vocabulary. Good and evil, right and wrong, just and unjust are action words while all the other evaluative discourse we use to make sense of our world, others, and ourselves seems to fall beyond the scope of moral discourse. This truncates our moral sensibilities. The focus on action words and evaluations of action is consistent with a picture of persons as solitary, substanceless wills who constitute their identity, even their world, in acts of choice. This makes it difficult to speak of the inner life or the continuity of the self over time, and thus our moral progress, other than through words about individual acts.

Murdoch pictures the moral life as the conversion of the self to the real guided by some object of attention, a conversion which entails the redirection of psychic energy. Attention expresses the "idea of a just and loving gaze directed upon an individual reality." This form of perception, and not unimpeded freedom, is, Murdoch notes, "the characteristic and proper mark of the active moral agent" (*Sovereignty*, 34). Drawing on Plato's analogy of the Cave, Murdoch describes persons as lost in illusions projected on the world who must, if they are to become morally better, turn and struggle from the cave in order, finally, to the see world, others, and self for what they are in the light of the sun, the Good. The moral life is about progress, a process of perfecting the agent through attention to what is real. Morally understood, the core of consciousness is attention, and its necessary object is the reality of the individual.

The heart of this position is Murdoch's claim that a person is compelled by obedience to the reality she or he can see. The real is sovereign over the self. Clarity of vision about the real organizes the system of psychic energy thus enabling the person to choose and to act rightly. The real is then the primary and irreducible source of intelligibility in life. And if it can be shown that the Good is real, then morality is irreducible and primary in human life. It is at this juncture that we are led to Murdoch's account of the Good and her defense of it as sovereign over all other concepts. If her argument is to hold, she must show that the Good is implicit in all acts of consciousness and that it is necessarily real.

In her famous essay "On 'God' and 'Good'," Murdoch defines God as "a single perfect transcendent non-representable and necessarily real object of attention" (*Sovereignty*, 55). She takes this to be the idea of God which has dominated traditional theism; it is what the word God symbolizes. Murdoch wants to argue that the Good has these same attributes. Once we have grasped her account of the problem facing ethics, we can see the reason for this equation of Good and what the old God symbolized. She wants to show that what claims one's attention is a reality transcendent to the subject, a reality in which value is necessarily real and singular. This object is non-representable and therefore not reducible to our systems of meaning or representation. The Good is also the transcendence of the singular against its reduction into a system of representations and manifests the metaphysical standing of value, that perfection is real. Insofar as all of this can be shown true, Murdoch will have established the categorical character of morality and reclaimed value as metaphysically basic in our conception of the world and ourselves.

In order to establish the irreducibility of goodness in our lives, Murdoch begins with a claim about the perception of things, persons, and activities. The Good is a unifying idea in human life insofar as we understand anything at all in terms of degrees of perfection. We constantly grade and evaluate events, persons, and activities with respect to some explicit or implicit idea of better or worse. These evaluative acts are unified around some idea of the Good. Yet this also means that the Good as such is indefinable because of the inexhaustible variety of the world. In the moral life, centered as it is on attention to the individual, the Good is connected with the pointlessness of virtue, that is, that moral virtue is good in itself and not a means to some other end, say the end of happiness. Thus, the Good spans our perception of the world and things in it and also the moral life. Murdoch's account of the Good unites in one grand vision a depiction of the world and the idea of virtue correlated to a claim about consciousness and attention. Her position, as she admits, is monistic. How then to establish the reality of the Good?

Murdoch attempts to justify her claim about goodness in terms of the ontological proof for the existence of God. This is possible, recall, because she equates Good with the attributes of God as a real, transcendent, perfect object of attention. She tries to show that understanding the Good entails affirming its necessary existence. Consistent with what we have seen, Murdoch reads the proof for God as rooted in our noticing degrees of goodness. As she puts it, the definition of God as noncontingent is "given body by our most general perceptions and experience of the fundamental and omnipresent (uniquely necessary) nature of moral value" (*Metaphysics*, 396). The proof is not about God but about the Good, that is, the necessarily real condition of possibility of our moral evaluations. "We gain the concept of this unique form of necessity," Murdoch argues, "from our unavoidable experience of good and evil" (p. 406). In making this move to the reality of Good, Murdoch frees the proof from the burden of establishing the necessary existence of a personal God and understands it to be a claim about moral value. What the proof of the Good designates, then, is an unconditioned structure which cannot be thought away in human life. Insofar as this is indeed the case, then moral philosophy "accommodates the 'unconditional element in the structure of reason and reality'" (p. 432). Ethics is a theology without God because Good is what the old God symbolized.

Murdoch's replacement of God with Good rests on a series of interrelated claims. First, she contends that "God" is the name of a supernatural person and that confusion arises if we try to extend the word "God" to cover any or all ideas of spiritual reality. She believes, second, that nothing is lost spiritually or morally by forgoing the idea of a supernatural person in favor of the Good. In fact, the ontological proof works to this end by showing that the concept of an existing personal being cannot meet the demands of necessary existence. Third, Murdoch insists that the Good is what the old God symbolized, especially the absolute, necessary moral claim upon humanity manifest in every experience of distinguishing degrees of perfection. And therefore, Murdoch, finally, frees religion from theism and defines it as "a mode of belief in the unique sovereign place of goodness or virtue in human life" (p. 426). This completes Murdoch's response to the problem of the loss of value as metaphysically basic and her proposal for a theology without God. She has shown the ubiquity of value in human consciousness and also the reality of Good.

I contend that "God" is not simply a name of a supernatural person, and, furthermore, that the Good does not exhaust the meaning of the divine. But as a step towards formulating a theological response to Murdoch's ethics, it is important to ask a basic but critical moral question. The question focuses on the object of moral concern, that is, the individual, and then forces us to consider the ground of morality in order to make sense of that object of concern. And as we have seen, Murdoch insists that the focus of morality is love and knowledge of individuals. The "central concept of morality," she writes, "is 'the individual' thought of as knowable by love, thought of in the light of the command, 'Be ye therefore perfect'" (*Sovereignty*, 30). This, then, is our question: What is the ground for this claim about the centrality of the individual? More pointedly, why ought the individual be an object of love and moral attention when any real, actual individual is always less than perfect? Was it not precisely the fact of contingency and imperfection that led Murdoch to reject a personal God in the favor of the impersonal Good? Why does not the same argument fall on actual, existing human beings? In a word, the question is about what confers value on individuals.

A number of well-known answers are possible to this question; Murdoch endorses none of them. It is important to see why she rejects these positions. First, it could be argued that we are to care for and know individuals as a means to the end of knowing the Good for ourselves. But if that is the case it would mean seeing persons as means to other ends; virtue, despite Murdoch's protest, would have a point. Second, maybe we are to respect and love persons only insofar as they approximate or represent perfection for us? But how would we know that our perception is without fault in making such evaluations? Murdoch is too aware of delusions that infest moral understanding to endorse this answer about the value of individuals. So, we are left to ask, again, what it is about the imperfect, contingent reality of persons that compels, even commands, our love. As far as I can tell, an answer to this question within the strict confines of Murdoch's thought might entail affirming a claim that cuts against her whole moral philosophy. Clarity on this point is then absolutely crucial to what I want to argue about God and morality.

As we have seen, according to Murdoch the mode of moral being is consciousness. Human consciousness, she further notes, is a one-making activity. We always try to organize our lives and our world into some coherent, meaningful whole; this is the metaphysical impulse endemic to the human mind. As Kant saw, consciousness is a synthetic activity. Plato insisted that we understand with respect to the Good. Murdoch is trying to make both of these claims. This one-making act with respect to some idea of perfection is found in creative, artistic activity. This is why art is so important for Murdoch. We are all artists, she insists. Of course, Murdoch is aware of how the mind can fabricate and love false unities.

She hopes to counter this tendency by establishing the reality of Good and exploring practices for transforming moral attention, practices like meditation and prayer.

What Murdoch has not examined is that the one-making of consciousness is itself an act of power. What are we to make of this fact with respect to what confers value on individuals and also the first principle of ethics? Two responses are possible: in terms I have used before one is an internalist answer while the other is externalist. First, we could argue that this act of power in consciousness, our cognitive one-making rather than willing, is value-conferring. The conferring of value must be understood internal to the agent, this idealist argument would go, because otherwise we could not make sense of why individuals, imperfect as we all obviously are, are fit objects of love and respect. What compels our respect and love is the reality of individuals as one-making creatures, that they have mind and thus some consciousness of the real with respect to goodness. To love individuals is to love the varied and complex ways in which goodness is known. What confers moral worth on persons is then an act of power, the one-making activity of the mind under the reality of Good. Power is creative of value, but it is the power of mind not will that is central in this idealist, as opposed to existentialist, account.

Murdoch insists on love and respect for persons as such and not the one-making acting of consciousness. And this must mean, as an externalist response to the question, that consciousness as such must not be value conferring. Even the value of the self is in some respect external to it; the Good is sovereign here as well. This is, I take it, Murdoch's point in saying that the self is seen by the good person as nothing, as transparent to the Good. The self in its one-making activity must be effaced if it is to be morally good although every act of consciousness potentially, maybe actually, works against this end. In other words, if consciousness were in fact value-conferring, then moral attention would be directed to what individuals share rather than the particularity of their existence. Idealism, like existentialism, ends by denying the complexity of individuals.

We have returned then to the point of departure for this inquiry, namely, the relation between power and value as the roots of morality and whether that relation is to be understood as internal to the agent, in willing or consciousness, or as somehow external to the subject. Murdoch rejects existentialist and idealist positions on precisely this point. Consciousness is directed towards the real, and human freedom only makes sense in that context. But then the question returns. What confers value on individuals? Murdoch has established the reality of Good, but what is the goodness of reality, especially the reality of individuals? This is the point, I judge, that a residue of the Christian insistence of the created worth of individuals plays its role in Murdoch's thought. Simply in virtue of being created, persons are worthy of respect and love. In the light of creation, one affirms that *esse qua esse est bonum*, to cite Augustine. But can we make sense of that claim without a creator, without God?

Let me now take up this question and with it Murdoch's claims about God and Good. For if I am right, a realist ethics which holds to the dignity of the individual on grounds other than an act of power within the self—be that the will or consciousness—is only possible by appeal to some idea of creation and thus also a creator. But that would mean that we cannot replace God with Good. It would mean, in other words, that the Good is not all that God symbolizes.

IV. THE SOVEREIGNTY OF GOD'S GOODNESS

I have been arguing that in our time the ground of value is increasingly defined in terms of power.[16] This means that value is under-

---

16. Value can be defined in naturalistic and relational terms. Value is the fittingness of being in relation to being insofar as this relation respects and enhances the integrity of an existent. The food that we consume is a value to us insofar as it does not thwart our needs, say by poisoning us. Disvalue is what demeans and destroys an existing being. As H. Richard Niebuhr has argued, value is not reducible to subjective evaluations; it is also not simply a property of entities. Value denotes a relation of being to being in terms of what completes or frustrates those involved. Given this account of value, what is morally right is any action or relation which respects and enhances the integrity of natural, personal, and social life. Right and wrong, and also moral duties, are determined and justified with respect to basic values rooted in the needs, capacities, and potentialities of specific kinds of beings, say human beings. Murdoch would seem

stood to be rooted in the capacity to bring about states-of-affairs which fulfill some person's or community's existence and this entails the further belief that value is increased through the increase of power, the capacity to bring about outcomes.[17] Because it is the case, as far as we know, that only human beings intentionally exercise power, this means that human beings, or at least human societies, are taken as the source of value. From this set of claims ethicists have drawn several conclusions. Value, it is argued, is not ontologically basic; power is basic. The constraints on power must then be found *internal* to those exercising power whether in will or consciousness, or at least in terms of some consensus between agents who exercise power. Insofar as this true, Platonism and Christianity along with their most basic affirmations are false. As we have seen, these are some of the deepest suppositions of late-modern cultures and also of contemporary ethics.

The question, again, is whether power is the ground of value in will or consciousness or if there are constraints placed upon the exercise of power by a good other than power itself. This question is morally basic insofar as all human beings are actual or potential

---

to agree with some version of this theory of value. She describes herself as a non-dogmatic naturalist in ethics. I take than to mean that morality cannot be severed from the question of what enables something to flourish. And it also means that in ethics we are intensely interested in exploring what kind of creatures we are and the world in which we live. For this account of value see H. Richard Niebuhr, "The Center of Value" in *Radical Monotheism and Western Culture* (New York: Harper & Row, 1961). Also see William Schweiker, "One World, Many Moralities: A Diagnosis of Our Moral Situation," *Criterion* 32, 2 (Spring 1993): 12–21.

17. By power I mean the capacity to respond to, influence, and shape reality. Power is not simply the capacity to control, coerce, or dominate persons or things. Power is, furthermore, not a thing. Rather, power, from the Latin *potere*, is to be able. It is that which enables things—like persons, moral values, the world—to come to be and to continue to exist in complexes of interaction. Power can take various forms, social and natural; it can be exercised legitimately or not, coercively or not. Access to power is access to the capacity to bring about states-of-affairs or outcomes. Freedom is the form of power crucial to the moral life, since freedom simply is the capacity to respond to, influence, and also shape reality. On this see Joseph Allen, "Power and Political Community" in *Annual of the Society of Christian Ethics* (Washington, D.C.: Georgetown University Press, 1993), 3–22.

agents who exercise the capacity to act for certain ends and also suffer the actions of others upon them. The connection of power and value is deep and cannot be eradicated from the human heart. It is the engine of human love, creativity and conflict, and also, I believe, what religions are about. Persons seek contact with value creating power in love, imagination, and action. This fact is basic to understanding realistically human existence.

What Murdoch has contributed to this inquiry is a careful analysis of the place of vision and perception in moral life. She has tried to show that our power, our love and freedom, is constrained and directed by our perception of reality. But her argument, I hope to show now, while indeed necessary is not finally sufficient for ethics. The problem centers on how the Good symbolizes the real. In order to show this, I want to move through the levels of reflection we traced in Murdoch's thought, that is, a conception of the first principle of ethics, justifying it with respect to ordinary experience, and, finally, how we picture the fundamental mode of moral being without a lapse into will or consciousness as value-conferring.

If my argument to this point has been at all persuasive, then the first principle of ethics must specify the relation of power and value in such a way that power is rendered subservient to the value of existing beings, beings like human individuals. An act of power is then not value-conferring; power has value when it respects and enhances finite existence. An ethics of the Good, as Murdoch presents it, finally does not have the conceptual resources to make this argument. This is so because of the symbolism of the Good itself. What do I mean? Murdoch insists that the Good is that in which the "light of truth is seen; it reveals the world, hitherto invisible, and is also a source of life."[18] But it is absolutely important to note that as the source of life the Good does not bind its power to finite, created life. The Good does not recognize or respond to what is other than itself. In other words, the Good does not symbolize the transformation of value creating power so that power respects and enhances finite life. And this is why, I believe, it is difficult for Murdoch to specify the ground for the value of the indi-

---

18. Iris Murdoch, *The Fire and the Sun* (Oxford: Clarendon Press, 1977), 4.

vidual. In grasping this point we have isolated the inner limits of the Good as a symbol of the real.

The transformation of power is central to the idea of God. That is, God is ultimate value creating power, a power which binds itself to the actual worth of finite existence. Clearly, this account of the divine is not the God of the philosophers, Murdoch's "single perfect real object of attention." That definition, as we have seen, is already loaded with an idea of perfection geared toward the Good. Yet I also do not mean the idea of God in much popular piety with its all too anthropomorphic conception of deity. The point in saying God is personal, in my judgment, is to make a claim about the irreducibility of creativity in our conception of life; it is not to designate a literal person. The deity in Christian faith is believed to be the unconditioned value creating power; the being of being itself. Yet because faith in God is articulated through a complex set of concepts and symbols, such as creation, the human as the *imago dei*, the priority of justice and mercy in the moral life, power qua power does not and cannot define the good. The word God symbolizes the connection of power and value in the divine reality so that power is in principle rendered subservient to what respects and enhances the integrity of non-divine existence.[19] But this means that power cannot be the first principle of ethics; power oriented towards respecting and enhancing existence is that principle. The word God enables us to grasp this insight.

This brings us to the second step in the argument. How are we to show within ethics that this is what theological discourse symbolizes? We can answer this question in the first instance with respect to ways of life which explicitly understand human existence in relation to the divine. If one looks at Christian and Jewish faith one finds that they are about a value creating power which in the act of identifying itself binds power to respecting and enhancing, even redeeming, finite existence, and, what is more, only that reality is the unconditioned, the absolute. The insight designated by the word God radiates throughout the whole of Christian faith

19. This is why sin or moral fault for this tradition is not simply a matter of ignorance or error, but the attempt by persons to usurp the divine as the unconditioned value creating power. Sin manifests itself in forms of exploitation and injustice.

and discourse. Take any concept or particular belief and it will lead back to this insight. This is found in ideas of covenant, redemption, creation, and the final reign of God. In Christianity this comes to focus on Christ, the individual in whose life power is made perfect.

Claims about God designate then a valuation of power, of the divine reality which enables things—like persons, moral values, the world—to come to be and to continue to exist in complexes of interaction and thus the very source of value. This is why God is irreducible and primary in understanding the world and human life. A theological ethics articulates the meaning and truth of the sovereignty of God's goodness, that is, the authority of value creating power to constitute our sense of what is unconditionally good. To direct one's attention toward God has the effect of transforming self-consciousness, one's construal of the world, and one's assessment of other persons. This is the claim, I take it, of Christian and Jewish faith. It is the center of these particular ways of human life.

Theological ethics must also show that this claim about God and how it symbolizes the first principle of ethics is true not only of Christian morality. Does the reality symbolized by the word God, the divine reality which is objective to the self, in fact resonate within the self, to the depths of self-being? In order to answer this question we must grasp the moral meaning of a seemingly obscure theological point. Theologians have long insisted that God's work, the divine act of power or will, enacts the divine nature. And yet the act of divine power, especially in creation and redemption, reconstitutes the identity of the divine—God is known as creator and redeemer. God's goodness, then, is the exercise of power which creates value but also reconstitutes the divine identity by binding its power to the worth of finite reality. This is why, in the biblical texts, the divine name is given within convenantal relations.

Morally speaking, this means that any exercise of power is always a response to something real, but the act of power also reconstitutes the identity of the agent. And this is why theistic discourse resonates in the self. In every creative act of one-making we too bind power of mind and will to the existence and continuation of a meaningful world and in doing so shape our own identities. In all actions and relations, we affirm or deny, implicitly at least, that power is always oriented beyond itself to what is real and meaningful. The problem, of course, is that the domain of the real and the meaningful, the world, can be limited to the ego. What then?

By interpreting human existence theologically one seeks to reconstitute the relation of power and value at the depths of human life. The power to act, the one-making power of human consciousness, and the power of human love and creativity are all transformed symbolically when God is the object of attention. This is because God symbolizes the real in terms other than the brute exercise of power. Moral progress or perfection can only begin with a transformation of the heart of human existence, with our longing for some contact with a value creating power in our attempt to render our lives and our world meaningful and intelligible. This is why Christians speak of sanctification as basic to the moral life. Without this transformation, value is collapsed back into power, the world into the ego, and the purpose of life is to serve whomever or whatever seems to possess power. Idolatry is always a form of slavery.

The point I am making is that insofar as we are agents, we seek a meaningful and intelligible world through the exercise of power. Given this, one needs in ethics an idea or symbol which designates the transformation of power with respect to the value of existence. This is to insure the worth of individuals and the world on grounds other than the exercise of human power and also to provide the symbolic means to transform moral understanding and thereby reorient human freedom. That idea or symbol is "God" and how it symbolizes the real. And all of this is missed if we assume that the Good is what God symbolizes.

Thus far in response to Murdoch, I have tried to show that the Good is not all that God symbolizes, that there are important differences in how God and Good symbolize the real, and that we can make sense of theistic discourse in terms of actual religious communities and human experience itself, especially our experience of being agents. The final step in my argument is to clarify what resonates in the self with respect to these claims about God. Murdoch, as we have seen, correlates Good and consciousness, the one-making act of mind with respect to our perceptions of grades of value. Is there anything analogous to that argument in the theological ethical position I have been presenting? There is and yet we can only designate it by reclaiming a concept missing in Murdoch's thought and much contemporary ethics. But we must also rethink this concept, the idea of conscience, beyond its interpretation in existentialism and also social psychology. Making this point about conscience will complete my argument for the sovereignty of God's goodness, since we will see how God is sovereign over the self and our drive for omnipotence.

In terms of traditional Christian morality, in virtue of being created, human beings know the moral law. Conscience is the witness to this law. In terminology I have been using, the core of consciousness, the one-making power of mind with respect to its evaluative capacity, is conscience which testifies that power is ultimately in service of finite existence. Conscience is not a faculty of mind; it designates our mode of being in the world as moral agents responding to the value of others. If we consider our experience as agents, we are grasped not only by our perception of better and worse. In our actions and relations, we are also grasped by the sense that some things simply ought to be and that what exists ought not to be wantonly demeaned or destroyed. The profound experience that some finite reality—a person, a child, a blazing sunset over a northern lake—ought to be and also ought not be demeaned or destroyed is a testimony to, an affirmation of, power's final, ultimate subservience to existence. This is an experience of the moral sense of creation, an awareness of the moral law; it is the witness of conscience.

Thus, conscience is not, as existentialist thinkers argued, the call of the human to itself, authentic existence to the inauthentic self. That is a purely internalist position, one which any realistic ethics rejects. Similarly, conscience is not only a name for the ways in which persons' moral convictions and identities have been formed by their communities. Rather, by conscience I mean the shape of our existence as responsive to the non-instrumental value of others. Conscience recognizes rather than confers value; it is the grasp of the other on the self and thus the grounds of our sociality itself. Conscience is the theological analogue to what Murdoch means by attention.

Once it is understood that experience testifies that power is ultimately in the service of existence, we find in the heart of human life, in conscience, a fundamental affirmation of the being of God. We can choose to conform our lives to this reality or to deny it. What has happened in our time—maybe all times—is not only a loss of a vision of the real. It is that conscience is blunted, deformed through social and ideological means, such that the claim of finite life to be respected and enhanced does not resonate within the self in its exercise of power. And this is a failure to grasp what is primary and irreducible as the source of intelligibility of our lives as agents. Given this, the moral life is in good measure about coming to know the reality witnessed to by conscience and living in conformity to it. As St. Paul puts it in Romans 12:2: "Do not be conformed to this world but be transformed by the renewal of your mind that you may prove what is the will of God, what is good and acceptable and perfect."[20] Through this transformation of conscience all things are valued in relation to God. The uniqueness of human persons, our irreducible moral worth, is that as created beings we do and may and must know what God symbolizes. Value is conferred in that we are created beings even as we are endowed with the capacity to respond to value other than the self, and, in doing so, transform and direct the exercise of power.[21]

V. Conclusion

I have been arguing that because we are beings who exercise power, make evaluations about how to live, and seek a meaningful existence, we need what the word God symbolizes if we are to articulate the first principle of ethics. Theological ethics symbolizes the real in such a way as to formulate that principle as the proper relation of value and power. I have tried to show this conceptually, in terms of our actual experience, and also with respect to how we are to picture the human. I have argued that God is the best

20. For a helpful discussion of this point see Hans Dieter Betz, "Christianity as Religion: Paul's Attempt at Definition in Romans," *Journal of Religion* 71, 3 (1991): 315–44.
21. For a fuller treatment of these issues see William Schweiker, *Responsibility and Christian Ethics* (Cambridge: Cambridge University Press, 1995).

symbolization of the real in ethics; conscience is the best picture of what it means to exist as a moral creature, the fundamental mode of moral being.

In making this argument, I have drawn insights from Iris Murdoch's thought. Like her, I have centered on the problem of how we understand the status of value other than the self and thus the depth of morality. Yet if I am right, we cannot rightly understand our contemporary situation or Murdoch's moral philosophy without attending to the relation between power and value. The fact that she does not address these matters is not an oversight. The centrality of the Good in her thought effaces the depth of this problem about power and value. The current situation is much more dangerous than Murdoch supposes; a correction of vision will not easily sever the equation of value with power. There are, in other words, limits to how the Good symbolizes the real.

Theological ethics has a complex set of concepts and symbols which addresses this problem and it does so through the very organizing center of faith, that is, the divine. By speaking of God's goodness, one can formulate the first principle of ethics in terms of the relation of power and value. This provides us a perspective from which to diagnose, criticize, and hopefully transform our situation. Thus, a theological perspective on the moral life isolates and answers problems in other moral positions. This is so, because it faithfully articulates the very structure of moral experience.

Iris Murdoch has helped us see that we are in search of an ethic capable of considering the ways in which religious matters permeate human existence in terms of the experience of the unconditioned claim of morality on our lives. In response to that search, Murdoch has proposed a theology without God. By engaging her work, I have sought in this paper to show what we need is an articulate, critical theological ethics fully engaged with the deepest problems of our age. This is because an ethics committed to the worth of persons is possible only given some moral sense of creation which resonates in the core of human life. And it is in this way, I judge, that God's goodness is sovereign over all other concepts, a sovereignty to which our existence as agents testifies.

Appendix
METAPHYSICS AND ETHICS

Iris Murdoch

What should a philosophical study of morals be like? This is a question concerning which there is a certain amount of doubt among modern philosophers. When I speak about modern philosophers and modern philosophy I shall be meaning that present-day version of our traditional empiricism which is known as linguistic analysis—and although a lot of what I have to say will be critical of recent developments in that tradition, the criticisms which I make will also come, I believe, out of the tradition. To understand current moral philosophy it is necessary to understand its history. And here it is convenient to begin from the moment when G. E. Moore made a certain distinction. Moore said we should distinguish between the question, what things are good? and the question, what does the word 'good' mean? On this second question Moore had important things to say. He claimed that 'good' was indefinable, and that previous moral philosophers, because they had failed to distinguish those two questions from each other, had fallen into the error of defining 'good', or 'valuable', in terms of some other non-valuable entity, whether a natural entity, such as pleasure, or a metaphysical entity, such as rationality. If asked, what *things* are good, one might indeed answer this question by pointing to pleasure or to rationality—but one could not answer the question what is *good itself* in this way. Moore convinced his readers of this very simply by pointing out that it made *sense* al-

---

Reprinted from *The Nature of Metaphysics*, ed. D. F. Pears (Macmillan, 1957), by permission of Macmillan Press, Ltd.

ways, given any proposition of the form 'X is good', to withdraw thoughtfully and ask—'But is X really good?' That is, the notion of 'good' could significantly be attached to or withdrawn from anything whatever, and the things to which it happened to be attached did not form part of its meaning.

This simple argument of Moore's produced a complete change of perspective in moral philosophy. It transformed the central question of ethics from the question, 'What is goodness?'—where an answer was expected in terms of the revelation of some real and eternally present structure of the universe—into the question—'What is the activity of "valuing" (or "commending")?', where what is required is to see what is in common to people of all ages and societies when they attach value to something. This phrase 'attach value' is itself significant of the change of attitude. The philosopher is now to speak no longer of the Good, as something real or transcendent, but to analyse the familiar human activity of endowing things with value. If we want to place the definitive breach with metaphysical ethics at any point, we can place it here.

Moore himself, however, was not wholly of the modern time in that although he pointed out that 'good' was not the second name of any other natural or metaphysical property, he could not rid himself of the conviction that it was nevertheless the name of *a* property, the unanalysable non-natural property of goodness, which inhered in certain actual states of affairs—so that although any proposition of the form 'X is good' could *make sense*, such a proposition would only be *true* if X really possessed the property of goodness.

Philosophers after Moore retained Moore's distinction of the two questions, and Moore's linguistic approach. They took it that the central question of ethics was the question 'What does "good" mean?'—but they refrained from answering the question 'What things are good?' and made it clear that this was a matter for the moralist, and not for the philosopher. Concerning the meaning of 'good', things then moved fast. What is known as the verficationist view of meaning, entering philosophy from the side of natural science, made a violent impact upon ethics. If the meaning of a proposition is the method of its verification, and if verification has to be in terms of observation of sensible events, then clearly ethical propositions could not have meaning in this way—and it was no use appealing to a mysterious property, not open to ordinary observation, to give them significance. Moore's non-natural property disappeared, in this more sceptical atmosphere, together with many other would-be metaphysical entities. Ethical propositions were clearly and firmly separated from other types of propositions and have remained so ever since. They were not, it was claimed, true or false, they did not state facts: they did not state *natural* facts, for the reason that Moore had given, and they did not state *metaphysical* facts, for the same reason, and also because there were none to state. It was then said that ethical propositions expressed emotion. They did not have *descriptive*, or factual, meaning, they had *emotive* meaning.

The emotive theory of ethics was not created as the result of a patient scrutiny of ethical propositions. It arose largely as the by-product of a theory of meaning whose most proper application was in other fields. The emotive theory was overthrown partly by a return to common sense; it was felt that, surely, ethical statements must somehow be regarded as rational, defensible by argument and by reference to fact. Partly, the theory disappeared as a result of two other philosophical developments: first, the notion that meaning should be analysed not in terms of method of verification, but in terms of *use*, and second, what might roughly be summed up as 'the disappearance of the mind'.

The notion that the meaning of a word is its use—a notion which in other fields we may associate with the name of Wittgenstein—did, I think, arise independently in the field of ethics, as a development and refinement of the emotive theory. Ethical statements were now said, not to express emotion, but to evoke emotion and more generally to persuade.

This is the view which we find most fully explained by Stevenson in his book *Ethics and Language*. Hard upon this development, however, and associated with the same change in our conception of meaning, there followed the revolution in our attitude to psychological concepts. When we speak of 'the mind', it was now maintained, we are not speaking of a set of inner entities such as faculties and feelings, which are open to introspection, we are speaking of observable actions and patterns of behaviour. We learn and we apply mental concept words on the basis of what we can openly observe. This new view, which was made widely known by Professor Ryle's book *The Concept of the Mind*, had consequences for moral philosophy. Previously a moral statement had been said to express an *attitude*, where this was conceived of in terms of the speaker's feelings, and, possibly his wish to influence the hearer's feelings. Now, if a moral statement was said to express an attitude, this was to be analysed rather in terms of the speaker's conduct, and his intent to influence the hearer's conduct. Moral statements had been treated first as exclamations and then as persuasions—now they were called imperatives or prescriptions or rules.

To adopt this analysis had the technical advantage of allowing the philosopher to express the essence of morality in a purely logical manner, without reference to either metaphysical or psychological entities, and in such a way that the old dilemma about whether moral remarks were subjective or objective was completely resolved. If a moral remark is not really a statement but a rule, then it cannot be subjective or objective, or true or false either. In this way two objections were met which had been made to Moore's ethics: it was now shown in the analysis that moral judgments were essentially practical (answers to the question 'What shall I do?') and not in any way factual. Whereas Moore had treated moral remarks as expressions of moral insight, not as instances of moral advice, and he had clung to the idea that they were still in some sense factual. The new analysis corrected both these points. There remained the question, concerning which Moore's view had also been far from satisfactory, of the *rationality* of ethical judgments. This was met by a further refinement of technique. The distinction between 'descriptive' meaning (meaning *via* reference to fact) and 'evaluative' meaning, as it was now called, which had previously been only a distinction made between types of proposition, was now pressed into the structure of individual moral words. The meaning of the word 'good', for instance, was to be divided into an evaluative and a descriptive part. The descriptive part would consist of reference to the facts in virtue of which the speaker called something valuable—and the evaluative part would consist of the prescription—'choose this one'. In this way the analysis could allow that a moral judgment might be discussed and defended by stating of facts—without itself becoming a factual statement.

Thus in a complex way, and by the successive correction of a series of theories, we have reached our present position—and the discussion goes on. This present position has, I think, been most clearly expounded in Mr. R. M. Hare's book *The Language of Morals*, and may be summed up as follows. A man's morality is seen in his conduct and a moral statement is a prescription or rule uttered to guide a choice, and the descriptive meaning of the moral word which it contains is made specific by reference to factual criteria of application. That is, in a moral statement we quasi-command that a particular thing be done, and are ready to say in virtue of what facts it ought to be done. We are also ready, if our moral statement is sincere, to do it ourselves in the appropriate circumstances. I think it is fair to take Mr. Hare's book as expressing the current position, although his book is under attack in many quarters. Most of these attacks, in my view, are upon the details of Mr. Hare's analysis and not upon its deep assumptions. What these assumptions are I shall discuss shortly.

Now this piece of our philosophical history might be described as the elimination of metaphysics from ethics. We are certainly now presented with a stripped and empty scene. Morality is not explained in terms of metaphysical concepts such as the rational will, nor in terms of psychological concepts such as moral feelings. It is not pictured by the philosopher, nor defended by philosophical arguments, as being attached to any real natural or metaphysical structure. It is pictured without any transcendent background. It is presented simply in terms of exhortations and choices defended by reference to facts. Now what has happened here exactly, and what have we been let in for? Let us look more closely.

The present view emerges from a very finely knit complex of mutual supporting arguments. To unravel this complex a bit, I suggest that we distinguish three types of argument on which this view may be said to rest. These are: *first*, a general critical argument to the effect that there are no metaphysical entities, *second*, a special critical argument, to the effect that even if there were, we could not base an analysis of morality upon them since it is impossible

Appendix: Metaphysics and Ethics

to argue from *is* to *ought*, from facts to values. *Third*, there are arguments, involving an appeal to our experience of morality, which support the various details of the analysis—the notion of guiding a choice, arguing, referring to facts, judging a man by his conduct, and so on.

About the first argument, which I shall call 'the anti-metaphysical argument', I shall be very brief. The criticism of metaphysics, which was always a part of our own tradition, and which was made systematic by Kant, is an established aspect of modern philosophy and has unavoidable implications for ethics. This is not to say, of course, that great moral conceptions such as 'the rational will' are senseless or useless, but simply that they cannot be established by certain familiar types of philosophical argument. This is a point I shall return to later. I go on now to argument number two.

This argument, which I shall call 'the anti-naturalistic argument', to the effect that we cannot derive values from facts is the most important argument in modern moral philosophy—indeed it is almost the whole of modern moral philosophy. Now this argument, as it has appeared in recent years, has a certain complexity about it. It is sometimes presented as if it were the exposure of a logical fallacy. When Moore called argument from 'is' to 'ought' 'the Naturalistic Fallacy' he implied just this—and in Mr. Hare's book the central argument, which is this same argument, is expressed in logical terms. To reach an imperative conclusion we need at least one imperative premise. We may also be encouraged to think of the argument in this way because of its original very striking formulation by Hume—and because Moore's formulation of it, which has so much caught our imagination, was made *à propos* of an obviously fallacious argument by John Stuart Mill: that is, Mill's argument that what in fact is desired is *ipso facto* what ought to be desired.

Now if the anti-naturalistic argument is designed merely to point out that a statement of value cannot be derived directly, and with no further help, from an ordinary statement of fact, then perhaps it may be called the exposure of a logical fallacy. But the trouble is that arguments of the crudity of Mill's argument are fairly rare in moral philosophy. If we want *pure* examples of this type of argument we are more likely to find them in the work of psychologists and sociologists than in the work of moral philosophers. What the great moral philosophers, in the past, have usually been doing is something much more complicated. They present a total metaphysical picture of which ethics forms a part. The universe, including our own nature, is like *this*, they say. Now this picture may be attacked by argument number one—that is straight philosophical criticism designed to show that the philosopher in question is not able to establish, by the argument he uses, the structure that he describes. But it is not so clear (although Moore, for instance, seems to have thought that it was) that such a picture of the place of morality can always be attacked by the second argument, the anti-naturalistic argument. Now it may be said—but surely the anti-metaphysical argument settles the matter. If we cannot establish transcendent metaphysical structures by philosophical argument then such structures cannot be the basis of ethics. But this is not so clear. What the moral philosopher professes to do nowadays is to analyse the essence of *any* morality, to display the logic of *any* moral language. But what place the concept of the transcendent may have in the structure of a morality is something which is *not* entirely settled by either the anti-metaphysical argument, or by the anti-naturalistic argument in its purely logical form. This narrow form of the anti-naturalistic argument I shall call 'the logical argument'. These arguments only prove that we cannot picture morality as issuing directly from a *philosophically established* transcendent background, or from a factual background. But this is not yet to say that the notion of *belief* in the transcendent can have no place in a philosophical account of morality.

Why has it been so readily assumed that the stripped and behaviouristic account of morality which the modern philosopher gives is imposed on us by philosophical considerations? I think this is because the anti-metaphysical argument and the logical argument have been very closely connected in the minds of those who used them with a much more general and ambiguous dictum to this effect: you cannot attach morality to the substance of the world. And this dictum, which expresses the whole spirit of modern ethics, has been accorded a sort of logical dignity. But, why can morality not be thought of as attached to the substance of the world? Surely many people who are not philosophers, and who cannot be accused of using faulty arguments since they use no arguments, do think of their morality in just this way? They think of it as continuous with some sort of larger structure of reality, whether this be a religious structure, or a social or historical one.

Now I suggest there is another type of answer to the question, why not attach morality to the substance of the world?—and that is a moral answer. If you do this you are in danger of making your morality into a dogma, you are in danger of becoming intolerant of the values of others, and of ceasing to reflect on your own values through taking them too much for granted. In short, if you start to think of morality as part of a general way of conceiving the universe, as part of a larger conceptual framework, you may cease to be reflective and responsible about it, you may begin to regard it as a sort of fact. And as soon as you regard your moral system as a sort of fact, and not as a set of values which only exist through your own choices, your moral conduct will degenerate. This fear of moral degeneration through lack of reflexion is to be found in many modern writers on ethics, notably in the work of Mr. Hare, whose book I have already mentioned. It is also to be found, more positively asserted, in many existentialist writers—and it may be found, at what I take to be one of its sources, in that great pamphlet of Liberalism, Mill's *Essay on Liberty.*

Now *this* sort of objection to picturing morality as part of a systematic understanding of the world is of a quite different type from the other objections. This is not a logical or philosophical objection, it is a straight moral objection to the effect that certain bad results follow in practice from thinking about morality in a certain way. We may agree with this. But to say it is of course *not* to say that morality cannot under any circumstances be part of a general system of belief about how the world is, or about transcendent entities. It is *not* to say that anything which involves such beliefs is not a morality—it is merely to maintain that the holding of such beliefs is morally and socially dangerous.

I am suggesting that modern philosophers have tended to take their stripped, behaviouristic and non-conceptual picture of morality as the only possible picture because they have joined the anti-metaphysical argument and the logical argument to a *moral* argument of a different type—a moral argument which properly belongs in the propaganda of liberalism. Why has this happened? I think it is not difficult to see if we consider the amount of support which what I have briefly called the behaviourstic view of morals can gain from a study of the actual morality of our own society. Of the three arguments which support the current view of morals, I have so far discussed the anti-metaphysical argument—and the anti-naturalistic argument, which I suggested should be divided into (*a*) a rather narrow logical argument, and (*b*) a much more general moral argument. I come now to the third argument, or group of arguments, the appeal to our general conception of what morality is like.

Now clearly, if this appeal is made with the morals of our own liberal society in mind, there is a great deal in the behaviouristic picture of morals which receives immediate confirmation. We, in our society, believe in judging a man's principles by his conduct, in reflecting upon our own values and respecting the values of others, in backing up our recommendations by reference to facts, in breaking down intuitive conclusions by argument, and so on. Our morality is, on the whole, conceptually simple. We approach the world armed with certain general values which we hold *simpliciter* and without the assistance of metaphysics or dogmatic theology—respect for freedom, for truth, and so on. We study the facts, and we make our choices in the light of the facts and our values. Our disagreements among ourselves concern the application of principles—our disagreements with other societies concern what principles to hold. There are, of course, persons and groups among us whose morality is *not* conceptually simple, but metaphysical and dogmatic (for instance, some Christians and all Communists)—but these people are in the minority. It is therefore the case that the logical formula presented by the modern moral philosopher is on the whole a satisfactory representation of the morality most commonly held in England. The simplest moral words ('good' and 'right') are selected for analysis, their meaning is divided into a descriptive and evaluative part, the descriptive part representing the factual criteria, the evaluative part representing a recommendation. And once the largely empirical disagreements about application of principles and classification of cases have been cleared up, ultimate moral differences will show as differences of choice and recommendation in a common world of facts. What the modern moral philosopher has done is what metaphysicians in the past have always done. He has produced a model. Only it is not a model of any morality whatsoever. It is a model of his own morality.

I want now to proceed with my discussion and to attempt to say more exactly what I think the philosopher's attitude ought to be towards what I have rather vaguely called conceptual or metaphysical frameworks within which morality may be placed. In order to do this I want to distinguish three different questions. These three questions are: *One*, Is morality to be seen essentially and by its nature centred on the individual, or as part of a general framework of reality which includes the individual? *Two*, What kinds of arguments could establish the existence of such a general framework? and *Three*, What should the method of the moral philosopher now be like? I shall consider them in order.

First—Is morality to be seen as essentially centred on the individual? Now our tradition of thought tends to take it for granted that morality must be self-contained; and we can also invoke here the patronage of Kant, who says that the moral will is autonomous, and that morality cannot be founded on anything but itself. But equally, if we can come out of the trees and see the wood for a moment, it is clear that this is only one type of view of morality—roughly a Protestant; and less roughly a Liberal, type of view. Kant himself is the source not only of this Liberal morality, but also of a modern version of its opposite, which I shall call, with an old name, Natural Law morality, and about which I shall have more to say in a moment.

If we consider our own assumptions here we may discover many ways in which our empiricist tradition goes with the view of the moral will as something essentially separate and autonomous. None of our philosophers, apart from the idealists, has presented any elaborately metaphysical view of ethics. This is not surprising. Ethics and epistemology are always very closely related, and if we want to understand our ethics we must look at our epistemology. I think the most important person here is Hume. It is from him more than anyone else that we have derived a philosophical tendency, which is still with us, to see the world in terms of contingently conjoined simples, to see it as a totality of ultimate simple facts which have no necessary connection with each other. In so far as we imagine that the world does contain necessities, and that real connections exist between these simple elements, this is merely the result of habit and custom, which are themselves the work of Nature. It is only in reflective moments that we can see the ultimately disjoined character of the world. It is habit which gives to us, according to Hume, both our objective material world, and our moral world. Moral attitudes are habits of sentiment built up in society, and they do not need, and cannot have, any greater sanction. Since Hume was conservative in morals and politics he had no objection to morality continuing to be a matter of habit. But since he was also the empiricist that he was, he presents this habit as covering up the world of disconnected facts that lies behind it. *This* is what reflection would discover, to the moral consciousness as to the scientific consciousness.

With this the stage is set for the history of ethics in this country. We oscillate between habit and reflection—the conservative side stressing habit, the progressive side stressing reflection. But notice still how much there is in common. Reflection is not metaphysical speculation, it is return to the facts. Burke, who was a great defender of tradition as a basis of morals, did not argue from a systematic or metaphysical background; indeed a rejection of the system was a part of his outlook. Tradition and custom were to be taken as facts, as present realities, which were to be respected as such. Our traditionalists have not been metaphysicians, and neither have our progressives. The ideals which have inspired our society have been utilitarian ideals. And the utilitarians, when they wished to break down habit and custom by reflection, did not refer us to any metaphysical structure, but referred us to certain simple values and, above all, back again to the facts. The oscillation between habit and reflection may be seen today in moral philosophy itself in the contrast between, for instance, Professor Ryle and Professor Oakeshott on the one hand, both of whom hold that morality is and ought only to be a matter of habit, and Mr. Weldon and Mr. Hare on the other, who hold that morality is a matter of studying the facts and then making a reflective choice.

So, I suggest that in answering the question concerning

whether morality is to be centred on the individual, we have been influenced partly by our own moral outlook and partly by our philosophical empiricism into assuming that it is of the *essence* of morality to be centred in this way. Nothing, we tend to assume, can *contain* the individual, except possibly his habits and his tradition, and these are merely facts like other ones, and capable of being reflectively examined. But this is only one way, roughly a Protestant, liberal, empiricist, way, of conceiving morality. What I have called Natural Law moralists—Thomists, Hegelians, Marxists— and less reflective persons who are camp followers of these doctrines, see the matter in a quite different perspective. The individual is seen as held in a framework which transcends him, where what is important and valuable is the framework, and the individual only has importance, or even reality, in so far as he belongs to the framework.

We may notice here some points of contrast between the Natural Law view and the Liberal view. On the Liberal view we picture the individual as able to attain by reflection to complete consciousness of his situation. He is entirely free to choose and responsible for his choice. His morality is exhibited in his choice, whereby he shows which things he regards as valuable. The most systematic exposition of modern liberal morality is existentialism. Contrast the Natural Law picture. Here the individual is seen as moving tentatively *vis-à-vis* a reality which transcends him. To discover what is morally good is to discover that reality, and to become good is to integrate himself with it. He is ruled by laws which he can only partly understand. He is not fully conscious of what he is. His freedom is not an open freedom of choice in a clear situation; it lies rather in an increasing knowledge of his own real being, and in the conduct which naturally springs from such knowledge.

I would emphasize here that the contrast which I am remarking is not just a contrast between two philosophies; it is a contrast between two types of moral outlook. And here it should be added that of course not everyone in our society holds the liberal view in a pure form. Indeed the man in the street, and this goes for most ordinary non-philosophical Christians, is often a sort of non-metaphysical objectivist. That is, he believes that moral values are real and fixed—that is why he is so scandalized by the emotivists and the existentialists—but he has no clear view of nature or of history which is to explain the fixing of the values—and in this respect of course he differs, for instance, from the Marxist.

The logical picture of morality, which our modern philosophy has presented us with, shows no awareness of the importance of the contrast of which I have been speaking. We have been led to adopt a method of describing morality in terms of which all moral agents are seen as inhabiting the same world of facts, and where we are unable to discriminate between different types of morality, except in terms of differences of act and choice. Whereas, I am arguing, it is possible for differences to exist also as total differences of moral vision and perspective. From the Liberal point of view it seems axiomatic that however grandiose the structure may be in terms of which a morality extends itself, the moral agent is responsible for endowing this totality with value. The Liberal concentrates his attention on the *point of discontinuity* between the chosen framework and the choosing agent—and it is this moment of discontinuity which the modern philosopher has tried to catch in a formula. But for the individual, whether he be a Marxist or a Christian, who takes up a Natural Law point of view the scene looks completely different. Here there is no axiom of discontinuity. The individual's choice is less important, and the interest may lie in adoration of the framework rather than in the details of conduct. And here if the Liberal philosopher just goes on insisting that the moral agent is totally free by definition and is responsible for endowing the framework with value, and that 'ought' cannot be derived from 'is', this merely results in a colossally important difference of outlook being left unanalysed.

I now pass on to the second question, what kind of argument can establish whether or not there exists a transcendent non-empirical framework within which morality is to find its place. Here I shall be brief. It seems fairly clear that much of the criticism of traditional metaphysics, which modern philosophy has made its task, must stand. In addition there is the task of criticizing types of modern quasi-philosophy or semi-scientific metaphysics which seek to present the human mind as enclosed within social, historical, or psychological frames. I have in mind a great variety of views deriving from a study of Marx, Freud, the behav-

Appendix: Metaphysics and Ethics 249

iour of calculating machines, and so on. It is in the criticism of such views that the logical argument (you can't derive 'ought' from 'is') is most often properly in place. The task of philosophy here may be said to be the definition and re-definition of human freedom *vis-à-vis* the various forces which, it is argued by arguments which are often more philosophical than empirical, may be said to threaten it. A recent example in this kind of defensive negative criticisms is Mr. Isaiah Berlin's lecture *Historical Inevitability*, in which, in accents which remind us of Kierkegaard's attacks on Hegel, he argues that the individual cannot be shown to be enclosed by any framework of inevitable laws. This definition of freedom, which it is so important for philosophy to concern itself with, is achieved partly by such negative criticism. Is it also to be achieved by more positive means? This leads me to the last and most difficult question.

It is not at all clear, to me at any rate, what sort of philosophical method should now be used in the study of morals and politics. It has been assumed by moral philosophers that they have to be descriptive analysts as well as critics, that is, that they are to produce some sort of positive philosophical characterization of morality; and it seems that this is a reasonable requirement. But how is it to be done? I think that the implications for ethics of doing philosophy by the linguistic method have not yet become entirely clear. Words are tricky things and must be handled with care. We must not be too impressed by them—on the other hand, we must take them seriously enough. I think philosophers were too impressed by words when they assumed that all that was needed to effect the change-over in ethics from the old to the new régime was to put the word 'good' in inverted commas. The analysis of this concept has been made the centre of modern ethics. This has been done partly under the influence of former metaphysical theories of ethics, and partly as a result of the concentration on act and choice, rather than descriptive or speculative discussion, as being the essence of morality. It has been assumed that moral argument always takes the form of pointing to facts, rather than the form of analysing or explaining concepts. On the current view, freedom is conceived as freedom of overt choice, and there is a corresponding lack of interest in differences of belief. Moral language is taken as closely related to choice—that it recommends to action is its defining characteristic—and all this can then be offered as an analysis of the meaning of the word 'good'. 'This is good' equals 'choose this'. But our freedom is not just a freedom to choose and act differently, it is also a freedom to think and believe differently, to see the world differently, to see different configurations and describe them in different words. Moral differences can be differences of concept as well as differences of choice. A moral change shows in our vocabulary. How we see and describe the world is morals too—and the relation of this to our conduct may be complicated.

We were too impressed by words when we assumed that the word 'good' covered a single concept which was the centre of morality. We were not impressed enough when we neglected less general moral words such as 'true', 'brave', 'free', 'sincere', which are the bearers of very important ideas. The concept of 'goodness', for reasons which it would be interesting to investigate, is no longer a rich and problematic concept. Whereas the concept of 'truth', for instance, contains tangles and paradoxes the unravelling of which would show us really interesting features of the modern world. It is in terms of the inner complexity of such concepts that we may display really deep differences of moral vision.

It is, of course, always the philosopher's task to study the writings of philosophers of the past impartially, and compare and contrast them with ourselves. There has been of late something of a tendency to read back into the great metaphysicians our own logical formulae, and to treat them as if they were trying ineptly to do what we have done successfully. But the main task is the task on which moral philosophy is in fact engaged—the analysis of contemporary moral concepts, through moral language. I have suggested that this task has been too narrowly conceived. We have not considered the great *variety* of the concepts that make up a morality. Nor have moral philosophers made any satisfactory frontal attack on the question of how belief in the transcendent may modify the meaning of ethical statements. This question, so far as it has come up, has mainly arisen as a by-product of criticism of theological statements.

Would this sort of analysis, in its more extended form, be itself a kind of metaphysics? In a way obviously not. It does not involve the postulation of transcendent entities established by philosophical arguments; on the contrary, it is critical of all such arguments, and if it speaks of such entities they are considered as objects of faith or belief. Modern philosophy is profoundly anti-metaphysical in spirit. Its anti-metaphysical character may be summed up in the *caveat:* There may be no deep structure. This is the lesson of Wittgenstein—and one which, incidentally, has not yet been taken enough to heart by those who want to reduce morality to a single formula.

On the other hand, to analyse and describe our own morality and that of others may involve the making of models and pictures of what different kinds of men are like. Moral philosophers in the past differed concerning what they supposed themselves to be doing. Some (*e.g.* Plato) attempted to reveal a truth which was not accessible to all men. Others (*e.g.* Kant) tried to analyse the morality of any ordinary conscientious person. Philosophers who attempted the latter have usually found themselves bound to coin new concepts in making the attempt, and have not in the past been shy of doing so. And it is here that description moves imperceptibly into moralizing. An instance of a modern moral philosopher, not in our tradition, who coins new and persuasive concepts in the course of offering a description is Gabriel Marcel. Indeed all the existentialists do this. So, in a more sober way, did some of our own fairly recent philosophical ancestors—A. E. Taylor and Joseph, for instance. Even, in a way, Moore. But we have been shy of such extensive description and shy of coining concepts because we are anxious not to moralize, and because we think that ethics should study the logical structure of moral language and have the neutrality of logic. If I am right, this has merely had the result that philosophers have done their moralizing unconsciously instead of consciously.

Philosophers have usually tended to seek for universal formulae. But the linguistic method, if we take it seriously, is by its nature opposed to this search. Logic, whatever that may be determined to be, has its own universality; but when we leave the domain of the purely logical we come into the cloudy and shifting domain of the concepts which men live by—and these are subject to historical change. This is especially true of moral concepts.

Here we shall have done something if we can establish with tolerable clarity what these concepts *are*. We should, I think, resist the temptation to unify the picture by trying to establish, guided by our own conception of the ethical in general, what these concepts *must be*. All that is made clear by this method is: our own conception of the ethical in general—and in the process important differences of moral concept may be blurred or neglected. Can the moral philosopher, once he stops being critical and begins to be positive, establish anything at all in the nature of a universal truth? If by universal truth is meant something which has a sort of logical universality, then I think the answer is no. The current would-be logical analysis of moral judgments is certainly not such a truth. The difficulty is, and here we are after all not so very far from the philosophers of the past, that the subject of investigation is the nature of man—and we are studying this nature at a point of great conceptual sensibility. Man is a creature who makes pictures of himself and then comes to resemble the picture. This is the process which moral philosophy must attempt to describe and analyse.

I think it still remains for us to find a satisfactory method for the explanation of our own morality and that of others—but I think it would be a pity if, just because we realize that any picture is likely to be half a description and half a persuasion, we were to deny ourselves the freedom in the making of pictures and the coining of explanatory ideas which our predecessors have used in the past. After all, both as philosophers and as moral beings we are concerned with the same problems with which they were concerned: What is freedom? Can it be shown that men are free? What is the relation of morality to social realities? What is the relation of morality to what we believe concerning God and the hereafter? It is a merit of modern philosophers to be more conscious than their predecessors of what the philosopher's activity is. We can become more patient and historical in analysing other moralities and more daring and imaginative in exploring our own without losing the benefit of that greater consciousness.

Select Bibliography

The following bibliography is intended to be useful primarily to readers of Iris Murdoch's moral philosophy. For a comprehensive bibliography, see John Fletcher and Cheryl Bove, *Iris Murdoch: A Descriptive Primary and Annotated Secondary Bibliography* (New York: Garland Publishing, 1994).

I. Works by Iris Murdoch

A. Philosophy, Criticism, and Letters

Acastos: Two Platonic Dialogues. New York: Viking Penguin, 1986.

"Against Dryness: A Polemical Sketch." *Encounter* 16 (January 1961): 16–20.

"Art Is the Imitation of Nature." *Cahiers du Centre de Recherches sur les pays du Nord et du Nord-Ouest* 1 (1978): 5–18.

"The Darkness of Practical Reason." Review of *The Freedom of the Individual,* by Stuart Hampshire. *Encounter* 27 (July 1966): 46–50.

"T. S. Eliot as a Moralist." In *T. S. Eliot: A Symposium for His Seventieth Birthday,* edited by Neville Braybrooke, 152–60. London: Rupert Hart-David, 1958.

"Existentialist Bite." Review of *Literature Considered as Philosophy,* by Everett Knight. *Spectator* (12 July 1957): 68–69.

"The Existentialist Hero." *Listener,* 23 March 1950, 523–24.

"The Existentialist Political Myth." *Socratic* 5 (1952): 52–63.

"Existentialists and Mystics." In *Essays and Poems Presented to Lord David Cecil,* edited by W. W. Robson, 169–83. London: Constable, 1970.

The Fire and the Sun: Why Plato Banished the Artists. London: Oxford University Press, 1977.

"Freedom and Knowledge." Symposium with S. N. Hampshire, P. L. Gardiner, and D. F. Pears. In *Freedom and the Will,* edited by D. F. Pears, 80–104. New York: St. Martin's Press, 1963.

"Hegel in Modern Dress." Review of *Being and Nothingness*, by Jean-Paul Sartre. *New Statesman* 53 (25 May 1957): 675–76.

"A House of Theory." *Partisan Review* 26 (Winter 1959): 17–31.

"Important Things." Review of *The Mandarins*, by Simone de Beauvoir. In *Encore: The Sunday Times Book*, edited by Leonard Russell, 299–301. London: Michael Joseph, 1963.

"Knowing the Void." Review of *Notebooks*, by Simone Weil. *Spectator* (2 November 1956): 613–14.

"Let Them Philosophise." Review of *Confessions of an Inquiring Spirit*, by S. T. Coleridge. *Spectator* (14 December 1956): 873.

"Mass, Might, and Myth." Review of *Crowds and Power*, by Elias Canetti. *Spectator* 209 (7 September 1962): 337–38.

"Metaphysics and Ethics." In *The Nature of Metaphysics*, edited by D. F. Pears, 99–123. London: Macmillan, 1957.

Metaphysics as a Guide to Morals. Allen Lane/Penguin Press, 1993.

"Midnight Hour." *Adelphi* (January–March 1943): 60–61.

"The Moral Decision about Homosexuality." *Man and Society* 7 (Summer 1964): 3–6.

"Negative Capability." *Adam International Review* 284–86 (1960): 172–73.

"Nostalgia for the Particular." *Proceedings of the Aristotelian Society* 52 (9 June 1952): 243–60.

"The Novelist as Metaphysician." *Listener* 43 (16 March 1950): 473–76.

"Philosophy and Beliefs." Symposium with Stuart Hampshire, Isaiah Berlin, and Anthony Quinton. *Twentieth Century* (June 1955): 495–521.

"Political Morality." *Listener* 78 (21 September 1967): 353–54.

"Rebirth of Christianity." *Adelphi* (July–September 1943): 134–35.

"Salvation by Words." *New York Review of Books* 18 (15 June 1972): 3–8.

Sartre, Romantic Rationalist. London: Bowes & Bowes, 1961.

"Socialism and Selection." In *Black Paper 1975*, edited by C. B. Cox and Rhodes Boyson, 7–9. London: Dent, 1975.

The Sovereignty of Good. London: Routledge & Kegan Paul, 1970.

"The Sublime and the Beautiful Revisited." *Yale Review* 49 (December 1959): 247–71.

"The Sublime and the Good." *Chicago Review* 13 (Autumn 1959): 42–55.

"Thinking and Language." Symposium with A. C. Lloyd and Gilbert Ryle. *Proceedings of the Aristotelian Society Supplement* 25 (1951): 25–82.

Untitled review of *The Ethics of Ambiguity*, by Simone de Beauvoir. *Mind* 59 (April 1950): 127–28.

Untitled review of *The Emotions: Outline of a Theory*, by Jean-Paul Sartre. *Mind* 59 (April 1950): 268–71.

"Vision and Choice in Morality." *Proceedings of the Aristotelian Society Supplement* 30 (1956): 32–58.

"Worship and Common Life." *Adelphi* (July–September 1944): 134–35.

B. Novels

Under the Net. London, 1954.
The Flight from the Enchanter. London, 1956.
The Sandcastle. London, 1957.
The Bell. London, 1958.
A Severed Head. London, 1961.
An Unofficial Rose. London, 1962.
The Unicorn. London, 1963.
The Italian Girl. London, 1964.
The Red and the Green. London, 1965.
The Time of the Angels. London, 1966.
The Nice and the Good. London, 1968.
Bruno's Dream. London, 1969.
A Fairly Honourable Defeat. London, 1970.
An Accidental Man. London, 1971.
The Black Prince. London, 1973.
The Sacred and Profane Love Machine. London, 1974.
A Word Child. London, 1975.
Henry and Cato. London, 1976.
The Sea, the Sea. London, 1978.
Nuns and Soldiers. London, 1980.
The Philosopher's Pupil. London, 1983.
The Good Apprentice. London, 1985.
The Book and the Brotherhood. London, 1987.
The Message to the Planet. London, 1989.
The Green Knight. London, 1993.
Jackson's Dilemma. London, 1995.

II. CRITICAL COMMENTARY

A. Monographs

Baldanza, Frank. *Iris Murdoch.* New York: Twayne Publishers, 1974.

Bloom, Harold, ed. *Iris Murdoch. Modern Critical Views.* New York: Chelsea, 1986.

Bove, Cheryl. *Understanding Iris Murdoch.* Columbia, S.C.: University of South Carolina Press, 1993.

Byatt, Antonia Susan. *Degrees of Freedom: The Novels of Iris Murdoch.* London: Chatto & Windus, 1965.

———. *Iris Murdoch.* London: Longman, 1976.

Conradi, Peter J. *Iris Murdoch: The Saint and the Artist.* New York: St. Martin's Press, 1988.

Dipple, Elizabeth. *Iris Murdoch: Work for the Spirit.* Chicago: University of Chicago Press, 1982.

Gerstenberger, Donna. *Iris Murdoch.* Irish Writers Series. Lewisburg, Pa.: Bucknell University Press, 1975.

Gordon, David J. *Iris Murdoch's Fables of Unselfing.* Columbia: University of Missouri Press, 1995.

Johnson, Deborah. *Iris Murdoch.* Brighton: Harvester, 1987.

Rabinovitz, Rubin. *Iris Murdoch.* Essays on Modern Writers, No. 34. New York: Columbia University Press, 1968.

Ramanathan, Suguna. *Iris Murdoch: Figures of Good.* New York: St. Martin's Press, 1990.

Spear, Hilda D. *Iris Murdoch.* Modern Novelists. New York: St. Martin's Press, 1995.

Todd, Richard. *Iris Murdoch: The Shakespearian Interest.* New York: Barnes & Noble, 1979.

———. *Iris Murdoch.* Contemporary Writers Series. New York: Methuen, 1984.

Wolfe, Peter. *The Disciplined Heart: Iris Murdoch and Her Novels.* Columbia, Mo.: University of Missouri Press, 1966.

B. Reviews and Essays

Allen, Diogenes. Review of *Metaphysics as a Guide to Morals. Commonweal* 120 (8) (23 April 1993): 24.

———. "Two Experiences of Existence: Jean-Paul Sartre and Iris Murdoch." *International Philosophical Quarterly* (June 1974): 181–87.

Antonaccio, Maria. Review of *Metaphysics as a Guide to Morals. Journal of Religion* 74 (20) (April 1994): 278–80.

Barrett, D. C. Review of *Metaphysics as a Guide to Morals*. *International Philosophical Quarterly* 34 (1) 133 (March 1994): 111–14.

Blackburn, Simon. "The Good and the Great." Review of *Metaphysics as a Guide to Morals*. *Times Literary Supplement*, 23 October 1992, 3.

Blum, Lawrence A. "Iris Murdoch and the Domain of the Moral." *Philosophical Studies* 50 (3): 343–67.

Eagleton, Terry. "The Good, the True, the Beautiful." Review of *Metaphysics as a Guide to Morals*. *Guardian*, 5 December 1993, 29.

Hacking, Ian. "Plato's Friend." Review of *Metaphysics as a Guide to Morals*. *London Review of Books*, 17 December 1992, 8–9.

Harrison, Bernard. Review of *Metaphysics as a Guide to Morals*. *Ethics* 103 (3) (April 1995): 653–55.

Kenny, Anthony. "Luciferian Moralists." Review of *The Sovereignty of Good*. *Listener* 85 (7 January 1971): 23.

Lewis, Tess. Review of *Metaphysics as a Guide to Morals*. *American Scholar* 62 (3) (Summer 1993): 466–70.

MacIntyre, Alasdair. "Good for Nothing." Article review of *Iris Murdoch: Work for the Spirit*, by Elizabeth Dipple. *London Review of Books*, 3–16 June 1982, 15–16.

———. "Which World Do You See?" Review of *Metaphysics as a Guide to Morals*. *New York Times Book Review*, 3 January 1993, 9.

O'Sullivan, Kevin. "Iris Murdoch and the Image of Liberal Man." *Yale Literary Magazine* 131 (December 1962): 27–36.

Pondrom, Cyrena N. "Iris Murdoch: An Existentialist?" *Comparative Literature Studies* 5 (December 1968): 403–19.

Rossi, Philip J. Review of *Metaphysics as a Guide to Morals*. *Theological Studies* 54 (4) (December 1993): 762–63.

Vickery, John B. "The Dilemmas of Language: Sartre's *La Nausée* and Iris Murdoch's *Under the Net*." *Journal of Narrative Technique* 1 (May 1971): 69–76.

Warnock, G. J. "The Moralists: Values and Choices." Review of *The Sovereignty of Good*. *Encounter* 36 (April 1971): 81–84.

C. Interviews

Bellamy, Michael. "An Interview with Iris Murdoch." In *Wisconsin Studies in Contemporary Literature* 18 (1977): 129–40.

Blow, Simon. "An Interview with Iris Murdoch." *Spectator* (25 September 1976): 24–25.

Bigsby, C. W. E. In *The Radical Imagination and the Liberal Tradition: Interviews with English and American Novelists*, edited by Heide Ziegler and Christopher Bigsby, 209–30. London: Junction Books, 1982.

Bibliography

Biles, Jack I. "An Interview with Iris Murdoch." *Studies in the Literary Imagination* 11 (Fall 1978): 115–25.

Bryden, R., with A. S. Byatt. "Talking to Iris Murdoch." *Listener* (4 April 1968): 433–34.

Chevalier, Jean-Louis. "Rencontres avec Iris Murdoch." *Centre de Recherches de Litterature et Linguistique des Pays de Langue Anglaise.* Université de Caen, France, 1978.

Haffenden, John. In *Novelists in Interview,* edited by John Haffenden. London: Methuen & Co., 1985.

Heyd, Ruth. "An Interview with Iris Murdoch." *University of Windsor Review* (Spring 1965), 138–43.

Kermode, Frank. "The House of Fiction: Interviews with Seven English Novelists." *Partisan Review* 30 (Spring 1963): 62–82.

Magee, Bryan. "Philosophy and Literature: Dialogue with Iris Murdoch." In *Men of Ideas: Some Creators of Contemporary Philosophy,* edited by Brian Magee, 262–84. New York: Viking Press, 1978.

Mehta, Ved. *Fly and the Fly Bottle: Encounters with British Intellectuals,* 51–57. Boston and Toronto: Little, Brown & Co., 1962.

Rose, W. K. "An Interview with Iris Murdoch." *Shenandoah* 19, 2 (Winter 1968): 3–22.

Slaymaker, William. "An Interview with Iris Murdoch." *Papers on Language and Literature* 21, 4 (Fall 1985): 425–32.

Contributors

Charles Taylor
    is professor of political science and philosophy at McGill University. He is the author most recently of *Sources of the Self: The Search for the Modern Identity* (1989) and *The Ethics of Authenticity* (1992).

Martha C. Nussbaum
    is professor of law and ethics at the University of Chicago Law School and Divinity School. She is the author most recently of *The Fragility of Goodness: Luck and Ethics in Greek Tragedy and Philosophy* (1986) and *The Therapy of Desire: Theory and Practice in Hellenistic Ethics* (1994).

David Tracy
    is Andrew Thomas Greeley and Grace McNichols Greeley Distinguished Service Professor of Catholic Studies at the University of Chicago Divinity School. His most recent books are *Plurality and Ambiguity: Hermeneutics, Religion, Hope* (1987) and *On Naming the Present* (1995).

Cora Diamond
    is William R. Kenan, Jr. Professor of Philosophy at the University of Virginia. She is the author of *The Realistic Spirit: Wittgenstein, Philosophy, and the Mind* (1991).

Maria Antonaccio
    is assistant professor of religious ethics at Bucknell University. Her dissertation at the University of Chicago is titled *Moral Identity and the Good in the Thought of Iris Murdoch*.

Elizabeth Dipple
> is professor of English at Northwestern University. She is the author of *Iris Murdoch: Work for the Spirit* (1982) and *The Unresolveable Plot: Reading Contemporary Fiction* (1988).

Franklin I. Gamwell
> is professor of religious ethics at the University of Chicago Divinity School. He is the author most recently of *The Divine Good: Modern Moral Theory and the Necessity of God* (1990) and *The Meaning of Religious Freedom: Modern Politics and the Democratic Resolution* (1995).

Stanley Hauerwas
> is Gilbert T. Rowe Professor of Theological Ethics at the Divinity School of Duke University. His most recent books are *The Peaceable Kingdom* (1983) and *Dispatches from the Front: Theological Engagements with the Secular* (1994).

William Schweiker
> is associate professor of theological ethics at the University of Chicago Divinity School. He is the author of *Mimetic Reflections: A Study in Hermeneutics, Theology, and Ethics* (1990) and *Responsibility and Christian Ethics* (1995).

Index

aesthetics, 54, 113, 117–24, 139, 191. *See also* art; beauty; perception; unity
agency, human. *See* freedom; human, picture of; individuality
Amis, Martin, 153
analytical philosophy. *See* philosophy, moral (analytical)
Anselm, Saint, 176, 184
anthropology. *See* human, picture of
anxiety, 42–45,74, 211
Arendt, Hannah, 175
Aristotle, 4–14, 51–53, 54, 57, 64–65, 70, 191–92, 204
Aristotleanism, 4–6, 51–57, 70, 192. *See also* Aristotle
art, xvii–xviii, 38, 42–53, 60, 66–72, 112–37, 140, 151, 167–68, 198–201, 208, 225. *See also* aesthetics; beauty; one-making; unity
atheism, 23, 191, 195
attention, 71–73, 82, 107–8, 136, 198, 223, 232–33. *See also* perception
Auden, W. H., 59
Augustine, Saint, 58–59, 69, 227
Austen, Jane, 122
autonomy. *See* freedom

Bakhtin, Mikhail, 68, 139, 143, 152, 168
Balthasar, Hans Urs von, 57
Barth, Karl, 55
Barthes, Roland, 148
Bataille, F.-H., 25–26
Bate, Jonathan, 145
Baudelaire, C. P., 25
beauty, 29–38, 63–64, 72–75, 108, 198–201, 215. *See also* aesthetics, art
behaviorism, 131, 196, 238–49
being, 55–56, 62, 132, 172–78, 185–86, 193, 202, 217–19, 227–30
benevolence, 6–12, 26–28, 31, 200, 212–13, 229–35
Berlin, Isaiah, 249
Bonaventure, Saint, 56–57
Bourke, Mermon, 190–92
Bradley, F. H., 54
Brown, Peter, 59
Buber, Martin, xv
Buddhism, 5, 14, 19–23, 69, 73–74, 146, 196
Burke, Edmund, 246
Burrell, David, 202–3

Callimachus, 145
Cavell, Stanley, 81

Chesterton, G. K., 93–95
Christ, 73, 194–208, 231. *See also* Christianity
Christianity, xii, 5–6, 11–26, 33–34, 51, 57–58, 73–75, 83, 102, 144–46, 161–67, 190–208, 209–35, 244–48. *See also* God; religion
Coetzee, J. M., 139
Collins, Cecil, 167
concepts, moral, xvi, 82–104, 127, 250–52. *See also* good, concept of
conscience, 210, 233–35
consciousness, xii–xiii, 11, 20–21, 60, 67, 82, 89–109, 113–19, 126–37, 139, 158, 172–79, 208, 214–32, 238–39, 245–52
consolation. *See* illusion
contingency. *See* individuality
Coreth, Emerich, 55
creation, 73, 154, 193–94, 200–208, 217–18, 227–35
creativity, 122, 225–32
Cupitt, Don, 195

Dante, 33–46, 52, 57
death, 20–28, 42–43, 65–66, 123, 164, 198, 201, 214
deism, 58
Deleuze, Gilles, 54
demonic, 19, 62
demythologization, 64, 140, 146, 177–79, 194–200, 209–35
Derrida, Jacques, 25–26, 49, 57, 62–69, 145
Descartes, René, 7, 195
determinism, social, 15, 139–47, 196, 206–8, 214–18, 238–52. *See also* unity
Dewey, John, 180
Dionysius, 56–57
disciplines, spiritual. *See* spirit, discipline of
dogmatism, 85, 243–44

Dostoevsky, Fyodor, 16, 142
Dworkin, R. M., 9

Eckhart, Meister, 74
egalitarianism, 6–7, 22–26, 146–47
ego. *See* consciousness
Eliot, George, 122
elitism, 6–7, 22–26, 146–47
Eluard, Paul, 96–98
Emerson, Caryl, 139
emotivism, 238–39, 248
empiricism, xviii, 110–37, 172, 236, 245–47
Enlightenment, European, 24–28, 87, 173. *See also* modernity
eros, 29–53, 60, 72, 164. *See also* love; sexuality
ethics. *See* philosophy, moral
evaluation, xvi–xvii, 14, 17, 103–7, 131–33, 153, 212–25, 232–35, 237–40, 247
existentialism, xiii, xvi, 114–18, 131, 196, 214, 217, 226–27, 233, 243, 247–48, 251

faith, 19–25, 139, 200, 204, 213, 230, 235, 242, 250–51
feminism, 141, 146–47
Fine, Arthur, 140–41, 151
Foot, Philippa, 84
form. *See* good, form or idea of; unity
Foucault, Michel, 25–36
foundationalism, 4, 15–16, 156
Fowles, John, 153
freedom, xiii–xiv, 9, 32–36, 44, 82–84, 90, 101–2, 114–17, 121, 198, 215–32, 244–52
Freud, Sigmund, 59–61, 66–70, 198, 220, 248

Gadamer, Hans-Georg, 57
gift, 56–57, 75, 177, 198, 204
Girard, René, 27, 165
God, xiii–xiv, 12–21, 55–62, 73–75, 139, 163–65, 171–89, 190–

208, 209–35. See also Christianity; ontological argument
Goldberg, Samuel, 102–3
good: absence of—see void; concept of, 79–709, 141, 155–61, 180, 236–52; form or idea of, xvii, 12–13, 19, 26–38, 47–51, 54–75, 132–34, 173–86, 198–201, 209–35 (see also Plato; Platonism); reality of, xiv-xvii, 173–89, 200–201, 209–35, 236–52 (see also naturalistic fallacy; ontological argument; realism, moral); self and, xii-xv, 3–28, 60–61, 129–34, 174, 209, 223–35 (see also spirit, pilgrimage of)
Grene, David, 65

Habermas, Jürgen, 4
habit, 17–18, 192, 208, 246–47
Hadot, Pierre, 70–71
Hare, R. M., 79, 84–95, 98–102, 240–43, 246
Hartshorne, Charles, 176, 184–89
Hegel, G. W. F., 54–55, 114–19, 185, 247–49
Heidegger, Martin, xiii, 10, 54–57, 62, 66
Hinduism, 146, 154–58
human, picture of, xi–xvii, 10–13, 27, 47–49, 82–90, 114–37, 172–75, 214–35, 248–52. See also consciousness; individuality
humanism, xiii, 13, 23–28
Hume, David, xvi, 106, 193, 241, 245–46
Hütter, Reinhardt, 204

ideology, 83, 140–41, 215, 234
idolatry, 19, 35, 201, 232
illusion, xvii, 22, 28, 34–53, 59–75, 81, 118–24, 136, 139–68, 172–79, 192–99, 207, 211–20

Index 263

imagination, xv–xviii, 138–40, 179, 190–92, 201, 208, 211, 222
imitation. See mimesis
individuality, xviii, 32–39, 45–53, 64, 86–92, 110–37, 141–45, 175–89, 197–208, 209–35, 246–47
Islam, 12, 21, 74

James, Henry, 141, 153
Johnson, Samuel, 79, 102
Jonas, Hans, 218
Joseph, H. W. B., 251
Joyce, James, 49–53
Judaism, 12, 74, 87, 146, 159, 193–94, 203, 230–31
judgment. See evaluation
justice, 6–12, 28, 163–65, 200, 213, 230

Kant, Immanuel, 4, 8, 13, 67, 73, 103–6, 114, 126–30, 172–89, 193, 199–202, 219, 225, 241, 245, 251. See also Kantianism
Kantianism, 6–7, 10, 15, 114–18, 131, 173–74, 180–81, 195, 226–27, 245. See also Kant, Immanuel
Kaufmann, Walter, 26
Kierkegaard, Søren, 69, 73, 249
Kinzie, Mary, 139

Leibniz, G. W., 184
Levinas, Emmanuel, 55–56
liberalism, xiii, 8–10, 85–88, 114–22, 243–48
life, 6, 18–28, 38, 110, 138, 156, 206–7, 215, 232
literary criticism, 138–51, 165
Lonergan, Bernard, 55, 71
love, 5, 13–28, 29–53, 72, 118–24, 182, 198–203, 209–35. See also eros; sexuality

Machiavelli, 101
MacIntyre, Alasdair, 55, 69, 173
Mackie, J. L., 15, 211
Macquarrie, John, 58
Magritte, René, 150
Maimonides, Moses, 203
Mallarmé, Stéphane, 25
Marcel, Gabriel, 251
Marion, Jean-Luc, 55–56
Marxism, 83, 115–16, 141, 146–47, 158, 244, 247–48
mathematics, 70–72
McGinn, Bernard, 58
meditation. *See* spirit, discipline of
metaphysics, xiv–xviii, 13, 47–53, 62, 72, 86, 110–17, 124–37, 171–89, 193–208, 211–35, 236–52. *See also* being
Mill, J. S., 20, 241–43
Miller, Jim, 26
Milosz, Czeslaw, 95–96
Milton, John, 154
mimesis, 11–18, 65–69, 143–44, 150, 156, 165, 197, 217–18
modernism, 143, 148
modernity, 13–28, 66, 118, 177, 195, 214–18, 227–28, 250. *See also* Enlightenment, European
Moore, G. E., xvi, 236–42, 251
moral philosophy. *See* philosophy, moral
morality, single-term. *See* philosophy, moral (analytical)
Morson, Saul, 139
mysticism, 192–99, 206
myth. *See* demythologization

Nagel, Thomas, 153
National Socialism (Nazism), 26, 86–89
natural law ethics. *See* realism, moral
naturalistic fallacy, xvi–xvii, 79–95, 102–9, 171–89, 236–52. *See also* good, reality of; realism, moral

neo-Platonism, 63, 70, 203
Newman, Charles, 152
Nietzsche, F. W., 4–5, 25–28, 54, 62–69
novel, form of, xi–xii, 37–53, 67–75, 110–37, 138–68
Nussbaum, Martha, 139

Oakeshott, Michael, 246
obligation, moral, 3–15, 93–94, 130–32, 209, 215–19, 233–44
O'Conner, Flannery, 208
Ogden, Schubert, 183
one-making, 126–37, 225–32. *See also* art; consciousness; unity
ontological argument, xiii, xvii, 19, 160, 171–89, 191, 199–202, 222–24
ontology. *See* being
ordinary life. *See* life
Ovid, 144–46

pain. *See* suffering
Paul, Saint, 234
Peirce, C. S., 144
perception, 7, 29–48, 92–94, 100–109, 121–33, 143, 174–75, 190–208, 216–35, 248. *See also* attention; illusion
Percy, Walker, 208
perfection, xiv, 133–34, 175–89, 201, 209, 222–35. *See also* good, form or idea of; ontological argument
philosophy, moral: analytical, xii–xvi, 3–18, 48, 54–55, 64, 79–109, 110–13, 125–27, 171–73, 195–98, 209–35, 236–52; first principle of, 211–35. *See also* metaphysics
pilgrimage, spiritual. *See* spirit, pilgrimage of
Pinsky, Robert, 139
Plato, 7, 12–13, 29–53, 54–75, 129–

30, 173–89, 200, 219–25, 251.
  See also Platonism
Platonism, xii–xiii, xvii, 14, 26, 40–
  53, 54–75, 172–82, 192, 203,
  209–35. See also Plato
Plotinus, 57–63, 155
pluralism, 19, 126, 146, 211
power, value of, 212–35
Powys, John Cowper, 143
practices, spiritual. See spirit, discipline of
pragmatism, xiii, 144, 180–89
prayer. See spirit, discipline of
principle, first. See philosophy, moral (first principle of)
Proclus, 63
Protestantism, 85–88, 245–47. See also Puritanism; Reformation, Protestant
Proust, Marcel, 48, 51, 101
Puritanism, 21–24
Pythagoras, 71

Rahner, Karl, 55
Rawls, John, 4, 7–9, 99
realism, moral, xiii–xvi, 114–16,
  133, 171–89, 200, 210–35,
  240–48. See also good, reality of
reason, 6–17, 63, 81–82, 94, 101,
  128–34, 161, 174, 181, 219,
  224, 236–40
Reformation, Protestant, 6, 21–24,
  58
religion, xi–xix, 5, 20–28, 43, 72–75,
  102, 126–27, 136–40, 167,
  176–89, 197, 209–10, 224,
  229, 243, 250. See also Christianity; demythologization; God; Islam; Judaism
Renaissance, Italian, 145
respect, 9, 13, 85, 205, 212–29,
  243–44
responsibility, 80–82, 98, 183, 216,
  243–48

Ricoeur, Paul, 59
Rorty, Richard, 55, 180
Ryle, Gilbert, 239, 246

Sartre, Jean-Paul, xiii, 56–57, 66,
  114, 117
Schleiermacher, F. D. E., 55
scholasticism, 58, 70
Schopenhauer, Arthur, 67
self. See consciousness; good, self and; human, picture of; individuality; spirit
sexuality, 29–53, 164, 198
Shakespeare, 142–45
Shklovsky, Victor, 143
sin, 34–39, 73, 194–98, 206, 213
Socrates, 29
sophists, 54
soul. See spirit
Spice, Nicholas, 147
spirit, 29–32, 44, 60–64, 70–71,
  158; discipline of, xiv, 19, 50–
  52, 67–75, 197, 206–8, 226; pilgrimage of, xiv–xv, xix, 59–75,
  86, 110, 129–37, 144–45, 174–
  86, 199, 206, 209, 221–22,
  232, 247
spiritual disciplines. See spirit, discipline of
Stevenson, Charles L., 238
stoicism, 70–73
structuralism. See determinism, social; unity
Suarez, Francisco de, 56
subjectivity. See consciousness
suffering, xviii, 5, 20–28. See also void
surrealism, 149, 155–56
system. See unity

Taylor, A. E., 251
Taylor, Charles, 195
teleology, xiv, 19, 182–89, 205–7
theism. See God
theology. See God

therapy. *See* spirit, pilgrimage of
Thomas Aquinas, Saint, 55, 63, 176, 191, 202–4. *See also* Thomism
Thomism, 17, 55–56, 116, 247. *See also* Thomas Aquinas, Saint
Tillich, Paul, 176–79, 185–86, 193
Titian, 145–46
Tolstoy, Nikolaevich, 122, 142–43, 155
totality. *See* unity
tradition, 55, 246–47
tragedy, 54–55, 65, 199
truth, xvii–xviii, 9, 37–46, 61–68, 74, 97–98, 111–12, 121–34, 140–44, 158, 174–80, 192, 200–202, 211, 222, 229, 237–52

unconditional aspect of morality, xvii, 6–10, 52, 67, 104, 124–25, 132, 176–86, 230–31. *See also* obligation, moral; ontological argument

unity, xvii–xviii, 55, 63–66, 110–37, 141, 151, 179–89, 198–99, 210–14, 247–49
utilitarianism, xiii, xviii, 4–16, 127, 196

violence, 27–28, 165, 218. *See also* power, value of
Virgil, 33
virtue, 11–14, 44–45, 117, 147, 164, 192, 198–99, 223–25
vision. *See* perception
void, xviii, 66–73, 136–37. *See also* suffering

Wat, Alexander, 95–103
Weil, Simone, xviii, 57, 67, 73, 200
Weldon, T. D., 246
Whitehead, Alfred North, 55, 173, 183–87
Williams, Bernard, 4, 12, 55, 83
Williams, Charles, 143
Wittgenstein, Ludwig, 67, 71, 87–88, 106–8, 192–95, 238, 251